ROSS GILBERT ANDERSON

# SUCCESSION

April 2005   House   up to £300 000
              furniture + furnishings   24 000
              cash   75 000 (if no kids)
                     42 0000 (if kids)

< June 2005   home   130 000
              (furniture + f)   22 000
              cash   58 000 (no kids)
                     35 000 (kids)

IHT nil rate band   £275 000

D1586131

**AUSTRALIA**
LBC Information Services
Sydney


**CANADA and USA**
Carswell
Toronto


**NEW ZEALAND**
Brooker's
Auckland


**SINGAPORE and MALAYSIA**
Sweet & Maxwell Asia
Singapore and Kuala Lumpur

*GREENS CONCISE SCOTS LAW*

# SUCCESSION

Third Edition

By

## D.R. Macdonald, B.A., LL.B.

*Solicitor, Senior Lecturer in Law, University of Dundee*

EDINBURGH
W. GREEN/Sweet & Maxwell
2001

First published 1990
Reprinted in 1993
Second edition 1994


Published in 2001 by W. Green & Son Limited
21 Alva Street
Edinburgh EH2 4PS

Typeset by LBJ Typesetting of Kingsclere

Printed in Great Britain by Athenaeum Press Ltd, Gateshead,
Tyne & Wear


No natural forests were destroyed to make this product;
only farmed timber was used and replanted.

A CIP catalogue record of this book is available from the British
Library.


ISBN 0414 014 367

# PREFACE

In this edition I have tried to take account of all relevant legal developments up to July 30, 2001. There still seems no immediate prospect of legislation to implement the Scottish Law Commission's 1990 reform proposals. However, in addition to the usual flow of case law there have been some important statutory changes: most notably the Requirements of Writing (Scotland) Act 1995.

The past year has seen the appearance of a valuable research resource in the form of *Meston's Succession Opinions* (ed. David O'Donnell). I have not cited specific passages in this book, but the wide range of its coverage means that it should always be considered as a source of further advice on practical executry problems.

My thanks go to those who have commented on previous editions, and to Alan Barr of Edinburgh University for his comments on executry taxation. Any defects in the resulting text are of course entirely my responsibility. I am also most grateful to the staff of Messrs W. Green & Son Ltd, particularly Neil McKinlay and Philippa Sladdin, for their ongoing assistance and encouragement.

Dundee
September 2001

# CONTENTS

*Page*

# Contents

# Contents

# TABLE OF CASES

# TABLE OF STATUTES

# TABLE OF STATUTORY INSTRUMENTS

# ABBREVIATIONS AND AUTHORITIES

| | |
|---|---|
| Anton | A.E. Anton & P.R. Beaumont, Private International Law (2nd ed., 1990) |
| Bankton, Inst. | Andrew McDouall, Lord Bankton, Institute of the Laws of Scotland in Civil Rights, 1751–3 |
| CTO | Capital Taxes Office |
| Clive | E.M. Clive, The Law of Husband and Wife in Scotland (4th ed., 1997) |
| Currie | J.G. Currie, The Confirmation of Executors in Scotland (8th ed., by E.M. Scobbie, 1995) |
| Elder | A.H. Elder, Forms of Wills, 1947 |
| Encyclopaedia | "Wills and Succession" in The Laws of Scotland: Stair Memorial Encyclopaedia, Vol. 25, by M.C. Meston and others, 1989 |
| Ersk., Inst. | John Erskine of Carnock, An Institute of the Law of Scotland (8th ed., 1871) |
| Ersk., Prin. | John Erskine of Carnock, Principles of the Law of Scotland (21st ed., 1911) |
| Gloag & Henderson | W.M. Gloag and R. Candlish Henderson, Introduction to the Law of Scotland (10th ed., by W.A. Wilson and A. Forte, 1995) |
| Goudy | H. Goudy, Law of Bankruptcy in Scotland (4th ed., 1914) |
| Halliday | J.M. Halliday, Conveyancing Law and Practice in Scotland (2nd ed., by I.J.S. Talman), Vol. 1 (1996) and Vol. 2 (1997) |
| Henderson | R. Candlish Henderson, The Principles of Vesting in the Law of Succession (2nd ed., 1938) |
| IHTA | Inheritance Tax Act 1984 (c. 51) |
| J.L.S. | Journal of the Law Society of Scotland |
| L.Q.R. | Law Quarterly Review |

| | |
|---|---|
| McBryde | W.W. McBryde, The Law of Contract in Scotland, 1987 |
| McDonald | A.J. McDonald, Conveyancing Manual (6th ed., 1997) |
| McLaren | John, Lord McLaren, Law of Wills and Succession (3rd ed., 1894); supplement by D.O. Dykes, 1934 |
| McMillan | A.R.G. McMillan, The Law of Bona Vacantia in Scotland, 1936 |
| Macphail | I.D. Macphail, Evidence, 1987 |
| Meston | M.C. Meston, The Succession (Scotland) Act 1964 (4th ed., 1993) |
| Miller | J. Gareth Miller, The Machinery of Succession (2nd ed., 1996) |
| Morley | M.F. Morley, Accounting for Scottish Executries and Trusts, 1984 |
| Morris | J.H.C. Morris, The Conflict of Laws (3rd ed., 1984) Murray C. de B. Murray, The Law of Wills in Scotland, 1945 |
| Parry & Clark | J.B. Clark. The Law of Succession (9th ed., 1988) |
| S.L.C. | Scottish Law Commission consultative memoranda: No. 69, Intestate Succession and Legal Rights; No. 70, The Making and Revocation of Wills; No. 71, Some Miscellaneous Topics in the Law of Succession; all 1986 |
| S.L.T. | Scots Law Times |
| Stair, Inst. | Sir James Dalrymple, Viscount Stair, Institutions of the Law of Scotland (Tercentenary ed., 1981) |
| Walker | N.M.L. Walker, Judicial Factors, 1974 |
| Walker, Prin. | D.M. Walker, Principles of Scottish Private Law (4th ed., 1988) |
| Walkers | A.G. Walker and N.M.L Walker, The Law of Evidence in Scotland, 1964 |
| Wilson | W.A. Wilson, The Scottish Law of Debt (2nd ed., 1991) |

Wilson & Duncan     W.A. Wilson and A.G.M. Duncan, Trusts, Trustees and Executors (2nd ed., 1995)

Further reading on specific topics is listed at the end of each chapter.

# CHAPTER 1

# PROOF OF DEATH AND OF SURVIVORSHIP

## INTRODUCTION

The law of succession governs how a person's property passes on **1.01** his death. Succession to property depends on proof or legal presumption that the person whose estate is to be distributed has died, and that the potential beneficiary has survived him. If an interest in property passes before death it is not a right of succession: it may instead involve a trust in favour of the beneficiary or an outright transfer by gift.[1]

While death and survivorship are essential to give the beneficiary **1.02** a vested—indefeasible—right, they are not always sufficient: vesting may be postponed till some later event such as the beneficiary's reaching a certain age. If the beneficiary dies before the date of vesting his right lapses. Conversely, if the beneficiary predeceases (dies before) the person from whom he would inherit, his offspring may step into his shoes and take his interest in his stead: this can result from the rules of representation (in intestacy) and the *conditio si institutus sine liberis decesserit* (in testate succession).[2]

## PROOF OF DEATH

**General requirements**

Death itself is an imprecise concept; questions of brain death as **1.03** opposed to physical death may arise in modern medicine. Issues of medical ethics aside, the position is ordinarily straightforward. Death must be proved in order to permit inheritance; the executor must aver precisely the date and place of death to obtain confirmation, and must prove this if challenged.[3] Under the Registration of

---

[1] An exception is the hybrid *donatio mortis causa*, a lifetime gift which only becomes irrevocable when the donor dies: see paras 5.33 *et seq.*

[2] Discussed at paras 4.45 *et seq.*, 4.70 *et seq.* and 10.59 *et seq.* For vesting see Chap. 11.

[3] Currie, 7.10–7.12.

Births, Deaths and Marriages (Scotland) Act 1965[4] an extract from
the Register of Deaths is "sufficient evidence of the death", but is
not conclusive proof.

### Disappearance: the legal background[5]

**1.04**    Difficulties arise where a person has disappeared and is not
heard of again. Scots common law had no rule presuming him to
have died after a period of seven years. There was a strong
presumption that life continued to the extreme limits of human
age: 80 or 100 years according to Stair.[6] To rebut it required proof
"beyond reasonable doubt"[7] or "positive proof",[8] a higher standard
than the ordinary standard in civil cases of proof on the balance of
probabilities. Rebuttal depended on the special circumstances of
each case: lapse of time was only one factor, insufficient by itself,
coupled with other evidence such as a dissipated or dangerous
lifestyle. So death was held proved in *Greig v. Merchant Company
of Edinburgh*[9] where a wife wished to claim a widow's pension: the
husband had been absent for 10 years; on medical evidence his
alcoholism would have killed him within that time. But in *Secretary
of State for Scotland v. Sutherland*,[10] where a husband had left his
wife and not been heard of for 42 years, he was presumed still alive
(though aged 72) on the grounds that this merely proved how
successful he had been in avoiding his wife.

**1.05**    Difficulty of proof aside, the common law was felt defective. Its
justification went once rapid modern communications made it
unlikely for someone to disappear completely for years yet still be
alive. It effectively quarantined the person's property for a generation. An action to declare death was probably only effective against
the parties to the action. If death could not be proved, the only
remedy was to appoint a factor *loco absentis* to administer the
missing person's estate.[11]

**1.06**    Legislation remedied some but not all of these defects. The main
problem was fragmentation of the legal rules, so that a person
might be treated as alive for some purposes and dead for others.
The Presumption of Life Limitation (Scotland) Act 1891[12] allowed
death to be declared after seven years' disappearance: but it
affected only succession to property, and permitted restitution to

---

[4] s.41(3).
[5] See generally Scot. Law Com. Report No. 34 (1974).
[6] Inst. IV. xlv. 17 (19thly).
[7] *Bruce v. Smith* (1871) 10 M. 130 at 133.
[8] *Fife v. Fife* (1855) 17 D. 951 at 954. See also *Tait v. Sleigh*, 1969 S.L.T. 227.
[9] 1921 S.C. 76; and see *X v. S.S.C. Society*, 1937 S.L.T. 87.
[10] 1944 S.C. 79.
[11] Still useful where the 1977 Act does not apply.
[12] Which replaced a more limited Act of 1881.

the disappeared person if he reappeared in the following 13 years. The Divorce (Scotland) Act 1938[13] allowed dissolution of a marriage, but had no effect on property rights. Neither Act gave a right to pension or life assurance benefits.

### The Presumption of Death (Scotland) Act 1977

The Act answers most criticisms of the previous law; common law actions are still competent but will be rare. By its main provisions: **1.07**

(1) A person may by court action be declared dead in two distinct situations: if he is thought to have died, or has not been known to be alive for a period of at least seven years. The first applies where there is some evidence of death (*e.g.* his plane disappears en route); the second where there is simple disappearance with nothing else pointing to death. **1.08**

The action may be brought by anyone having an interest: such as a spouse, or a potential beneficiary, or the Lord Advocate for the public interest. Both the Court of Session and the sheriff court may have jurisdiction on grounds of the domicile or habitual residence of the missing person or his spouse (if that is the pursuer). The sheriff may—and must if the Court of Session so directs on application by a party to the action—remit the case to the Court of Session if the issues are important or complex (section 1).

(2) Proof is on the balance of probabilities. If death is proved, the decree states its date and time; if it is uncertain when within a period of time the person died, the end of the period is chosen. In the case of seven or more years' disappearance, death will be held to occur at the end of the day seven years after he was last known to be alive (section 2). **1.09**

The decree may also determine domicile at death and any question relating to any interest in property resulting from the death—*e.g.* where A's right to B's estate depends on the missing person C's death.

The court may appoint a judicial factor to manage the deceased's property, whatever its value. Thus, unlike ordinary appointments of judicial factors, there is no financial limit on the sheriff court's power. Note that if no decree is possible within the seven-year period, because there is no proof of death, the main remedy is to have a factor *loco absentis* appointed over the property until the period is up.[14]

(3) The decree is effective and conclusive against any person and for all purposes, including the acquisition of rights to any person's property. It thus applies to insurance and social security benefits. It **1.10**

---

[13] s.5.
[14] See N.M.L. Walker, *Judicial Factors*, pp. 2–29.

dissolves the missing person's marriage, even if the spouse did not bring the action (section 3).[15]

**1.11**    (4) Suppose in fact the missing person did not die, or died at a different date from that stated: (a) despite the decree the person remains liable for any crimes he has committed (section 3(4)); (b) the marriage remains dissolved by the decree and is not revived by its subsequent recall or by the person's reappearance (section 3(3), 4(5)); (c) supposing the spouse remarried without a decree dissolving the first marriage, it is a defence to a bigamy charge that for the seven years preceding the remarriage he had no reason to believe the missing person to be alive (section 13); (d) anyone having an interest may apply to have the decree varied or recalled (section 4(1)).

**1.12**    (5) The policy of the Act is to protect rights acquired under a decree—especially by a spouse—and to limit the missing person's right to recover his property if he reappears. So variation or recall will not automatically affect property rights acquired under the decree, but:

(a) If application for variation is made less than five years after the decree, the court may make "such . . . order . . . as it considers fair and reasonable in all the circumstances" (section 5(3)). Thus it may order restitution in kind or in cash. The order does not affect income accruing between the decree and its variation, nor the rights of third parties who acquired property for value.

(b) Special rules govern trusts and insurers. When making payments after a decree of death, insurers may (and trustees normally must) obtain insurance against its possible variation (section 6). If the court varies the decree, so far as practicable it will only order restitution of trust property still in the trustees' hands or, if previously distributed, its value when distributed. Insurers may recover capital sums—not annuities or periodical payments—if "the facts . . . justify", *e.g.* the sums were paid in error. (Note that insurance policies need not permit payment on a decree of death; they may require proof of accidental death.)

(c) The court may, on application by a trustee or a person entitled to aliment from the missing person, declare property not to be recoverable under a variation order (section 7).

(d) The court may order that inheritance tax be repaid to anyone entitled to a repayment (section 8).

---

[15] For criticism of this rule, see 1977 S.L.T. (News) 217.

(6) To obtain confirmation an executor formerly required to aver **1.13** a precise date of death. The Act makes this unnecessary. If the person disappeared in Scotland, the decree is automatically effective for confirmation. An analogous foreign decree is sufficient (though not conclusive) evidence of death (section 10); the executor may use it in his averment (section 11). Similar rules apply to death in or loss from a ship, aircraft, hovercraft, or offshore installation (section 11).

(7) To ensure due publicity, (a) anyone possessing relevant **1.14** information must disclose it if he knows that an action for decree or variation has been raised, unless rules of privilege, confidentiality or public interest apply; this duty applies explicitly to the D.S.S. (section 9); (b) decrees and variation orders are entered by the Registrar General in the Register of Deaths (section 12).

## PROOF OF SURVIVORSHIP

### General

For a beneficiary to inherit from the deceased, it must be proved **1.15** on the balance of probabilities that he survived him. "Survivance is in every case a matter of proof, and . . . when a claimant whose claim depends on proof of survivorship is unable to establish the fact of survivance, his claim necessarily fails."[16] Scots law requires no minimum period of survivance: a matter of seconds, if proved, is sufficient; once the beneficiary thus acquires a vested right of succession, on his own subsequent proven or presumed death that right passes to his own representatives as part of his own estate.[17]

The rule applies generally to testate and intestate succession. A **1.16** special case is a survivorship destination, whereby property is owned in the names of "A and B and the survivor", the share of the first to die passing by accretion to the other on his death. Conversely a right of succession may depend on proof of another potential beneficiary predeceasing: this may occur in intestacy (the doctrine of representation), testacy (the *conditio si institutus sine liberis decesserit*), or under the express terms of a will (such as a legacy to X "if Y dies in my lifetime" or "to Y whom failing to X").

Failure to prove survivance may have drastic effects. A legacy **1.17** will lapse, unless the *conditio* or the rules of accretion apply, and the sum will fall into residue or intestacy; failing intestate heirs the Crown will take as *ultimus haeres*.[18]

---

[16] *Drummond's J.F. v. Lord Advocate*, 1944 S.C. 298 at 302 *per* L.J.-C. Cooper.

[17] If (more rarely) vesting is postponed to a later date, the beneficiary's right is extinguished if he dies in the interval. For vesting, see Chap. 11.

[18] See paras 10.50 *et seq.* (accretion), 10.59 *et seq.* (the *conditio*), and 10.74 (residue).

### Common calamities

*(a) Common law*

**1.18**  Rigid insistence on this principle caused problems whenever it was uncertain in what order two or more people died: especially where they died in one "common calamity" such as a bomb blast. Evidence may be slight—disappearance in a shipwreck at an unknown moment within some period of time—and medical speculation necessary as to the precise time of death. At common law, in the absence of proof, there was no presumption as to who died first.

**1.19**  A trio of cases illustrates the effect of the rule. In *Drummond's J.F. v. Lord Advocate*[19] a husband, wife, and children died in a bomb blast. The wife died intestate: her husband would inherit if he survived, but since there was no evidence of order of death and no other heir the Crown took as *ultimus haeres*. In *Mitchell's Exx v. Gordon*[20] a husband, wife, and daughter died in an aeroplane crash; two children, and the daughter's son, survived them. Could the grandson claim his mother's share in the husband's intestacy (by representation) and under the wife's will (by the *conditio si institutus*)? His claims failed: both required proof of his mother's predeceasing the spouses (which was lacking); the share went to the surviving children. In *Ross's J.F. v. Martin*[21] two sisters made separate but identical wills each leaving property to the other and to a charity if the other predeceased her. They died, the order uncertain, in a gas leak. The charity argued that the wills should be construed as one and the legacy implemented to give effect to the testators' intention: this argument failed because the words of the will were clear; the legacy failed and the intestate heirs inherited.

*(b) Statute*

**1.20**  It was generally felt that any presumption of survivance was better than none. English law now lays down two: the general rule is that where the order of death is uncertain the younger is taken to survive the older,[22] but where spouses die together and the older is intestate then neither is taken to survive the other.[23] *Hickman v. Peacey*[24] took "uncertain" to cover "virtually simultaneous": exact simultaneity is most unlikely.

---

[19] 1944 S.C. 298.
[20] 1953 S.C. 176.
[21] 1955 S.C. (H.L.) 56. *Wing v. Angrave* (1860) 8 H.L.C. 183 is an analogous English case.
[22] Law of Property Act 1925, s.184.
[23] Administration of Estates Act 1925, s.46(3). The aim is to stop a husband's estate going to his wife's relations.
[24] [1945] A.C. 304.

In Scots law the Succession (Scotland) Act 1964 now lays down a **1.21** general rule with two exceptions:

(1) Where two persons die in circumstances indicating that they **1.22** died simultaneously or rendering it uncertain which, if either, survived the other, then the younger is presumed to survive the elder for all purposes of succession to property, legal and prior rights (section 31(1)(b)). However;

(2) Where the persons are husband and wife, it is presumed that **1.23** neither survived the other (section 31(1)(a)). Note that this gives no answer where, as in *Ross's J.F.*, "predecease" is required; survivorship destinations raise a similar point since they assume that one spouse survived the other.

(3) Where the elder left a legacy in favour of the younger or (if **1.24** the younger fails to survive) to a third person, and the younger dies intestate, the elder is presumed for the purposes of that legacy only to survive. For all other purposes the ordinary rule applies (section 31(2)). One is intestate if one leaves any part of one's estate undisposed of by will (section 36(1)).

The Act talks of "two persons". If a group is involved, it must be **1.25** analysed "in twos": each person's survivance of each other must be separately determined.

The Act only applies if proof of survivance is not possible. Proof **1.26** is on the normal civil standard, balance of probabilities: *Lamb v. Lord Advocate*[25] rejected the idea, floated in *Hickman*, that a higher standard is ever required. Mere speculation not amounting to proof is insufficient.[26]

The Scottish Law Commission suggests two possible reforms[27]: **1.27**

(1) A presumption of "predecease" rather than "survivorship". **1.28** This would cover the point in (2) above; property held under a destination would pass in separate shares to each owner's heirs.

(2) A minimum period of survivance by the beneficiary: five days **1.29** unless the deceased by will specified another period. In practice many wills already include a "survivorship clause" to require 30 days' survivance, failing which a third person inherits. Otherwise the beneficiary inherits even if his death ensues minutes later: this has tax disadvantages and scarcely reflects the testator's true intentions.

### Revenue law

If A is proved or presumed to survive B, inheritance tax (IHT) is **1.30** in principle due on both A's and B's death. This would be unjust if they in fact die in one accident (albeit minutes apart), even though

---

[25] 1976 S.L.T. 151.

[26] *Re Beare* [1957] C.L.Y. 1361.

[27] Report No. 124, paras 5.1–5.7. English law now requires an intestate's spouse to survive for 28 days: Administration of Estates Act 1925, s.46(2A), inserted by Law Reform (Succession) Act 1995, s.1.

quick succession relief[28] will apply to B's death reducing his IHT. Two rules remedy this:

**1.31** (1) If it cannot be known which, of two or more persons who died, survived the other(s), they are deemed to die at the same instant.[29] Now IHT is due on the estate immediately before death. So the effect is that property inherited by B from A suffers tax only on A's death, since it is not deemed part of B's estate for this purpose.

**1.32** (2) Suppose under A's will property is held for B on condition he survives for a specified period less than six months, and it is transferred to him then (if he survives) or to an alternative beneficiary earlier (if he dies). Tax is due as if the transfer were made on A's death, *i.e.* once only and not also on B's death during the period.[30] This is why a will should include a "survivorship clause".

POSTHUMOUS CHILDREN[31]

**1.33** Rights of succession are normally determined at the deceased's date of death. But where he leaves a child who is conceived but as yet unborn, it may be treated as actually born to allow it to inherit. "A child in the mother's womb is esteemed as already born, in all things that concern its own interest"[32]; *qui in utero est, pro jam nato habetur*.[33] The principle is not confined to succession: the child may have a remedy in delict for antenatal injury, either to itself directly or by the loss of a relative.[34]

**1.34** The rule derives from Roman law and has rarely been disputed. It applies to wills, to entitlement to legal rights,[35] and to intestacy; the 1964 Act made no apparent changes. So, in *Cox's Trs v. Cox*[36] where property was divided among "the descendants alive at the time of my death", that class included posthumous descendants unless expressly or impliedly excluded by the terms of the will.

**1.35** The rule has two limits. First, the child must ultimately be born alive. Secondly, the rule cannot be invoked in the interests of a third person, but only if the child gains some direct benefit by it. So it was refused in *Elliot v. Joicey*,[37] where A's property was to be

---

[28] Inheritance Tax Act 1984, hereafter "IHTA 1984", s.141. See para. 12–53.
[29] IHTA 1984, s.4(2).
[30] IHTA 1984, s.92.
[31] See Meston (1970) 15 J.L.S. 33.
[32] Bankton, Inst., I. ii. 7.
[33] Erskine, Inst., III. viii. 76.
[34] See Scot. Law Com. Report No. 30 (Cmnd. 5371), "Liability for Antenatal Injury".
[35] *Jervey v. Watt* (1762) Mor. 8170.
[36] 1950 S.C. 117.
[37] 1935 S.C. (H.L.) 57.

held "in trust for [B] absolutely . . . in the event of [B] leaving any issue . . . surviving." In the House of Lords' view "surviving" would not normally mean "posthumous": but, crucially, even if *pro jam nato* were applied that would benefit B's estate and not necessarily his issue. The issue would benefit only indirectly (by B's will) or not at all, if B were insolvent.

**Further reading**

M.C. Meston, "Succession Rights of Posthumous Children" (1970) 15 J.L.S. 33.

Scottish Law Commission: Report No. 34 (1974), "Presumption of Death".

"Common Calamities and the Presumption of Death", 1963 S.L.T. (News) 101.

"Presumption of Death", 1977 S.L.T. (News) 217.

# CHAPTER 2

# ENTITLEMENT TO INHERIT

## INTRODUCTION

**2.01**  Many legal systems recognise various factors which debar a person from inheriting on intestacy or under an otherwise valid will. Commonly someone who witnesses[1] or writes out[2] a will—or his spouse—may not take benefits under it. That point, where relevant in Scotland, makes the entire will formally invalid.[3] Otherwise Scots law debars only the "unworthy heir". Its former discrimination against adopted and illegitimate children, tending to recognise only legitimate blood-relationships, has now largely been removed by statute.

## THE UNWORTHY HEIR

### General

**2.02**  Civil law systems identify various circumstances personal to a beneficiary which make him unworthy to inherit; common law systems treat this question in terms of public policy. South African law, for instance, has several types of unworthiness, such as adultery, concealing a will, or unlawful killing. Whatever the early Scots rules (such as barring inheritance by wayward fornicating daughters[4]), the present Scots law derives largely from three overlapping sources: the Parricide Act 1594, English rules of public policy and the Forfeiture Act 1982.

### The Parricide Act 1594

**2.03**  "Quhatsumeuir he be that hes slayne or sail heireftir slay his father or mother guidschir or guddame and hes bene alreddie or salbe heireftir convict be ane assyise The commitaris of the said

---

[1] England: Wills Act 1837, s.15.
[2] South Africa: see Corbett *et al.*, *The Law of Succession in South Africa*, p. 74.
[3] Only in the case of notarial execution of a will: see paras 6.45 *et seq.*
[4] *Regiam Majestatem*, 11.49.

cryme and his posteritie in linea recta salbe disheresit in all tyme
heireftir fra thair landis heretages takis possessionis and the samyn
sall apertene to the nixt collaterall and narrest of blude quha
vtherwayes micht succeid falyeing of the richt lyne."

The precise scope of the Act is unclear,[5] but is so limited that the **2.04**
Act has never actually been successfully used to disinherit anyone.
Conviction of murder is required: so in *Oliphant v. Oliphant*,[6]
where a man killed his mother but escaped and was legally
declared fugitive, the Act did not apply. Succession to moveables is
apparently not affected. Only killing of parents or grandparents is
covered: not spouses. Finally, the Act disinherited the murderer
and his descendants: but the analogous concept in treason cases of
"corruption of the blood" has since been abolished,[7] and that may
restrict the Act to disinheriting the murderer himself. His own
children would then inherit as if he had predeceased the victim.

**Public policy**

English law has evolved principles of public policy to prevent **2.05**
criminals inheriting or taking other benefits from their victims. The
modern rule is relatively recent: prior to the Forfeiture Act 1870
the property of convicted felons was forfeited to the Crown. Scots
law has adopted the English rule, without necessarily rejecting the
idea of "personal unworthiness" as a rationale for debarring a
killer from inheriting from his victim.[8]

*(a) The scope of the rule*

To what crimes does the rule apply? The principle has been **2.06**
variously stated. In the classic case of *Cleaver v. Mutual Reserve
Fund Life Association*[9] it was said that "no system of jurisprudence
[will enforce] rights directly resulting to the person asserting them
from the crime of that person." In that case a woman, entitled
under the Married Women's Property Act 1882 to the proceeds of
life assurance taken out by her husband in her favour, murdered
him. She was debarred from taking the proceeds; they thus formed
part of the husband's estate and passed to their children. This
broad rule would not normally cover crimes committed accidentally
or by an insane person.

The rule is usually stated more restrictively. Lord Esher M.R. in **2.07**
*Cleaver* spoke simply of "the person who commits murder". The
problem area is manslaughter or culpable homicide. The courts

---

5 Bankton, Inst., II. 331; Erskine, Inst., IV. iv. 47.
6 (1674) Mor. 3429.
7 Criminal Justice (Scotland) Act 1949, s.15(1).
8 See most recently *Hunter's Exrs, Petrs*, 1992 S.L.T. 1141.
9 [1892] 1 Q.B. 147 at 156, *per* Fry L.J. See also *Re Crippen* [1911] P. 108 at 112.

were quick to exclude the rule where drivers (even if convicted of manslaughter) claimed insurance against death caused by their reckless or careless driving.[10] But in succession cases they preferred to treat manslaughter as an absolute bar to inheritance.[11] So in *Re Giles, Deceased*[12] a woman guilty of her husband's manslaughter on grounds of diminished responsibility could not inherit: "neither the deserving of punishment nor carrying a degree of moral culpability has ever been a necessary ingredient of the crime". As regards the question of moral culpability that is still true, so provocation is disregarded, but the manslaughter test has been redefined. In *Gray v. Barr*[13] the Court of Appeal stressed that the crime "varies infinitely in its seriousness" and in exceptional cases will not debar:

2.08    "The logical test is whether the person seeking the indemnity was guilty of deliberate, intentional and unlawful violence or threats of violence . . . however unintended the final death of the victim may have been."

2.09    This is now the Scottish position. In *Burns v. Secretary of State for Social Services*[14] a woman, provoked by her husband's violence, stabbed him; she pled guilty to culpable homicide. Approving *Gray*, the Inner House held her debarred from claiming a widow's allowance: the stabbing was intentional and the provocation was irrelevant. No reference was made to the only previous Scottish decision, *Smith, Petr*,[15] where *Gray* was not cited and the rule was held to be absolute if there was a conviction for murder or culpable homicide.

2.10    Conviction is not essential, so the rule applies although the killer escapes or commits suicide. The killing must be proved: the standard of proof is less stringent than in criminal law, but "the more serious the allegation, the more cogent is the evidence required to . . . prove it".[16] A conviction raises a presumption of guilt in subsequent civil proceedings, which the killer must rebut[17]; but conversely the court need not accept acquittal as conclusive of innocence.[18]

*(b) The effect of the rule*

2.11    (1) The rule has automatic effect: a court declarator is useful but not essential. It applies, within succession, to intestacy, legal rights, wills, and rights deriving from survivorship (such as special destina-

---

[10] *Tinline v. White Cross Ins. Ass. Ltd.* [1921] 3 K.B. 327. See MacGillivray & Parkington, *Insurance Law* (9th ed.), 14.34 *et seq.*
[11] In the estate of *Hall* [1914] P. 1.
[12] [1972] Ch. 544 at 552.
[13] [1971] 2 Q.B. 554 at 569, approving [1970] 2 Q.B. 626 at 640; not cited in *Giles*.
[14] 1985 S.L.T. 351.
[15] 1979 S.L.T. (Sh. Ct) 35.
[16] *Re Dellow's Will Trusts* [1974] 1 All E.R. 771.
[17] Law Reform (Miscellaneous Provisions) Act 1968, s.22(5).
[18] As in *Gray v. Barr* [1971] 2 Q.B. 554.

tions). It also prevents the killer being appointed executor[19] or taking insurance and social security benefits arising from the death.[20]

(2) The disqualification covers the killer or any person claiming **2.12** through him, such as his executors or beneficiaries if he dies. Others with independent claims are unaffected. So in *Cleaver* the couple's children inherited directly from the murdered husband rather than through his guilty wife. Similarly a third party who takes insurance benefits as an assignee for value, or under a trust, has an independent claim.[21]

(3) Foreign laws generally treat the killer as predeceasing the **2.13** victim[22] so that his claim passes to the person next entitled under the victim's will or intestacy. The position in England is similar. In *Re Callaway*[23] S killed her mother C, her son, and herself; C had left her estate by will to S. The Crown argued that it vested in S and, she being barred from taking, went to the Crown as *bona vacantia* (ownerless property); but it was held that the legacy lapsed and it went to the heir on intestacy, S's brother.

Until recently it was supposed, in the absence of authority, that Scots law also treated the killer as predeceasing the victim. *Hunter's Exrs, Petrs* disapproved that view, on the logic that "such a rule of public policy should be carried no further than is necessary to achieve its object".[24] Clearly in *Hunter* the killer could not take a legacy from the victim (his wife). Her will named alternative legatees in the event of his predeceasing her. The court held that they would not inherit: the destination-over could not operate because there had been no "predecease". Public policy simply required that the killer be ignored: the legacy thus lapsed and passed to the victim's heirs on intestacy.

There may be no necessary conflict with the actual decision in *Callaway*, which was concerned with the Crown's rights and produced the same outcome (intestacy) as in *Hunter*. Given similar facts Scots courts might reach the same result. *Hunter* turned on the words of the will; arguably, given a legacy "to X [killer] whom failing Y" (with no requirements of X's predecease), Y should inherit.

(4) Does the rule prevent the killer inheriting from the victim's **2.14** heir, or apply only to inheritance directly from the victim? South Africa, for instance, debars only if the heir is a close relation.[25] There is no Scots authority.

---

[19] *Re Crippen* [1911] P. 108.
[20] *Burns v. Secretary of State for Social Services*, 1985 S.L.T. 351.
[21] MacGillivray, n.10.
[22] *e.g.* Ireland, Succession Act 1965, s.120(5).
[23] [1956] 2 All E.R. 451.
[24] 1992 S.L.T. 1141 at 1143, *per* L.J.-C. Ross.
[25] *Steenkamp v. Steenkamp*, 1952 (1) S.A. 744 (T).

### (c) Suicide

**2.15**   Can a suicide's estate benefit from his life assurance policy? Two quite distinct issues arise[26]:

**2.16**   (1) The construction of the policy. It may explicitly or impliedly exclude suicide, *e.g.* by requiring accidental death, or cover only insane suicide. Or it may allow only an assignee for value to claim: this was the point in *Ballantyne's Trs v. The Scottish Amicable Life Assurance Society*[27] where the suicide's wife could claim because, in return for his assigning her the policy benefits, she had agreed not to claim divorce for his adultery.

**2.17**   (2) Public policy. This only arises if the assurance policy allows a claim for the suicide. In England suicide was a crime until 1961, and on that basis the personal representatives' claim was struck down in *Beresford v. Royal Insurance Society Ltd*[28]; again an assignee for value could claim. But suicide is no longer a crime, "the principles of public policy on which the courts act change over the generations",[29] and *Beresford* would not now be so decided. It never was a crime in Scotland, so public policy is probably irrelevant: (1) is the only issue.[30]

### (d) Law reform

**2.18**   The Scottish Law Commission favours new rules to replace public policy and the Parricide Act.[31] These would cover murder and culpable homicide; lesser crimes resulting in two or more years' imprisonment would debar from claiming legal rights. Conviction would be essential. The criminal would be treated as predeceasing his victim, but survivorship destinations would be ignored.

### The Forfeiture Act 1982

**2.19**   The Act alleviates the effect of the public policy "forfeiture rule", but not of the Parricide Act:

**2.20**   (1) The Act applies if a person unlawfully kills another: so suicide is excluded. It applies where that person would, but for the forfeiture rule, acquire an interest in property: either by will, legal rights, intestacy, nomination, *mortis causa* donation, special destination, or trust. Analogous regulations cover social security bene-

---

[26] See MacGillivray, n.10, 14.71 *et seq.*
[27] 1921 2 S.L.T. 75.
[28] [1938] A.C. 586.
[29] *Re Giles, Decd.* [1972] Ch. 544 at 552.
[30] On this view Gow, 1958 S.L.T. (News) 142 is outdated. But the question might arise in respect of assisting another's suicide: see (in England) *Dunbar v. Plant* [1998] Ch. 412 (C.A.) where relief was granted under the Forfeiture Act 1982.
[31] Report No. 124, paras 7.1–7.14. See also Chap. 15 below.

fits.[32] The Act applies only to inheritance, so excludes rights to insurance benefits or appointment as the victim's executor (sections 1, 2(3), 2(4), 4).

(2) A court may modify the effect of the forfeiture rule only if **2.21** "satisfied that, having regard to the conduct of the offender and of the deceased and to such other circumstances as appear to the court to be material, the justice of the case requires the effect of the rule to be so modified in that case" (section 2(2)). So the victim's adultery or provocation is relevant.

Apparently the court can modify but not completely exclude the rule. This was doubted in *Re K, Deceased*,[33] was not decided in *Paterson, Petr*[34] but was confirmed in *Cross, Petr*.[35] In recent cases the courts have, depending on the circumstances, allowed the killer to inherit up to 99 per cent of the victim's estate.[36]

(3) Where "a person stands convicted of an offence of which **2.22** unlawful killing is an element" the court may modify the rule only if the case is brought within three months after the conviction. Where he "stands convicted of murder" the rule may never be modified (sections 2(3), 5). These provisions will not apply if the killer dies before he can be convicted; the rule may still be modified to benefit his estate. The Scottish Law Commission tentatively suggests a six month time limit starting from the date when the succession opens to the killer.[37]

### The Conjugal Rights (Scotland) Amendment Act 1861

This creates a type of statutory "unworthiness" for marital **2.23** misconduct. All property acquired by a wife after she obtains a decree of separation *a mensa et thoro* (*i.e.* judicial separation) will pass, if she dies intestate, to her heirs and representatives as if her husband were dead (section 6). If her husband deserts her and she obtains an order to protect property which she acquires by her own industry, that has the effect of a decree of separation (sections 1, 5).[38] If the spouses start living together again the rule ceases to apply.

---

[32] See Ogus & Barendt, *The Law of Social Security* (4th ed., 1995), pp. 408–410; S.I. 1982 No. 1792, S.I. 1984 No. 451, S.I. 1999 No. 1495.

[33] [1985] 2 W.L.R. 262 at 275–276.

[34] 1986 S.L.T. 121; only modification was asked for.

[35] 1987 S.L.T. 384.

[36] *Jackson, Petr*, 1989 G.W.D. 22–947; *Gilchrist, Petr*, 1990 S.L.T. 494.

[37] Report No. 124, paras 7.21–7.27.

[38] See Clive, 14.008.

ADOPTED CHILDREN

**General rules**

**2.24**    Before 1964 adoption had no effect on the adopted child's rights of succession. He retained his rights in respect of his natural parents, and—except by specific provision by will—did not succeed to the adopter's estate.

**2.25**    The Succession (Scotland) Act 1964 reverses the position. In both testate and intestate succession (and also deeds disposing of property *inter vivos*) an adopted person is treated as the child of the adopter and of no one else. So he will not inherit from his natural parents. To avoid doubt, "succession" explicitly includes claims to legal and prior rights (section 23(1)).

**2.26**    This rule does not apply to succession to those dying before September 10, 1964, nor to titles or coats of arms (sections 23(4), 37(1)). Otherwise it is general: it applies for all purposes of succession, not just between parents and issue. But the effect was that the child had no rights at all if the natural parent died after, but the adopter before, September 10, 1964. To remedy this, where the adopter died then and the natural parent died after August 3, 1966, a child is treated as the natural parent's child for purposes of succession to his estate.[39]

**2.27**    Special rules govern the child's relationship with collaterals—brothers, sisters, and their descendants. If adopted by two spouses jointly he is deemed brother of the whole blood to any child or adopted child of them both. Otherwise he is a half-brother: *e.g.* if adopted by one spouse, or by a single parent, or where one spouse had a child by a previous marriage (section 24(1)). In determining seniority between children, the child is deemed born on the day of adoption, or (purely as between children adopted on one day) on the true date of birth (section 24A).

**2.28**    If a child is adopted more than once, only the last adoption is relevant for succession after that date (section 24(3)). Where adoption is revoked—as may occur if an illegitimate child's parents adopt it but later legitimise it by marrying—the revocation does not affect existing rights of succession.[40]

**Deeds**

**2.29**    The above rules apply to deeds executed after September 10, 1964. In addition section 23(2) contains special provisions.

**2.30**    (1) If a deed is executed after an adoption order, references in it to the adopter's child include the adopted person, references to the

---

[39] Law Reform (Miscellaneous Provisions) (Scotland) Act 1966, s.5.
[40] Legitimation (Scotland) Act 1968, s.6(2).

natural parents' child exclude him, and references to persons related to the child are construed as if he is the adopter's child "unless the contrary intention appears".

(2) Whatever the actual date of execution (provided it is after **2.31** September 10, 1964), where a provision is effective on a person's death then the deed is deemed executed on that date. So adoptions in the intervening period after actual execution are covered. Note that that date may, paradoxically, be after the testator's death: *e.g.* A's legacy to "B's children if they survive B" includes B's adopted children.

(3) References may be express or implied. This will cover the **2.32** rules of accretion and the *conditio si institutus*, or references to "parents".

The meaning of section 23(2) and its relationship to the general rule (section 23(1)) have caused debate.[41] In particular, what is the effect of A's legacy to "my child B, failing whom B's issue"? "Issue" are descendants: is A's adopted grandchild included? On one view he is not: section 23(2) governs wills (but not intestacy); "issue" ordinarily includes only biological relations, and its use in a will displays a "contrary intention" to exclude the Act. Such a view, if correct, frustrates the purpose of the Act, and it has been cogently argued that "issue" impliedly covers adopted children and that "contrary intention" requires a positive exclusion of the Act. The Scottish Law Commission's proposals will clarify the problem by inserting a new section 39A in the Adoption (Scotland) Act 1978.[42] In the meantime however the Law Society of Scotland feels that in view of the doubt on the point a will should ideally make explicit reference to adopted grandchildren.

## ILLEGITIMATE CHILDREN[43]

### Introduction

The trend in the past century has been towards the elimination **2.33** of discrimination against illegitimate children. In a wider context this has been encouraged by the European Convention on Human Rights.[44] Until 1986 reform was piecemeal; even now the concept has not been abolished, and the old law is still relevant.

---

[41] *e.g.* (1965) 10 J.L.S. 95; (1969) 14 J.L.S. 204; (1979–81) J.L.S. (Workshop) lxxv, 159, 182.

[42] Report No. 124, paras 9.1–9.2. For a recent case on the interpretation of s.23(2) see *Salvesen's Trs, Petrs*, 1992 S.C.L.R. 729, 1993 S.L.T. 1327.

[43] See generally Scot. Law Com. Report No. 82 (1984).

[44] Articles 8 and 14. See *Marckz v. Kingdom of Belgium* (1979–80) 2 E.H.R.R. 330.

**Intestate succession**

**2.34** At common law an illegitimate child was *filius nullius*; a stranger in blood to both his parents, with no right to inherit from anyone.[45] In 1926 mother and child were allowed to inherit from each other if either died intestate with no legitimate issue.[46]

**2.35** The Law Reform (Miscellaneous Provisions) (Scotland) Act 1968 gave child and parents reciprocal rights to inherit. He could claim legitim[47]; his issue could represent him if he died.[48] But the rights went no further: they did not extend to other relations (such as brothers); the child, not being "lawful issue", could not himself represent a predeceasing parent. If the child died it was presumed (rebuttably) that his father did not survive him. Furthermore, a deceased's executors were (and still are) protected from liability if they distribute his estate without checking that he left no illegitimate children (section 7).

**2.36** The Law Reform (Parent and Child) (Scotland) Act 1986 virtually abolishes the effects of illegitimacy. "The fact that a person's parents are not or have not been married to one another shall be left out of account in establishing the legal relationship between the person and any other person" (section 1(1)). The child can now inherit from anyone as if legitimate. But:

**2.37** (1) The Act will not apply to succession to titles and honours (section 9(c)), or to deaths, before December 8, 1986. It only affects previous Acts if it explicitly repeals or amends them; the Succession (Scotland) Act 1964, among others, is amended to delete references to illegitimacy[49] (Schedules 1, 2).

**2.38** (2) The presumption of non-survivance by the child's father is abolished; the executors' protection is extended to cover all undiscovered paternal relatives of the child (Schedule 1, paragraph 10).

**Testate succession**

**2.39** At common law the child could, in effect, only inherit by will if expressly named: it was strongly presumed that descriptive terms such as "children" included only legitimate people.[50] By the Law Reform Act of 1968, in construing a deed executed after November 25, 1968 to determine who is entitled to benefit under a provision in it, both legitimate and illegitimate relationships are included

---

[45] Erskine, Inst., III. x. 8; *Clarke v. Carfin Coal Co.* (1891) 18 R. (H.L.) 63.
[46] Legitimacy Act; extended to heritage by Succession (Scotland) Act 1964.
[47] *i.e.* legal rights; see paras 4.34 *et seq.*
[48] *i.e.* if he would have inherited from someone had he survived, they would inherit in his place. See paras 4.70 *et seq.*
[49] In particular ss.4 and 10A are completely deleted.
[50] *e.g. Mitchell's Trs v. Cables* (1893) 1 S.L.T. 156.

"unless the contrary intention appears" (section 5). The provision extends to inheritance under the *conditio si testator*, the *conditio si institutus*, and accretion,[51] but not to titles or honours or to interpretation of statutes.

Under the 1986 Act illegitimacy is irrelevant in construing deeds **2.40** (section 1(2)). This is wider than the 1968 Act: it is not confined to inheritance and will, say, cover entitlement to be appointed executor. But it does not apply to deeds executed before December 8, 1986 (which the common law or 1968 Act still govern), nor to later deeds which make reference to illegitimacy. So a testator may still exclude illegitimate children from his will. They may always claim legitim, which no will can defeat.[52]

The concept of illegitimacy has not stayed static over time. Its **2.41** definition has altered. There may be a question as to when to judge a legatee's legitimacy: when the will was made, the testator dies, or (if later) the legatee potentially inherits? The problem is discussed later.[53]

### SPECIAL TYPES OF PROPERTY

### General

Special rules of law restrict the ability to inherit certain classes of **2.42** property. This has nothing to do with concepts of unworthiness, but reflects the idea that the rights in question are in some way personal to the deceased and, if transmissible at all, should normally pass only to members of his immediate family. The details are beyond the scope of this work.

### Transmissibility of obligations

*Delict*

Where someone suffers injury to himself or his belongings, he **2.43** may—depending on the nature of his loss—claim compensation for two reasons: for *patrimonial loss* (*i.e.* financial, by damage to earning capacity or property) and *solatium* (pain and suffering). Claims for patrimonial loss pass without restriction on his death, by will or intestacy as appropriate. Claims for solatium, until recently, lapsed with his death; now, however, they too are transmissible. There are two restrictions: first, that both types of claim can cover only loss incurred in the period between injury and death; secondly, that (in actions for defamation) claims for solatium lapse with death unless the deceased had already raised a court action.[54]

---

[51] See paras 7.32 *et seq.*, and 10.50 *et seq.* respectively.
[52] See paras 4.34 *et seq.*, 9.01 *et seq.*
[53] See paras 10.18–10.21.
[54] Damages (Scotland) Act 1976, s.2 amended by Damages (Scotland) Act 1993, s.3. See Stewart, *Delict* (3rd ed., 1998), paras 11.23–11.30; Maguire, "The Damages (Scotland) Act 1993", 1993 S.L.T. (News) 245.

*Contract*

**2.44**     Whether contractual rights and obligations lapse on the death of one of the parties, or transmit to his beneficiaries, depends largely on whether (first) the contract makes express provision for the event, and (secondly) whether there is *delectus personae* (that is, the contract is treated in law as peculiarly personal to the deceased). A contract of employment, for instance, will lapse if the employee dies.[55]

**Leases**

**2.45**     A lease passes to the deceased's executor along with the rest of his estate. Who can inherit then depends on whether the terms of the lease prohibit its transfer.[56]

*Intestacy*

**2.46**     An express prohibition (which is usual) bars transfer except with the landlord's consent. If there is only an implied prohibition, or no prohibition at all, the executor can transfer to the person entitled to inherit on intestacy.

*Bequests of leases*

**2.47**     The landlord's consent to transfer is required only if the lease contains an express prohibition on transfer.

*Special types of lease[57]*

**2.48**     For agricultural and residential leases, close relatives of the deceased have statutorily-defined rights of inheritance. In an agricultural lease, this permits bequest to a relation who would potentially be entitled to inherit if the tenant died intestate; but the landlord can object to the legatee, and if the Land Court uphold the objection the lease will end. For residential leases the right is usually restricted to the surviving spouse.

**Further reading**

B. Davis, "Ex Maleficio non Oritur Actio?", 1969 S.L.T. (News) 49.

---

[55] See McBryde, *The Law of Contract in Scotland* (1987), Chap. 24. In *Lady Taylor v. Brunton*, 1998 S.L.T. (Sh. Ct) 72 a deceased husband's agreement to let someone continue living in his house was enforceable against his widow. For problems of proof see 5.51 below.

[56] See McAllister, *Scottish Law of Leases* (2nd ed., 1995), p. 87; Meston, pp. 95, 109–113; Succession (Scotland) Act 1964, ss.16, 29.

[57] Agricultural Holdings (Scotland) Act 1991, ss.11–12; Housing (Scotland) Act 1988, s.31; Housing (Scotland) Act 1987, s.52. See McAllister, n. 56, pp. 191–197, 239–240, 252–253; Gill, *Law of Agricultural Holdings in Scotland* (1990), Chaps 33–34.

J.A.M. Inglis, "Succession and Special Destinations" (1986) 31 J.L.S. 151.

A.J. McDonald, "Adopted Persons" (1965) 10 J.L.S. 95.

"Issue and Adopted Children" (1979—81) J.L.S. (Workshop) lxxv, 159, 165, 172, 182, 191, 206.

M.C. Meston, "Bastards in the Law of Succession", 1966 S.L.T. (News) 197.

M.C. Meston, "Illegitimacy in Succession" (1986) 31 J.L.S. 358.

"Succession and Public Policy" (1986) 31 J.L.S. 246.

M.C. Meston, *The Succession (Scotland) Act 1964* (4th ed., 1993), Chap. 7.

# CHAPTER 3

# PAYMENT OF DEBTS

## Introduction

**3.01**     A deceased person's debts do not die with him. His estate remains liable for them after it passes into the hands of his executor.[1] This is the principle of "passive representation". If he objects to that liability he may of course simply decline to be executor. He is liable for all the deceased's debts if he deals with the estate without obtaining confirmation of his title—"vitious intromission"—but provided he has confirmation his liability is limited to the value of the estate confirmed to.

**3.02**     On the same principle beneficiaries are liable, up to the value of their inheritance, for debts unpaid by the executor. Such liability is in fact rare: creditors cannot sue beneficiaries if the executor had sufficient funds when the estate was distributed and yet they failed to claim from him. *Menzies v. Poutz*[2] illustrates the effect of the rule where it applies: a widow was sequestrated four years after getting confirmation to her husband's estate; it then transpired he had also been bankrupt; his creditors had a preferential claim in her bankruptcy.

**3.03**     So the executor, after gathering in the deceased's property, must pay all known debts before anything—even income—goes to beneficiaries.[3] It is unnecessary (though common) to stipulate this by will. He should, by advertisement if necessary, take steps to ascertain all debts due; he may, but need not, require creditors formally to constitute debts by court decree. Having paid out all known debts he may, a year at most after the death, start paying beneficiaries.

**3.04**     If the executor knows or should know that the estate is absolutely insolvent, and is likely to remain so, he must within a

---

[1] See McLaren on *Wills*, Vol. II, pp. 1280 *et seq.* and 1301; Wilson & Duncan, paras 34.01–34.27.

[2] 1916 S.C. 143.

[3] *Heritable Securities Investment Association Ltd v. Miller's Trs* (1892) 20 R. 675.

reasonable time take steps to have a judicial factor or trustee in bankruptcy appointed. Otherwise any dealing with the estate constitutes vitious intromission and he may be liable for all the deceased's debts.[4]

## Time of payment

Before modern bankruptcy law emerged, creditors could enforce **3.05** payment on the principle "first come, first served". Slower creditors might find the debtor's property already exhausted. The trend in modern times has been to put creditors on a more equal footing. In line with that, since 1662[5] debts intimated to the executor within six months after death ordinarily rank equally: they have equal priority. He cannot be compelled to pay within that period; if he does so he is personally liable to other creditors if the estate turns out to be insufficient to pay them as well. After the six months he may if satisfied the estate is solvent pay creditors in order as they claim, and he is not personally liable to later claimants if he has paid out all the assets in good faith to earlier ones.

Conversely, certain "privileged debts" may be paid within the six **3.06** months even if other creditors cannot be paid in full. This is because those debts have a preference if the estate is declared bankrupt. The category was developed by the courts, but should now be read subject to the modern statutory rules of bankruptcy; some of the older examples are obsolete.

## Order of payment[6]

Debts must be paid in the following order. Each class of debt **3.07** must be paid in full before the next class. Within each class debts rank *pari passu* (equally),[7] so the same proportion is paid of each if they cannot all be paid in full.

### (a) Expenses of sequestration

If the estate is bankrupt, the outlays and remuneration of the **3.08** interim trustee and the permanent trustee (in that order) must be paid first.[8]

### (b) Deathbed and funeral expenses

These are privileged debts[9] and are payable ahead of all others, **3.09** even debts secured over the deceased's general property.[10]

---

[4] Bankruptcy (Scotland) Act 1985, s.8(4). See McBryde, *Bankruptcy*, pp. 32–33, 41 and 236–238.

[5] Act of Sederunt, February 28, 1662.

[6] See McBryde, *Bankruptcy*, pp. 205 *et seq.*; Wilson, *Debt*, paras 23.11, 29.4 *et seq.*

[7] *e.g. Peter v. Monro* (1749) Mor. 11852 (funeral expenses).

[8] Bankruptcy (Scotland) Act 1985, ss.51(1)(a), (b).

[9] *Sheddan v. Gibson* (1802) Mor. 11855.

[10] *Rowan v. Barr* (1742) Mor. 11852 (Landlord's hypothec); *Drysdale v. Kennedy* (1835) 14 S. 159.

**3.10** "Deathbed" covers medical expenses of the deceased's last illness, such as medicines and doctors' fees.[11] Funeral expenses include cremation.[12] Mourning clothes for the widow are also a privileged debt, which is not discharged by the widow accepting a provision by will "in satisfaction of all claims"[13]; no cases refer to widowers, but mourning debts are in any event now rare and the Scottish Law Commission favours their abolition.[14]

**3.11** The expenses must be reasonably incurred. In old cases, now outdated, the test was suitability to the deceased's social rank; but simple extravagance should still disallow the debt. Take *Glass v. Weir* where, out of a £300 estate, £8 was spent on spirits for a four-day drinking spree: the court cut this to a more sober £3.[15] The position of a gravestone is unclear. One old case suggests that it is a funeral expense if reasonably incurred.[16] The cost is now deductible for purposes of inheritance tax.[17] It is also (if reasonable) a claimable funeral expense in calculating a claim for reparation by a relation of a deceased injury victim.[18] It is best to make specific provision by will, and essential if trustees are to make ongoing payments for its upkeep.

**3.12** Reasonably incurred costs of obtaining confirmation and of executry administration rank along with funeral expenses.[19]

*(c) Secured debts*

**3.13** A creditor holding a security over the deceased's property can enforce it at any time. He can of course sue for the balance of his debt, ranking according to the normal rules as privileged, preferred, or ordinary according to its nature.

*(d) Preferred debts*

**3.14** Some of these were classed as privileged at common law. Various statutory preferences—such as assessed taxes and rates—were abolished by the Bankruptcy (Scotland) Act 1985. Two main types now exist[20]:

**3.15** (1) Taxes and social security contributions due in respect of specified periods: *e.g.* PAYE, VAT, car tax, and betting duty. In

---

[11] *Sanders v. Hewat* (1822) 1 S. 333 (new ed. 370).
[12] Cremation Act 1902.
[13] *Griffiths' Trs v. Griffiths*, 1912 S.C. 626.
[14] Report No. 124, para. 9.3.
[15] (1821) 1 S. 163 (new ed. 156). See now Bankruptcy (Scotland) Act 1985, s.51(1)(c).
[16] *Moncrieff v. Monypenny* (1713) Mor. 3945: the point was not directly decided.
[17] Inland Revenue Statement of Practice 7/87.
[18] Damages (Scotland) Act 1976, s.1(3); *Prentice v. Chalmers*, 1985 S.L.T. 168.
[19] Bankruptcy (Scotland) Act 1985, s.51(1)(c).
[20] Bankruptcy (Scotland) Act 1985, Sched. 3; S.I. 1986 No 1914. As regards payment within the six months, see Wilson & Duncan, 34.08–34.10.

most cases the period is 12 months immediately before death; the Inland Revenue can no longer—as before—pick the year most advantageous to it.

(2) Employees' wages for four months before the employer's **3.16** death, up to a maximum of £800; or money advanced (by, say, a bank) to pay wages and actually used for that purpose.

### (e) Ordinary debts

There are innumerable types: debts arising from delict, restitu- **3.17** tion, or contract. Expenses relating to the birth of the deceased's posthumous child form one rare example.

A spouse or child may be able to claim aliment as a debt from **3.18** the estate. This has three distinct aspects:

(1) Temporary aliment after the death of the father or husband, **3.19** or (probably) the wife.[21] This is strictly speaking not a privileged debt, and has no preference over ordinary creditors; but if the estate is not manifestly insolvent the executor may pay reasonable aliment within the six months without having to reimburse creditors if it later turns out insolvent.[22] The purpose is to provide support till the estate can be distributed: so it lasts for six months after the relative's death[23] and is due irrespective of the value of any legacies or inheritances. One may lose one's entitlement if one has clearly renounced it, or if one is otherwise well provided for during that period.

(2) Continuing aliment rests on a general principle that "in every **3.20** case the representatives of a person deceased . . . are, out of [their] succession, liable in aliment to those whom the deceased himself was under a natural obligation to maintain".[24] Though it is sometimes termed a debt (and so has priority over legal rights[25]) it is payable after ordinary debts and—unlike them—cannot delay payment of legacies. The claim is primarily against beneficiaries to the extent that they are enriched by inheritance, and only against the executors while the estate is still in their hands. It is equitable: it lasts for as long as one needs support, but fails if one expressly renounces one's rights or receives a fair and adequate share of the deceased's estate.

The Scottish Law Commission considers whether the concept should be abolished, but makes no recommendations.[26]

(3) These claims are a continuation of the deceased's obligation **3.21** to aliment his family. But if the estate is bankrupt unpaid aliment

---

[21] Married Women's Property (Scotland) Act 1920, s.4.
[22] *Barlass v. Barlass's Trs*, 1916 S.C. 741.
[23] Or, in older law, till the next term day of Whitsunday or Martinmas.
[24] Erskine, Inst. (3rd ed.), I.vi.58 (note by Lord Ivory). Nearly all cases involve widows or children.
[25] *Anderson v. Grant* (1899) 1 F. 484.
[26] Report No. 124, paras 9.4–9.10. For the current law see Clive 30.010 *et seq.*

cannot be claimed unless it is quantified by court decree or by a legally binding obligation evidenced in writing, and—in cases involving spouses—they were divorced or living apart.[27]

INCIDENCE OF DEBTS

### General

**3.22**    A creditor may demand payment of his debt from any part of the estate, whether heritable or moveable. But the type of debt determines which part of the estate must ultimately bear liability for it. The part which pays the creditor will be repaid so far as possible from the part primarily liable.

**3.23**    Before 1964 this involved reimbursement between those to whom the deceased's property passed: the executor (moveables) and (for heritage) the heir at law or heir of provision. Under the Succession (Scotland) Act 1964 the property now goes to the executor,[28] but the old rules governing incidence of debts were expressly preserved.[29] They now have two purposes. They allocate a debt to heritage or moveables: this is important in calculating the moveable estate available for legal rights. Secondly, a debt may be payable out of a specific item (and thus the beneficiary taking the item bears the cost) or out of the residue of the general estate.

### Heritable and moveable debts

**3.24**    The basic principle is that "the personal estate is the primary fund for the payment of unsecured obligations, as the real [heritable] estate is for the payment of obligations secured on heritage or attached to it".[30] Moveable debts are paid out of moveables, heritable out of heritage. So heritable debts reduce the assets available for some prior rights, and moveable debts those available for legal rights.[31]

**3.25**    Ordinary debts arising from delict or contract are moveable. This includes the unpaid price of heritage under a contract of sale (conversely, a house is a heritable asset of the estate even though a real right has not yet been obtained by registration). Arrears of feu duties and rent, and obligations of warrandice in respect of land, are moveable. The rationale is that they are all normally paid out of cash funds.

**3.26**    A debt is heritable if declared a real burden or if secured over heritage. A standard security over a house (a mortgage) is the

---

[27] Bankruptcy (Scotland) Act 1985, Sched. 1, para. 2(1).

[28] With exceptions, like property subject to special destinations.

[29] 1964 Act, s.14(3).

[30] McLaren. Vol. II, p. 1305.

[31] For prior rights see paras 4.19 *et seq.*, for legal rights paras 4.34 *et seq.*

obvious example: it will reduce the surviving spouse's prior right in the house.[32] Restitutionary obligations to recompense someone for improvements to land are also heritable, as are "rights having a future tract of time" such as annuities.

Complications arise if two securities exist for one debt—one **3.27** being moveable (such as a life assurance policy) and one heritable (a standard security). The debt must be deducted from moveables and heritage in proportion to the two securities' respective values. Similarly, if there are two borrowers (typically a couple buying their house as co-owners) each is liable for half the debt. Now in practice the life policy provides the cash to pay off the whole debt: whereas, as we have seen, for succession purposes only a proportion of the debt should be set against the policy. To adjust matters, the rest of the debt should, as appropriate, be deducted from the heritage or recovered from the other borrower.[32a]

Where a debt is secured over a particular asset—heritable or **3.28** moveable—whoever inherits the asset takes *cum onere* (subject to the debt). He must pay the debt if he wants the asset. Take *Stewart v. Stewart*[33]: an insurance policy had been assigned to a bank in security for a loan; the legatee only took the policy after repayment of the loan. The same goes for a loan secured over a house: even if an insurance policy provides funds to pay it off (as is common) the legatee must in principle reimburse the estate.[34]

**Provisions in wills**

A well-drafted will may specify what assets debts should be paid **3.29** out of. It may thus alter the normal rules of incidence, by (say) passing certain items to beneficiaries "free of debts" or instructing that debts be paid out of the residue or some other part of the estate. The courts have evolved various rules to decide the effect of such provisions. The question is to ascertain the testator's intention as expressed in the will: the mere fact that executors for convenience pay debts out of particular assets will not itself alter their ultimate incidence.

(1) There must be express words or clear implication: **3.30**

"The heritable and the moveable succession must respectively bear the debts and burdens appropriate to each, unless the testator in his settlement gives express directions to the

---

[32] As defined in Succession (Scotland) Act 1964, s.8(6)(d).
[32a] There may however be evidence that the deceased intended the policy to bear the whole debt and pay off the other borrower's share: *Christie's Exr v. Armstrong*, 1996 S.L.T. 948.
[33] (1891) 19 R. 310.
[34] For the effect of mortgages and insurance policies see Gretton (1987) 32 J.L.S. 303, (1988) 33 J.L.S. 141; Dalgleish (1987) 32 J.L.S. 423.

contrary, or gives directions with reference to the disposal of his means and estate which by clear and necessary implication plainly shew that a particular . . . debt is to be paid out of that part of his succession upon which it would not fall but for these directions."[35]

Several of the reported cases concern annuities, which under normal rules are paid out of heritage. In *Breadalbane's Trs v. Duke of Buckingham*[36]—one of a string of cases which helped impoverish the vast Breadalbane estates—trustees were to pay the "whole free proceeds" of certain lands; those lands were unaffected by the annuity, which thus was a burden on the other heritage. But one may, as in *Gordon v. Scott*,[37] implicitly or expressly instruct annuities to be paid out of the residue of the moveable estate.

**3.31**  (2) If the will expressly states that debts are to be paid out of a particular asset, the rest of the estate is freed of liability. The legatee to whom the asset goes must pay the debt. If a will directs debts to be paid from the residue of the estate, the other assets bear the burden only to the extent that the residue is insufficient for full payment.

**3.32**  (3) Wills frequently contain a general direction to executors to "pay all my just and lawful debts". That by itself does not alter their ordinary incidence: it merely makes explicit the executors' legal duty. So where a debt is secured over heritable assets which are left in a legacy, the direction does not free the legatee of liability to pay. The same rule governs moveables, but has been doubted.[38] More is required in order to transfer liability to the general estate: "express directions are not essential, but the inference must be irresistible and the intention clear beyond all doubt".[39]

### Inheritance tax

**3.33**  Inheritance tax is a debt of the estate. It is chargeable on the value of the deceased's estate immediately before his death after deducting his debts and funeral expenses. Executor and beneficiaries are both liable to account for the tax attributable to the estate (respectively) confirmed to or inherited; the executor is liable first because he must account to the Capital Taxes Office for the tax before he can obtain confirmation, normally doing both along with

---

[35] *Gordon v. Scott* (1873) 11 M. 334 at 337, *per* Lord Kincairney.

[36] (1842) 4 D. 1259.

[37] n. 35. Contrast *Smith's Trs v. Smith*, 1912 1 S.L.T. 484 where the heritable estate bore the burden.

[38] By Lord Dunedin in *Reid's Trs v. Dawson*, 1915 S.C. (H.L.) 47 at 50; *cf. Stewart v. Stewart* (1891) 19 R. 310. See also *Brand v. Scott's Trs* (1892) 19 R. 768.

[39] *Muir's Trs v. Muir*, 1916 1 S.L.T. 372.

the standard Form C1 inventory. A will cannot alter the rules of accountability. The incidence of inheritance tax on particular assets is a separate issue: that can be altered by will.

Subject to any contrary intention shown in the deceased's will, **3.34** inheritance tax attributable to the deceased's United Kingdom property which vests in his executors (excluding trust property) is a testamentary expense. Thus it will normally fall on the residue of his estate. Where it is not a testamentary expense it must "where occasion requires" be repaid to the executor by the beneficiary who takes the assets to which the tax is attributable.[40]

These rules do not distinguish between heritable and moveable **3.35** property. It was originally thought that specific legacies of heritage—but not moveables—bore their own tax, so that the legatee must reimburse the executor for the pro rata share of tax attributable to that asset. That had been the rule for estate duty. But it was decided in *Cowie's Trustees, Petrs*[41] that inheritance tax falls on the general estate rather than the specific asset: only if the testator by will says otherwise must the legatee bear the tax.

The testator may expressly leave a legacy "free of tax". Tax must **3.36** of course be paid in respect of it (unless it is exempt, such as a gift to a spouse) but it is paid not by the beneficiary but by the executor out of the residue. Special rules dictate how the appropriate amount of tax is calculated.[42] A share of the residue may be left "free of tax", but not the whole residue—as there then would be nothing to pay tax from. "Free of tax" provisions are interpreted as referring to tax payable only in respect of the testator's own death, and not future tax charges (*e.g.* on a liferenter's death).

### Special destinations

A special destination is a provision in a property title stating who **3.37** takes it on an owner's death. In the usual survivorship destination (property owned in the names of "A and B and the survivor") a deceased's share passes automatically to the survivor when he dies; it does not vest in the executor. Under other special destinations the deceased's share vests in the executor purely to enable it to be conveyed to the person entitled under the destination.[43] Because (unlike other assets) the property does not vest in the executor for the purpose of paying the deceased owner's debts, it was decided in *Barclays Bank Ltd v. McGreish*[44] that the successor takes it free of debts: therefore the creditor cannot sue him.

The decision was heavily criticised.[45] It is irrelevant whether the **3.38** property passes via the executor: it is part of the deceased's estate

---

[40] IHTA 1984, s.200 (accountability), s.211 (incidence).
[41] 1982 S.L.T. 326; *sub nom. In Re Dougal* [1981] S.T.C. 514.
[42] See Capital Taxes Encyclopaedia, paras B 6.01–B 6.21.
[43] Succession (Scotland) Act 1964, s.18(2).
[44] 1983 S.L.T. 344.
[45] *e.g.* Morton, 1984 S.L.T. (News) 133, Gretton, 1984 S.L.T. (News) 299.

albeit it devolves automatically rather than by will. The successor is an "heir of provision" and—just as before 1964—creditors should be able to sue him to the value of his inheritance. That reasoning was adopted, and *McGreish* overruled, in *Fleming's Tr. v Fleming*.[46]

**Further reading**

Elder, *Forms of Wills* (1947), pp. 20–21, 46–47, 56–57.
McLaren, Vol. I, pp. 126–129, Vol. 11, pp. 1280–1329.
Meston, Chap. 3, *passim*.
Special Destinations: see 1984 S.L.T. (News) 133, 180, 299; (1984) 29 J.L.S. 154.

---

[46] 2000 S.L.T. 406

# CHAPTER 4

# INTESTATE SUCCESSION

## BACKGROUND

A person dies intestate if he does not dispose of his property by **4.01** will. In any society the rules of intestate succession are of great importance. They may govern the bulk of deaths—perhaps two thirds of Scots people die intestate. They may, depending how equitable they are, influence whether people make wills or not. Furthermore they embody broad principles as to how a society considers property should be disposed of on death. It might, for instance, revert to the state; it might go to the deceased's dependants. It may or may not be permissible to opt out of these rules entirely and make a will disposing of one's property in a different way. The modern Scots law is contained in the Succession (Scotland) Act 1964, which radically altered the old rules. But the Act is not a comprehensive code, and one important aspect of intestate succession—the protected "legal rights" of spouse and children—derives not from it but from the old common law.

The pre-1964 law had two striking features. **4.02**

(1) *Heritable and moveable property.* Different rules governed **4.03** their disposal. Moveables passed to the executor for distribution to the beneficiaries; heritage passed directly to the person entitled to succeed, the heir-at-law. In each case the order of succession was, broadly: descendants; if none, collaterals (such as brothers); if none, paternal ascendants (father, grandfather, and so on).[1] Inheritance depended on blood relationship: except in legal rights—discussed below—the spouse was traditionally excluded. If no blood relation existed, the Crown succeeded as *ultimus haeres*.[2]

Beyond that there were two main differences, due to the rules **4.04** for heritage deriving from feudal society: their rationale was to transfer the property undivided to a male heir. First, heritage involved primogeniture: the oldest male heir took everything.

---

[1] This greatly over-simplifies the scheme. See Currie (7th ed., 1973), p. 102.
[2] *i.e.* literally "last heir".

Moveables were divided equally among a class of people: *e.g.* children. Second, and more important today, was "representation". If an heir died before the intestate person, his own heirs "represented" him: they stood in his shoes and inherited in his place. Representation of all heirs was infinite in the case of heritage: a great-grandchild, say, could take under it. Representation was more limited for moveables, and non-existent for legal rights.

**4.05**    (2) *Legal rights*. Scots law recognised various protected rights of inheritance known as "legal rights". Those affecting heritage gave a surviving spouse income arising from the property: these were "terce" (for the widow) and "courtesy" (for the widower). They were abolished in 1964. Those affecting moveables, *jus relictae* (for the widow), *jus relicti* (for widower) and legitim (for children), are discussed later in this chapter.

Reform was long overdue. In 1911 the surviving spouse was given a limited protected right to inherit, over and above legal rights. The proposals of the Mackintosh Committee in 1950 led ultimately to the Succession (Scotland) Act 1964.

THE SCOPE OF THE ACT

**General policy**

**4.06**    The Act sets out to improve the position of the surviving spouse: it gives her *prior rights* to the intestate estate.[3] It preserves the stress on blood relationship, but extends that to relations on the mother's side. As amended, it now gives adopted and illegitimate children virtually the same rights as others. Finally, it applies the same legal machinery to heritage and moveables—both normally pass through the executor—and gives much the same rights to inherit, with one unfortunate exception: legal rights only apply to moveables.[4]

**4.07**    The Act is not retrospective, and applies to deaths on or after September 10, 1964. It does not apply to titles, coats of arms, and honours; these remain governed by the old law. Until 1968 it did not apply to crofting tenancies.[5]

**Intestate estate**

**4.08**    Three definitions should be borne in mind.

**4.09**    (1) The "estate" is "the whole estate, whether heritable or moveable . . . [or both] belonging to the deceased at the time of his death or over which [he] had a power of appointment . . . [and] the

---

[3] For fuller discussion see below at paras 4.19 *et seq.*
[4] s.1. See Chap. 2, above; Chap. 13, below.
[5] ss.37(1)(a), (d), (e), 37(2).

interest of a tenant under a tenancy which was not expressed to expire on his death". Special rules govern powers of appointment and special destinations.[6]

(2) One dies intestate by "leaving undisposed of by testamentary **4.10** disposition the whole or any part of" one's estate, and the "intestate estate" is initially that undisposed-of part.[7]

(3) A testamentary disposition includes any deed taking effect on **4.11** the intestate's death "whereby any part of his estate is disposed of or under which a succession thereto arises".[8]

The effect, taking the rules together, is as follows. **4.11a**

(i) The Act applies to partial intestacy, where a will (intentionally or not) validly disposes of only part of the estate. It ignores the part which is left by will, except that the cash prior right is set off against legacies. But one can claim legal rights out of testate and intestate estate quite independently of the Act: a will cannot defeat them.

(ii) A special destination is a clause in the title to property, such as a house, governing its passage on death. If the clause deals with the event of the intestate's death, this is not "intestate estate"— whoever put the clause in the title. The reason is that "disposal" is not restricted to actions by the intestate person: it covers instructions made by earlier owners. All this assumes the destination had not been evacuated, *i.e.* revoked: if it had, it passes on death according to the ordinary rules of succession.

(iii) A power of appointment is a provision in a will authorising someone else, the donee of the power, to dispose of one's own property in a certain way. In effect one to some extent delegates one's will-making power. If on the donee's death the power is unexercised and passes to someone else, then (in the case of heritage) the property falls outwith the donee's estate. Otherwise it falls under his estate, but is not intestate estate.

(iv) A *mortis causa* lifetime gift,[9] though not a will, is a testamentary disposition for the purposes of the Act.

### Artificial intestacy

Intestacy can come about after the deceased's death even though **4.12** he left a will. That may happen by accident or deliberately.

A legacy may be ineffective for some reason. It may be so **4.13** imprecise that the beneficiary cannot be identified: it then lapses for uncertainty. It may be contrary to public policy. The legatee may have died. The will should ideally say what is to happen to the

---

[6] s.36(2).
[7] s.36(1).
[8] s.36(1).
[9] See paras 5.33 *et seq.*

item on that event. Normally it makes specific provision for disposal of the "residue", the remainder of the estate after payment of debts and legacies: the item should then fall into the residue. But if it does not—there is no residue clause—the item is undisposed of by the will. It then falls into intestacy and the rules in the 1964 Act apply.

**4.14**    Similarly the legacy may be intrinsically valid but lapse because the legatee does not take it. He may simply disclaim it. If he claims legal rights he cannot take a benefit under the will: he must choose between them. That is "approbate and reprobate".[10] Again in each case intestacy results if the will names no one else to inherit on that event.

**4.15**    The odd effect is shown in *Kerr, Petr*.[11] A widow was left all her husband's fairly small estate; there was no other provision in the will. She would have been better off under intestacy. The reason was that if she took under the will, she could not claim prior rights (it not being intestate estate) or legal rights (approbate and reprobate forbade her) but her children could claim legal rights (as indefeasible by will): so she would not in fact get the whole estate. If she took under intestacy, she could claim prior rights; those have preference over legal rights and in her case would use up the whole estate. So a will cannot defeat legal rights, but intestacy can to the extent of prior rights. She disclaimed her benefit under the will, got prior rights, and took the whole estate; the children got nothing.

**4.16**    *Kerr* will not always be useful. The size of prior rights depends on the types of assets in the estate—house, furniture, and cash. If the estate is large, there is a surplus over prior rights and there may be no cash benefit in disclaiming the will. If the will contains a residue clause, or a "destination-over" whereby someone else inherits if the widow disclaims, there is no intestacy.

**4.17**    One course, under current law, is to make a simple will as in *Kerr*. The widow can decide herself in due course whether she is best taking the legacy or prior rights.[12]

### Order of dividing the estate[13]

**4.18**    As a result of the Act there are six stages in distributing an intestate person's estate. They must be carried out in a set order. Because some rights are exigible from heritage and others from moveables, the deceased's heritage and moveables must be quantified separately until after stage (e):

---

[10] See paras 9.08 *et seq.*
[11] 1968 S.L.T. (Sh. Ct) 61.
[12] For such post-death rearrangements and their tax effects see paras 5.54 *et seq.*
[13] For examples see Meston, app. 2; Hastings, *Expenses*, app. 3.

(a) Payment of debts;

(b) Prior rights: right to dwelling-house (section 8(1));

(c) Prior rights: furniture and plenishings (section 8(3));

(d) Prior rights: right to cash (section 9);

(e) Legal rights;

(f) Free estate (section 2).

## PRIOR RIGHTS[14]

Prior rights are an innovation of the Act, though under the **4.19** Intestate Husband's Estate (Scotland) Acts 1911 to 1959 a spouse had a more limited right of succession where no children survived. They apply in favour of a surviving spouse, but only on intestacy (unlike legal rights). They prescribe after 20 years[15]: they cease to be legally enforceable.

### Dwelling-house

The surviving spouse has a right to the deceased's dwelling **4.20** house or, depending on its value, cash in lieu. Four questions must be asked:

(1) Had the deceased a "relevant interest" in the dwelling-house **4.21** in question? He must have been owner or tenant. Rent Act tenancies are excluded (they have similar parallel rules). If the tenancy was worded to end with the death, there is no interest for the spouse to inherit.[16]

"Dwelling-house" includes a part of a building occupied as a separate dwelling: *e.g.* a flat. It also includes garden and amenity ground attached to the house itself, so the spouse gets that too.

(2) Was the surviving spouse ordinarily resident in the house at **4.22** the date of the death? Where the deceased lived is immaterial. If the spouse was ordinarily resident in two such houses (*e.g.* town house and country cottage) she must choose one only, but has six months after the death to do so.

(3) What was the value of the deceased's interest? If over **4.23** £130,000[17] the spouse will receive that amount in cash instead. If the value is disputed, it is to be fixed by arbitration by one arbiter chosen by agreement or by the sheriff for the area where the deceased was domiciled at his death or (if that was abroad or unknown) for Edinburgh.

---

[14] See generally Clive, 30.025 *et seq.*
[15] Prescription and Limitation (Scotland) Act 1973, s.7 and Sched. 1, para. 2(f).
[16] See also s.36(2).
[17] Set by S.I. 1999 No. 445, under s.8(1); previously £110,000.

The interest is valued under deduction of heritable debts secured over it, *i.e.* mortgages. So the spouse gets the house less the amount of the mortgage, while any surplus insurance proceeds which pay it off on death are not hers but are an asset of the estate. In effect she may have to reimburse the estate if she wants the house at its full value.

**4.24**    (4) Is the interest, though worth under £130,000, an exception to the rule? If so the spouse gets cash to the value of the interest.

There are two such exceptions: where the dwelling-house forms part of property that the deceased tenanted; and where it forms part or all of property used by the deceased to carry on a business, and the value of the estate as a whole would be likely to be substantially diminished by disposing of the house separately from the other business assets.

### Furniture and plenishings

**4.25**    This right applies where the estate includes the furniture and plenishings of a house where the spouse was ordinarily resident at the date of death. The spouse is entitled to receive them or, if they total over £22,000,[18] items coming in total to that sum.

**4.26**    Again arbitration is possible. If there is more than one such house the spouse has six months to choose from which house to take the contents: she cannot pick and choose from both. This election is quite separate from that as respects the dwelling-house under section 8(1): the contents can be from a different house; indeed (by contrast with the former election) the house need not itself be part of the deceased's intestate estate, provided the contents themselves are.

**4.27**    Furniture and plenishings include "garden effects, domestic animals, plate, plated articles, linen, china, glass, books, pictures, prints, articles of household use and consumable stores". That is not an exhaustive definition; it may be a nice question in some cases whether an item falls within the list. They exclude articles and animals used at the date of death for business purposes, money and securities, and heirlooms. An "heirloom", rather unhelpfully, is "any article which has associations with the intestate's family of such nature and extent that it ought to pass to some member of the family other than the surviving spouse".

### Monetary right

**4.28**    The surviving spouse has the right to a sum of cash from the intestate estate (section 9). This is in addition to the rights to house and furniture, which have priority and must be dealt with

---

[18] S.I. 1999 No. 445; previously £20,000.

first: the "intestate estate" available for purposes of section 9 is that available after satisfaction of debts and section 8 prior rights.

**4.29** The sum is currently £35,000 if the deceased left surviving children and £58,000 if he did not.[19] The spouse will also receive interest on the sum from the date of death till actual payment: the rate is fixed from time to time by the Secretary of State, and is currently seven per cent.[20]

**4.30** If the spouse is entitled to receive a legacy from the deceased's estate, that must be set off against the cash sum (unless the legacy is of a "section 8–type" dwelling-house or of furniture and plenishings in it). That contrasts with the section 8 prior rights: house and furniture prior rights need not be set off against corresponding legacies.

**4.31** Note that "legacy" is widely drawn to cover, say, special destinations and *mortis causa* gifts: "any payment or benefit to which a surviving spouse becomes entitled by virtue of any testamentary disposition". The set-off is calculated on the value at the date of death.

**4.32** All the three prior rights are independent of each other; they are not simply aspects of a cash fund. So what the spouse gets depends very much on precisely what mix of assets was in the estate.

**4.33** If any surplus estate is left after payment of prior rights, the next stage is to calculate legal rights due out of the moveable property.

## LEGAL RIGHTS

### Nature of legal rights

**4.34** Legal rights are a distinctive feature of Scots law. They are probably a relic of an old form of "community of property" within the family: a person could not dispose of his property on his death just as he liked; his spouse and children had some claim on it. Freedom of testation over part of the estate—the "dead's part"—was probably a later innovation. Such rules were once more widespread, and still exist in an updated form in many Civilian legal systems. English law, by contrast, moved long ago to allow complete freedom of testation, and has only relatively recently reintroduced a limited form of family protection.[21]

**4.35** As such, legal rights are more like debts than ordinary rights of succession.[22] They are paid after ordinary debts, but before ordinary rights of succession. They apply in both testacy and intestacy,

---

[19] S.I. 1999 No. 445; previously £30,000 and £50,000 respectively.
[20] Law Reform (Miscellaneous Provisions) (Scotland) Act 1980, s.4; S.I. 1981 No. 805.
[21] Wills Act 1837; Inheritance (Provision for Family and Dependants) Act 1975.
[22] *Naismith v. Boyes* (1899) 1 F. (H.L.) 79.

and cannot be defeated by will: so they protect the family against disinheritance. If the will cuts them out they can claim legal rights instead; the provisions in the will are abated—reduced—to the extent necessary to make property available to pay legal rights. Even if they are left legacies they can elect for legal rights instead; in that case they lose the legacies. The rights are automatic: they need no court application. Spouse and children are thus far better protected than in England, where discretionary payments require application to the courts.

**4.36** The property available for legal rights depends on whether the deceased left a surviving spouse, or children, or both. *Jus relictae* gives the widow one-third of the moveable estate (if descendants survive) and one-half otherwise; similarly *jus relicti* for the widower. Legitim (the "bairns' part") gives children (and their offspring by representation if they die first) one-third of the moveable estate in aggregate, or one-half if there is no surviving spouse. The remaining one-third or one-half is the "dead's part": he can make a will over that without fear of challenge from spouse or children, and if he does not it becomes the "free estate" for distribution under the rules of intestacy.

**4.37** In principle the claimant's right is to cash, not to particular assets from the estate. The executor can hand over assets, but failing agreement among all concerned he can sell and transfer the proceeds. But if the assets fetch more than their death value the rights must be revalued[23] and capital gains tax may be due.[24]

### Heritable and moveable property

**4.38** Legal rights are exigible only from moveable property. For that reason heritable and moveable assets and debts of the estate must be segregated on paper at the stage of paying debts and distributing prior rights.

*(a) Types of property*[25]

**4.39** Usually it is obvious whether an item is heritable or moveable. Some types of property have special rules, and others are, by a quirk of history, legal chameleons—heritable for one purpose and moveable for another. The main examples are:

**4.40** (1) Heritable securities: such as a standard security over a house, *i.e.* a mortgage. Their treatment depends on whether one is dealing with the estate of the creditor or the debtor. As regards the creditor they are moveable for most purposes, except—to be perverse—(a) taxation, which may affect the incidence of IHT; and

---

[23] Allan (1988) 33 J.L.S. 130; see para. 4.58.
[24] Scobbie (1987) 32 J.L.S. 341; see paras 12.71 *et seq.*
[25] See Meston, pp. 58–60. For legacies see paras 10.70 *et seq.* below.

(b) legal rights. So investments in heritable securities are not subject to legal rights.[26]

More normally one is dealing with the estate of the debtor: the person who has taken out the mortgage. Heritable debts are in principle set against heritable assets, unless (in testacy) the will alters their incidence. If the lenders also had a life assurance policy (covering the sum due) assigned to them in security of the same debt, one must calculate what proportion it bears to the total amount of the two securities: that proportion of the debt is treated as moveable, the rest being a heritable debt. The policy security thus reduces the estate subject to legal rights.

**4.41** (2) If the deceased had sold heritage but not received the price, the right to the price is moveable under the doctrine of conversion. If he has bought but not paid, the asset is heritable but the debt (the price) is moveable.

**4.42** (3) Suppose the deceased had, when he died, a vested right under someone else's will. That right is an asset of his estate. In the case of a specific legacy, if the item itself was moveable so is his right to it. With general legacies the legatee usually only has a right to cash (and no right to insist on delivery of particular assets), which is moveable whatever the deceased's original property was.

### (b) The effect of prior rights

**4.43** The prior right to a house is plainly deducted from heritage; that to furniture, from moveables. When cash is paid in lieu of the house, it seems that should also be taken off heritage.

**4.44** If the monetary provision were all taken out of moveables, that would deplete the legitim fund and would be unfair on the children. So it is deducted from heritable and moveable assets in the same proportions that they form of the estate at that stage. Note that that is purely a paper calculation so that one can value what is available for legal rights. In practice the monetary right may be satisfied by giving the spouse heritable assets: that is a matter of choice (either on the executor's part or by mutual agreement between all the beneficiaries) and is immaterial for calculating legal rights.

### Entitlement to legal rights

#### (a) Representation

**4.45** Suppose a child was entitled to legitim but died before his parent leaving a grandchild. Before 1964 the child's legal rights would simply have been extinguished. The 1964 Act allows the grandchild

---

[26] Titles to Land Consolidation (Scotland) Act 1868, s.117, as amended by Succession (Scotland) Act 1964, Sched. 3.

to "represent" the child: to step into his shoes and inherit his claim. So section 11(1), as amended, provides:

**4.46**    "Where a person dies predeceased by a child who has left issue who survive the deceased, and the child would, if he had survived the deceased, have been entitled . . . to legitim out of the deceased's estate, such issue shall have the like right to legitim as the child would have had if he had survived the deceased."

**4.47**  This originally applied only to legitimate children, but the distinction has now been completely abolished in intestacy.[27] The idea is analogous to the *conditio si institutus sine liberis decesserit* in wills. But there is no representation under *jus relictae* or *relicti*: if there were, a stepchild of the deceased, unrelated to him by blood, could claim; and that would run contrary to the whole ethos of the 1964 Act.

**4.48**    The problem then is how to divide legitim if there are several claimants. Suppose A left two children B and C; B survives and has a grandchild D; C has died leaving two grandchildren E and F. There are two possible modes of dividing the legitim fund. One is per capita division: equal shares of one-third each. The other is *per stirpes* division. A *stirps* is a branch of a family tree; *per stirpes* division would divide the fund at the level of B and C so that B takes half and E and F take a quarter each. (The problem also arises in wills, where the question is often where the will places the head of the *stirps*.)

**4.49**    Section 11(1) by itself suggests *per stirpes* division. In fact it is governed by section 11 (2) which orders per capita division in some cases. The net effect is as follows:

**4.50**    (1) If all the descendants have the same degree of relationship to the deceased, division is equal—per capita. So (above) if B and C both die, D, E and F each get a third.

**4.51**    (2) Otherwise division is at the level of the nearest surviving relation to the deceased—*per stirpes*. So if B is alive, he takes half and E and F take a quarter each. D gets nothing because representation only operates on B's death.

*(b) Date of calculation and payment*

**4.52**    The existence of legal rights is ascertained at the date of death. Spouse or children then alive acquire a vested right, which passes to their executors if they die before payment. Several factors can delay payment. Debts take some time to be paid; claimants may claim late. A child cannot make a valid binding election till aged

---

[27] Law Reform (Parent and Child) (Scotland) Act 1986, s.1.

18, and the executors will need to retain funds to cover a possible election at that point.

Interest accrues from death to the date of payment,[28] unless **4.53** (perhaps) the delay was the claimant's fault.[29] The rate is not fixed: it is what the sum earned or could have earned by prudent management.[30]

Similarly the estate available for payment is that at the date of **4.54** death, after deducting moveable debts, IHT, funeral costs and executry expenses to obtain confirmation and realise assets.[31] Later insurance or pension payments made directly to a widow or child (as opposed to the executors) are not part of the estate: the recipient's claim derives from the policy, not from legal rights.

There are two moot points: **4.55**

(1) A dies; B, a legatee, elects for a legacy instead of legal rights. **4.56** Later another legatee dies before his legacy vests: that legacy lapses and the asset falls into intestacy. Legal rights are now due from it if it was part of the estate at A's death[32]; B's election affects only the *testate* estate.

(2) Income from the estate was accumulated as ordered by a **4.57** testamentary trust. The accumulation later becomes illegal and any further income falls into intestacy. The income was not part of the death estate, so is probably not subject to legal rights; but the caselaw is undecided.[33]

At what date are legal rights valued? In principle it is the date of **4.58** death, so one uses the figures inserted for IHT and confirmation; but *Alexander v. Alexander's Trs*[34] illustrates an exception. A widow and child wanted to claim legal rights in place of legacies; the assets had been sold soon after the death at a lower value than that estimated for tax purposes. The court held that the realised and not the estimated value is used if executors sell assets in due course without delay. On the other hand later profits or losses resulting from the executors' administration have no effect on the valuation for legal rights.

### (c) *Collation* inter liberos

The purpose of collation is to ensure equality in the distribution **4.59** of the legitim fund among claimants. If one claimant has received advances from the deceased during his life, other claimants can

---

[28] *Kearon v. Thomson's Trs*, 1949 S.C. 287.

[29] *Wick v. Wick* (1898) 1 F. 199.

[30] The Scottish Law Commission proposes a fixed rate, initially seven per cent to parallel that currently payable on prior rights; Report No. 124, paras 3.28–3.29. For discussion see Meston, pp. 53–54.

[31] *Russell v. Att.-Gen.*, 1917 S.C. 28.

[32] *Naismith v. Boyes* (1899) 1 F. (H.L.) 79.

[33] *cf. Moon's Trs v. Moon* (1899) 2 F. 201, *Wilson's Trs v. Glasgow Royal Infirmary*, 1917 S.C. 527. See Wilson & Duncan, 9.60–9.62.

[34] 1954 S.C. 436; *Gilchrist v. Gilchrist's Trs* (1889) 16 R. 1118.

require the advances to be notionally added to the fund. So it applies only when there is more than one claimant: one cannot insist on non-claimants collating and so increase the legitim fund.[35]

**4.60** Not all advances need be collated. An advance of heritable property is irrelevant. An advance in discharge of the natural duty to maintain and educate the recipient need not be collated[36]; similarly remuneration under a contract. Nor need a loan by the deceased (that will be an asset of the estate anyway) or one made on the express basis of being in addition to legitim. But advances in order to set the recipient up in the world—say, to furnish a home of his own—or in business must be collated.

**4.61** The method is to add the advance to the fund (on paper); divide equally among claimants; and deduct the advance from the recipient's resulting share. If that gives him a minus quantity he need not actually repay anything; he simply gets no legitim. Envisage four claimants A, B, C, and D: £50,000 is available; A had an advance of £10,000. The legitim fund is £60,000: A gets £5,000 and the others £15,000 each.

**4.62** The 1964 Act, in conjunction with representation, allows collation of advances to a predeceasing child who is being represented (section 11(3)). The representer must collate an "appropriate proportion" of such advances. The problem is that the representer's per capita share of legitim may not be the same as the child's would have been, and that the Act does not define "appropriate proportion". The Act gives no clear answer.[37]

### Extinction of legal rights

*(a) Discharge during deceased's lifetime*

**4.63** Before 1964 it was possible for parents to discharge their children's legal rights by means of an antenuptial marriage contract. *Callander v. Callander's Exr*[38] shows just how inequitable this could be. The *quid pro quo* in the marriage contract was to set up a trust fund whose income would go to the children. Many years later the trust was wound up by a deed. A son argued that as a result his legitim should revive: the Lords found no support for that in the words of the deed.

**4.64** Since the 1964 Act only the person entitled to legitim can discharge it. That was always so with spouses. But pre-1964 discharges remain in force (section 12).

**4.65** The effect is that the estate available for legal rights is divided between claimants as if the person giving the discharge had died before the deceased.

---

[35] *Coats' Trs v. Coats*, 1914 S.C. 744.
[36] Erskine, Inst., III. ix. 24.
[37] Meston at 1967 S.L.T. (News) 195 suggests solutions.
[38] 1972 S.C. (H.L.) 70.

## (b) Renunciation after deceased's death[39]

**4.66** The effect is that legal rights are calculated as if the discharger was a claimant, but his share then falls into the free intestate estate. So renunciation, unlike pre-death discharge, does not increase the other claimants' shares.

**4.67** Formerly a child under 18 could not make a binding discharge or renunciation. The minimum age is now 16, and the executor cannot delay payment if claimed.[40] The executors must retain sufficient funds in case he decides to claim at that age. However executors should be cautious in taking a discharge from a child aged 16 or 17. The child can challenge it until he is 21 and have it set aside if it can be shown to be a "prejudicial transaction" (the test is whether a reasonably prudent adult would have entered the transaction).[41] A straightforward receipt for legitim will cause no difficulties: the child suffers no prejudice. But suppose the child renounces legal rights in part or in full, or opts for a legacy less than his legitim entitlement. In that case there is potential prejudice. The executors may be wise to seek court ratification of the discharge.[42]

**4.68** However in calculating legitim for IHT purposes the executors can make a provisional election within two years after the death; failing that IHT is assessed as if legitim was claimed; but whichever they choose the assessment can be reopened to reflect what the child finally decides at 18 (or, at latest, before he is 20).[43]

## (c) Prescription

**4.69** Legal rights, like prior rights, prescribe—lapse—if not claimed in 20 years after becoming enforceable. That refers (as appropriate) to the date when the deceased died, or when intestacy arose, or (given the reduction of the age of legal capacity) the date when the legitim claimant becomes 16.[44] The period runs even if the entitled person is incapax.

### THE FREE ESTATE

**4.70** The free estate is what is left after debts have been paid and prior and legal rights satisfied. If the deceased left no surviving spouse or children, it comprises the whole estate.

---

[39] See Election at paras 9.08 *et seq.*

[40] Age of Legal Capacity (Scotland) Act 1991, s.1(b).

[41] Age of Legal Capacity (Scotland) Act 1991, s.3, to the Court of Session or Sheriff Court.

[42] Age of Legal Capacity (Scotland) Act 1991, s.4. See Barr & Edwards, 1992 S.L.T. (News) 77. Similar difficulties arise in relation to paying a legacy to a child of 16 or 17.

[43] IHTA 1984, s.147. The Inland Revenue may allow a later decision. The age limits were not altered by the 1991 Act.

[44] Prescription and Limitation (Scotland) Act 1973, s.7, Sched. 1, para. 2(f). See also Meston, p. 67.

**4.71** The estate is distributed in the order laid down in section 2(1). One simply goes through each successive class of relations till one finds someone entitled to inherit. One must exhaust each category of relative before going on to the next. There is no limit except the practicality of tracing a genealogical link (legitimate or not): anyone, however distant, may inherit.

**4.72** Each category in section 2(1) is read subject to sections 5 and 6 which provide for infinite representation of a deceased beneficiary, and for division per capita and *per stirpes* in that process. For instance (in (3) below) nephews and nieces, and their own descendants, have preference over (4); (6) gives cousins preference over (7). Sections 5 and 6 apply to all beneficiaries except the deceased's parents and spouse: this will (for instance) prevent someone inheriting who is a child of one's spouse but is not related to oneself—*i.e.* a stepchild. The law still stresses a blood tie with the deceased person. The "parent" exception stops one's half brother (or sister) taking that parent's share by representation; he/she can (as discussed below) in some cases inherit a share in his/her own right as a collateral.

**4.73** The order of succession (subject to representation) is:

    (a) children;

    (b) parents *and* brothers or sisters (if someone survives from both classes): each class takes half the estate;

    (c) brothers or sisters (if no parents alive);

    (d) parents (if no brothers or sisters alive);

    (e) spouse;

    (f) uncles and aunts, both maternal and paternal;

    (g) grandparents;

    (h) grandparents' brothers or sisters; and so on.

**4.74** Those in (3), (6) and (8) are examples of *collaterals*: brothers and sisters of the intestate or of an ancestor. They are classified as being of the whole blood (sharing both parents with the intestate or ancestor) or half blood (sharing one). The first class has preference over the second; but among the second it is immaterial whether the parent was their mother or father (section 3).

**4.75** Currently co-habitants inherit nothing under intestacy; all beneficiaries (except a spouse) must be blood relations of the deceased. The Scottish Law Commission proposes[45] that a co-habitant be

---

[45] Report No. 135, Family Law (1992), paras 16.24–16.37.

able to apply for a court order of financial provision if the deceased has not left her (or him) reasonable financial provision in the circumstances. Applicant and deceased must have been living together "as husband and wife" immediately before the death. The award would be discretionary—not automatic—taking into account (*inter alia*) the size of the estate and other claims on it; whether they had children (either of their own or who were treated as children of the family); other provision coming to the applicant from the death (*e.g.* insurance); and contributions made, or economic disadvantage suffered, by the applicant.

If no relation is found, the estate goes to the Crown as *ultimus* **4.76** *haeres*. The Queen's and Lord Treasurer's Remembrancer, an official who is now the same person as the Crown Agent, takes possession of the estate without obtaining confirmation. He will advertise for possible relatives, but anyone who knows of one must tell him. He will then pay the debts and the balance goes to the Treasury. But unrelated people who apply for money from the funds may be paid at his discretion. At one time these were often illegitimate relations (who then had no right to inherit); now it may be someone such as a housekeeper who has a moral claim.[46]

LAW REFORM

The core of the Scottish Law Commission's proposed reforms is its **4.77** radical restructuring of the present categories of prior rights and legal rights. The spouse will receive a simple cash amount, varying according to the size of estate; and she has the option to take her spouse's interest in the matrimonial home and furnishings in part or total satisfaction of that amount. The children (if any) receive the rest. A separate system of "legal shares" will apply to testate estate only, fulfilling the present function of legal rights in protecting spouse and children against disinheritance.[47]

**Further reading**

N.R. Allan, "Legal Rights" (1988) 33 J.L.S. 130.
A. Barr & L. Edwards, "Age of Legal Capacity—Further Pitfalls", 1992 S.L.T. (News) 77.
Clive, *Husband and Wife* (4th ed., 1997), Chap. 30.
Meston, "Collation of Advances by Ancestors", 1967 S.L.T. (News) 195.
Meston, *The Succession (Scotland) Act 1964* (4th ed., 1993), Chaps 4–6.

---

[46] See Wilson & Duncan, 31.28; Currie, 6.57.
[47] Report No. 124, Parts II & III. For details see Chap. 15.

CHAPTER 5

# WILL SUBSTITUTES

**5.01** Scots law recognises a number of methods whereby, without making a will, one may provide for succession on death. Various types of lifetime deed may contain provisions which have a testamentary effect.

SPECIAL DESTINATIONS

## Types of special destination

*(a) General*

**5.02**   The purpose of a destination is to regulate the order in which people own property. The type found in wills is the destination-over, which provides for a substitute beneficiary to succeed either after an original institute or in his place if he fails for some reason to inherit.[1] The special destination, by contrast, occurs in documents of title which regulate the ownership of property during the maker's lifetime and also its inheritance on his death. It is thus not a testamentary writing but it has a testamentary effect: it supersedes the rules of intestate succession without the need to make a will. It may relate to moveables or, more commonly, heritage.

**5.03**   The usual type is a survivorship destination: property is taken in the name of "A and B and the survivor of them"; this frequently occurs when spouses buy their matrimonial home. It is loosely analogous to the English "joint tenancy". Rarer types specify named individuals—"A then B then C"—or a class—"my male heirs".

**5.04**   The essence of the special destination is that it alters the ordinary rules of intestate succession; otherwise, after all, it would have little point. But for the destination each person's share would pass straight to their beneficiaries. It is "special" in that it deals with a particular item of property as opposed to the grantor's whole estate. A destination to "heirs" is not special: they would

---

[1] See Murray, pp. 138–141; below, paras 10.35 *et seq.*, 11.31–11.34.

take on intestacy anyway. Judicial definitions are rare, but that in *Cormack v. McIldowie's Exrs*[2] is important and controversial:

> "I ... regard a special destination as one in which the **5.05** particular property in the deed is disponed to the particular person (or persons) specifically nominated by the granter, without regard to the normal operation of the law of succession on intestacy."

That formulation apparently excludes "class" destinations, and has **5.06** been challenged for that reason.[3] The case concerned an agricultural tenancy: the court feared that including "class" destinations would, absurdly, take most tenancies outwith the scope of the 1964 Act.

### (b) Types of property

At one time one could not dispose of heritable property by will, **5.07** but only by a *de praesenti*—immediate—lifetime conveyance. One way to circumvent this was to include in that conveyance a special destination stating to whom the property passed after the buyer's death. Its *raison d'être* vanished when wills of heritage were allowed in 1868,[4] but it is still used for convenience.

One may also find destinations in any document of title for **5.08** moveable property. *Connell's Trs v. Connell's Trs*[5] illustrates their scope. That case confirmed that a bond—a document constituting a debt—may contain a destination. So may shares in companies.

Contrast a deposit receipt—a receipt for money deposited in a **5.09** bank. Often the depositor includes on it names other than his own. That is convenient: it gives those named on it the right to uplift the money from the bank. But it is not a document of title: it does not prove who owns the money.[6] In principle only the depositor himself is owner. So if he puts a destination on the receipt it has no testamentary effect: the survivor can uplift the funds but must pay them on to the depositor's executor as part of his estate.[7] So in *Dinwoodie's Exx v. Carruthers' Exr*[8] X and Y respectively provided £50 and £400 of a deposit; despite a survivorship destination, X as survivor only owned what he had put in, Y's executors getting the rest.

[2] 1975 S.C. 161, at 177 *per* L.J.-C. Wheatley.
[3] Halliday (1977) 27 J.L.S. 16; see Scot. Law Com. Memorandum No. 71, para. 3.24 and Report No. 124, paras 6.10–6.14, reversing the principle in *Cormack* (but proposing special rules to achieve similar results for destinations in leases).
[4] Titles to Land Consolidation (Scotland) Act 1868, s.20.
[5] (1886) 13 R. 1175.
[6] The same applies to names on a bank account.
[7] *Connell's Trs*, n. 5; *Crosbie's Trs v. Wright* (1880) 7 R. 823.
[8] (1895) 23 R.234.

**5.10**   There is a further problem with share certificates. In England a simple joint holding by "A and B" implies a survivorship destination though none is expressed; in Scotland that is not so. But the English rule apparently applies to shares held by Scots in English companies. The rule has been doubted, and does not apply to Government stock, which is deemed British rather than English.[9]

*(c) The effect of special destinations*

**5.11**   Because a destination is contained in a lifetime conveyance but has testamentary effect, one should distinguish its effect during life and on death. Consider the typical case where A purchases property in the name of "A and B and the survivor".

**5.12**   In bare principle A, as buyer, remains full owner of that property during his lifetime; B has no rights till the destination operates on death. Merely taking title in another's name gives them no immediate rights: delivery of the document—or an equivalent act—is also essential. Failing delivery, the destination still operates on A's death because testamentary provisions need no delivery, but B has no half share while A lives:

**5.13**   "The doctrine of special destination is that if (1) anyone takes the documentary title to property or securities (including shares), which he has acquired in his own right or out of his own means, in favour of some other person (either solely or jointly with himself. . .), and (2) if such title remains in the possession of the acquirer undelivered to such other person during the acquirer's lifetime, then such title is held to constitute a valid nomination of such other person as successor of the acquirer in [that] property—to the extent of the whole, if the title is in favour of [the other] solely or as survivor."[10]

**5.14**   Heritage is registered in the Register of Sasines or Land Register: that is the legal equivalent of delivery, so A and B are at once common owners. Non-delivery is much more likely with documents of title to moveables: suppose A keeps them in his files till he dies? Some actions are deemed equivalent to delivery, but there is no closed list. What is needed is "a dealing with the document in such a way as to put it out of the power of the [grantor] to deal with it".[11] Confusingly, registering shares in a company register has been accepted in some cases but not others.[12]

---

[9] *Connell's Trs*, n. 5; *cf. Cunningham's Trs v. Cunningham*, 1924 S.C. 581, *Colenso's Exr v. Davidson*, 1930 S.L.T. 359.

[10] *Dennis v. Aitchison*, 1923 S.C. 819 at 825 *per* L.P. Clyde; affirmed 1924 S.C. (H.L.) 122.

[11] L.P. Dunedin in *Carmichael v. Carmichael's Exx*, 1920 S.C. (H.L.) 195 at 201, where intimating an insurance policy to a beneficiary was sufficient.

[12] *Inland Revenue v. Wilson*, 1928 S.C. (H.L.) 12; *cf. Dennis v. Aitchison*, above.

Assuming delivery (or the equivalent), A and B are common **5.15** owners of the property while they both live. Each is full owner of a *pro indiviso* half share (*i.e.* a notional proportional share of the undivided property), and has an unrestricted right to dispose of it *inter vivos*; neither has any rights over the other's share. That was clear in *Steele v. Caldwell*,[13] where the husband put his wife out of the house and sold his half-share to strangers who took up residence: the wife could not stop that. (The Matrimonial Homes (Family Protection) (Scotland) Act 1981 would now protect her right to occupy the house, but as regards ownership the principle remains.) Having said that, in one maverick case[14] three children A, B and C were treated as joint owners: the special factor was supposedly an agreement that they could use the property for life as a family home. For that reason none of them could have sold their share without the others' consent.

### (d) Operation of destination on death

Before 1964 heritage passed on death directly to the person **5.16** entitled to succeed: the heir-at-law or, in the case of special destinations, the heir of provision. The 1964 Act abolished the machinery of "service of heirs"; under the Act both heritage and moveables ordinarily pass to the executor for distribution to beneficiaries.

Special rules for destinations were thus necessary. In principle **5.17** heritage subject to an unrevoked special destination is not part of a deceased's estate under the Act (section 36(2)(a)): so it does not go to the executor for ordinary distribution. But title must pass to the heir somehow. With survivorship destinations his title is automatic by virtue of survivance: nothing need be done. With other types the property vests in the executor purely for him to have it conveyed to the person entitled under the destination (section 18(2)).

### Revocation of special destinations

### (a) Revocability

We have seen that a destination can be defeated by lifetime **5.18** dealings: *Steele v. Caldwell*. In principle one may also evacuate— revoke or defeat—it by will. One cannot of course affect other co-owners' shares by so doing.

Two factors bar revocation; both depend on who paid the **5.19** purchase price of the property. First, the destination may be regarded as contractual because the two co-owners contributed

---

[13] 1979 S.L.T. 228, followed in Smith v. MacKintosh, 1989 S.C.L.R. 83.
[14] *Munro v. Munro*, 1972 S.L.T. (Sh. Ct) 6.

equally to the price, as in *Perrett's Trs v. Perrett*[15]: "each took the chance of getting the half of the other, and accordingly ... the property stands upon its own destination and is not carried, and could not be carried, by any testament whatsoever ... this destination could [not] have been altered except by joint consent of the spouses". Alternatively they may contribute in kind by pooling property, as in *Shand's Trs v. Shand's Trs*.[16] Secondly, if one co-owner paid the whole price he can revoke, but the co-owner who paid none cannot: the destination is a condition of the "gift". Similarly if both co-owners had a gift from a third person, neither can revoke.[17]

**5.20**   Inevitably the words of the conveyance are crucial evidence. They will narrate who paid the purchase price; they may, as in *Shand's Trs*, go further and refer to an agreement. But they are not always accurate. In *Hay's Trs v. Hay's Trs*[18] this was admitted, so extrinsic evidence was allowed to prove who actually paid the price. *Hay's Trs* was special: in *Gordon-Rogers v. Thomson's Trs*[19] there was no such admission, the words of the conveyance (as a probative deed) were conclusive, and extrinsic evidence was not allowed to contradict them. Thus if a special destination is to be contractual it is important that the deed makes express mention of who has contributed the purchase price.

*(b) Revocation*

**5.21**   Supposing a destination can be revoked, "evacuated": has it been? The old common law was vague, relying on presumptions in an attempt to discover the testator's intention. If the testator himself created the destination (say by having it inserted when he purchased the property) he did not revoke it by a general settlement[20]: the two were read together insofar as reconcilable. If he did not create it (because he took the property by gift from the creator, or by succession under the destination) the general settlement did revoke it. If the destination postdated the will it plainly was not revoked. (A postdated codicil to an earlier will probably had no effect unless it itself affected the destination.)[21]

**5.22**   These presumptions could be displaced by circumstances. First, a later will might be irreconcilable with the destination. It might

---

[15] 1909 S.C. 522 at 527 *per* L.P. Dunedin. See also *Marshall v. Marshall's Exr*, 1987 S.L.T. 49; similarly *Smith v. MacKintosh*, 1989 S.C.L.R. 83.

[16] 1966 S.C. 178.

[17] *Renouf's Trs v. Haining*, 1919 2 S.L.T. 15; *Brown's Trs v. Brown*, 1943 S.C. 488.

[18] 1951 S.C. 329.

[19] 1988 S.L.T. 618.

[20] *i.e.* a will of his whole estate.

[21] *Thoms v. Thoms* (1868) 6 M. 704; *Perrett's Trs*, n. 15; *Cunningham's Trs v. Cunningham*, 1924 S.C. 581; *Murray's Exrs v. Geekie*, 1929 S.C. 633.

dispose of property which was expressly or tacitly known to be subject to the destination, as in *Hay's Trs* or *Dennis v. Aitchison*.[22] Secondly, it might revoke the destination. But the usual revocation of "all previous testamentary writings made by me" would not do: while a destination has testamentary effect, it is not in a testamentary document.[23] Other circumstances might be relevant evidence of the testator's intention: for instance his actings, but not his oral statements of intention.[24]

The old law still applies to wills executed before September 10, **5.23** 1964: the testator's date of death is immaterial. Under section 30 of the 1964 Act, a testamentary disposition executed on or after that date will not evacuate a special destination unless it contains a specific reference to the destination and a declared intention on the part of the testator to evacuate it. This is strictly construed[25]: implied revocation thus disappears.

Special destinations between spouses, like wills, are not revoked **5.24** by divorce. Even if one spouse transfers his share to the other in a divorce settlement, the destination will still operate in his favour if the other dies before him.

Thus it is important to ensure that evacuation of a special **5.25** destination is not overlooked where appropriate. Failure to do so will constitute professional negligence. Given that the destination often concerns the most valuable item owned by spouses—the matrimonial home—a mistake may radically affect their own beneficiaries' rights of inheritance. A spouse, drafting a later will, may not realise that the destination disposes of her share in the house in a quite different way from what she now intends; another intended beneficiary may thus fail to inherit, as in *Weir v. J.M. Hodge & Son*.[26]

## Law reform

Special destinations have complex and confusing rules, and their **5.26** very concept is widely considered outdated. The Scottish Law Commission's proposals will largely abolish all except survivorship destinations. Evacuation will be made easier, even where the destination is contractual; and "class" destinations—the problem in *Cormack*—will be brought within the definition.[27]

At present destinations only exist if express in the title deed: **5.27** Scots law does not imply them among co-owners. (Contrast the

---

[22] Above at n. 10.
[23] *Murray's Exrs v. Geekie*, n. 21, but note doubts in *Colenso's Exr v. Davidson*, 1930 S.L.T. 359.
[24] *Murray's Exrs*; *Colenso's Exr*.
[25] *Stirling's Trs v. Stirling*, 1977 S.C. 139; *Marshall v. Marshall's Exr*, 1987 S.L.T. 49.
[26] 1990 S.L.T. 266. For the solicitor's liability to disappointed beneficiaries see paras 6.70–6.72, below.
[27] Report No. 124, Part VI. See also Chap. 15 below.

rules for joint property and joint tenancies in Scotland and England respectively.) The Commission decided against introducing automatic destinations.

Nominations[28]

**5.28**  A nomination is a document of a testamentary nature and is akin to a special destination. It relates to funds deposited by someone, or credited to him, with certain official savings or benevolent bodies. It gives the nominee the right to those funds after the nominator's death without the need for an executor to obtain confirmation to them.

**5.29**  Nominations are based purely on statute, and the rules governing each individual type depend on the particular statute allowing it. The most important current types relate to friendly societies, industrial and provident societies, and trade unions. Obsolete types include National Savings Certificates and the National Savings Bank (before May 1, 1981) and the Trustee Savings Bank (before May 1, 1979); nominations made prior to those dates are still valid. The current maximum sum is £5000[29]; there is no limit for TSB and National Savings funds.

**5.30**  The formalities of execution differ from those for wills. Normally they require the nominator to sign—a mark being permitted for National Savings only[30]—and to deposit the form with the society. One witness may be required, who cannot be the nominee. The nominator must be aged over 16: a concession for England (where 18 is the usual limit for wills) but more stringent than for Scots wills. However, if a document is invalid as a nomination for lack of age or formality, it may still be valid as an ordinary Scots will.

**5.31**  A nomination falls if the nominator marries or the nominee dies. It can only be revoked by the prescribed statutory formalities, and not by a will (though that may convert the nominee's right from being beneficial to purely administrative). The rule seems clear, though in the only two relevant cases some doubts were expressed.[31]

**5.32**  On the other hand, a nomination simply allows the nominee to get payment of the fund. It does not decide whether his right is beneficial (he owns the funds) or, like a deposit receipt, merely administrative (so that he must pay them over to the executor). The second is rare; a later will, while not revoking the nomination, can have this result if the relevant regulations permit it.[32]

[28] See Currie, 13.10–13.18.
[29] Administration of Estates (Small Payments) Act 1965, ss.2, 6; S.I. 1984 No. 539.
[30] *Morton v. French*, 1908 S.C. 171.
[31] *Ford's Trs v. Ford*, 1940 S.C. 426; *Clarke's Exr v. Macaulay*, 1961 S.L.T. 109.
[32] *Young v. Waterson*, 1918 S.C. 9.

## Donation Mortis Causa

**Definition and characteristics**

The classic case of a *mortis causa* donation was *Morris v.* **5.33**
*Riddick*.[33] Morris, terminally ill, gave Riddick a deposit receipt for
£300, endorsed it in Riddick's name, and gave him a note for the
bank to that effect; the gift was on the footing that he did not
recover. This was not a legacy; it was held to be a donation *mortis
causa* so that the sum went to Riddick and was not part of Morris's
estate. Lord President Inglis defined donation *mortis causa* as:

> "a conveyance of an immoveable or incorporeal right, or a **5.34**
> transference of moveables or money by delivery, so that the
> property is immediately transferred to the grantee, upon the
> condition that he shall hold for the grantor so long as he lives,
> subject to his power of revocation, and, failing such revoca-
> tion, then for the grantee on the death of the granter . . . if the
> grantee predecease the granter the property reverts to the
> granter, and the qualified right of property which was vested in
> the grantee is extinguished by his predecease."

The *mortis causa* donation is thus a hybrid between a legacy and **5.35**
lifetime gift; it shares characteristics of both. Unlike a legacy it is
effective at once, though conditional on death ensuing; it requires
delivery, but not writing unless—as with land—the type of property
demands writing for effective transfer. In that sense it is no
different from an ordinary lifetime gift. Like a legacy the gift is
revocable during the granter's lifetime, and the recipient's right is
not complete unless he outlives the donor. For that reason the
donor's creditors can still treat the item as part of his property (*e.g.*
for purposes of diligence or bankruptcy). The gift is payable after
legal rights but before ordinary legacies, even if as a result there is
no estate available for legacies.

**Essential requirements**

Three elements are essential. They are interrelated, so strong **5.36**
evidence of one may make up for weak evidence of another.

(1) The donor must act in contemplation of his death. There **5.37**
need not be fear of imminent death, but if there is it points the
more strongly to *mortis causa* donation rather than a legacy.[34]

(2) There must normally be delivery. Scots law in principle insists **5.38**
on delivery to transfer property rights—mere agreement being

---

[33] (1867) 5 M. 1036 at 1041. For a comparative survey of the concept see A.
Borkowski, *Deathbed Gifts* (1999).
[34] *Blythe v. Curle* (1885) 12 R. 674; *Aiken's Exrs v. Aiken*, 1937 S.C. 678.

insufficient—with wills and sale of goods the two main exceptions to the rule. But the requirement is flexible, and less stringent for *mortis causa* than *inter vivos* donation. Inevitably deposit receipts illustrate the point. Formal delivery is unnecessary, but there must be some act sufficient to transfer ownership which the law may treat as equivalent to delivery. One equivalent is intimation to the bank. Contrast *Macpherson's Exx v. Mackay*,[35] where the bank included the donee's name on the receipt, with *Gray's Trs v. Murray*,[36] where the donor inserted the name himself without the bank knowing and never notified this.

**5.39** (3) There must be *animus donandi*, intention to make an immediate (but revocable) gift rather than a legacy. Whenever property is handed over there is a strong presumption against donation (it might be sale or loan instead) which needs clear and unequivocal evidence to rebut.[37] In practice this may be a crucial element when, in (2), there has not been formal delivery.

Proof is the main problem since the donor's intention rarely appears explicitly in writing. "Accordingly, in almost all cases, the true quality of the donor's *animus* has to be inferred from implications drawn from his conduct, and the circumstances which surround his acts."[38] Documentary evidence is certainly important, but rarely conclusive: inserting a payee's name on a deposit receipt may suggest gift but may equally be done with pure administrative convenience in mind. But, as in *Aiken's Exrs v. Aiken*,[39] oral evidence of the donor's actions or statements of intention may suffice if coupled with the terms of the document.

LIFE ASSURANCE

**General rules and joint policies**

**5.40** If A takes out a life assurance policy on his own life it is normally payable to his executors and so forms part of his estate to be distributed on death according to will or intestacy. But if someone else, B (say a spouse or child) is beneficiary under the policy, then (even if A pays the premiums himself) the proceeds go direct to B and they are excluded from A's own estate. They thus escape IHT and legal rights.

**5.41** A can achieve that result by taking the policy out in B's favour to start with, or by assigning it later. Often the policy is taken out

---

[35] 1932 S.C. 505; also *Crosbie's Trs v. Wright* (1880) 7 R. 832.
[36] 1970 S.L.T. 105.
[37] *Brownlee's Exr v. Brownlee*, 1908 S.C. 232.
[38] *Macpherson's Exx*, above, *per* L.P. Clyde at 513–514.
[39] 1937 S.C. 678; see also *Morris v. Riddick*, above. For Commission proposals regarding *donatio mortis causa* see Report No. 124, paras 9.12–9.16.

jointly in order to benefit whichever of A and B survives longer: supposing A dies first then (depending on its terms) the proceeds may go (i) to his estate, (ii) directly to B, or (iii) they may be payable only to B's estate when B dies. Methods (i) and (ii) are usual to pay off a mortgage, (iii) to pay IHT on spouse B's death.

**Policies written in trust**

Alternatively a husband may take the policy in trust for spouse **5.42** or children as beneficiaries. The most important example occurs under the Married Women's Policies of Assurance (Scotland) Act 1880.[40] At that time wives had limited powers to own property, and the main purpose of the Act was to give them funds which were protected from the husband's creditors. That is still the effect, though its original rationale is long gone, and the Act now applies equally in favour of husbands.

Unlike an ordinary trust, an 1880 Act policy is effective at once **5.43** without the need for delivery or intimation to the beneficiary.[41] It need not refer to the Act by name, but must be written in favour of spouse and/or children. "Children" now includes illegitimate or adopted ones, but not stepchildren. The spouse who takes out the policy is deemed trustee with the usual powers under the Trusts (Scotland) Act 1921.

Beneficiaries acquire immediate irrevocable vested rights under **5.44** the policy. If adult they can assign or renounce them.[42] If the wife divorces, she may be able to keep her rights. If she dies before her husband, her rights will either pass to her executors as part of her estate, pass to a child (if the policy has a destination-over to it), or revert to the husband (if they were conditional on her surviving).[43] It all depends how the policy is worded.

MARRIAGE CONTRACTS

Marriage contracts are made between a couple either before their **5.45** marriage—antenuptial—or after, in order to regulate their respective property rights and those of their children and, in some cases, strangers. They were once much commoner than now. They were a way to protect a wife's property rights at a time when, on marriage, her moveable property passed by law to her husband; but now that marriage has few automatic effects on spouses' property rights[44] they are rare.

---

[40] s.2, as amended by Married Women's Policies of Assurance (Amendment) (Scotland) Act 1980.

[41] *Allan's Trs v. Inland Revenue*, 1971 S.L.T. 62.

[42] Married Women's Policies of Assurance (Amendment) (Scotland) Act 1980, s.3(1).

[43] *Barclay's Trs v. Inland Revenue*, 1975 S.L.T. 17.

[44] Married Women's Property Act 1920; Family Law (Scotland) Act 1985, ss.24, 25.

**5.46** In the normal way a marriage contract sets up a trust which provides for wife, child, or others. A provision is irrevocable if truly contractual and if the beneficiary is within the consideration of the marriage; otherwise it is purely testamentary, so revocable. So provisions in favour of spouses or their descendants are presumed irrevocable unless a power to revoke is expressly reserved. But the terms of the deed may give others a contractual and indefeasible right: as in *Mackie v. Gloag's Trs*[45] in favour of children of the wife's previous marriage.

**5.47** If a spouse makes a gift under a marriage contract he will probably receive nothing explicitly in return. If so it is a *gratuitous alienation* to an *associated person*; as such it can be challenged if he is sequestrated—made bankrupt—within five years. The rule applies to other gifts between spouses, but not to insurance policies under the 1880 Act.[46]

MISCELLANEOUS

**5.48** Rather as a testator may bind himself irrevocably to leave property to someone, so a legatee with a vested right may bind himself to deal with the legacy in a certain way. He may, for instance, agree to re-transfer it in a way that the testator had wanted. That transfer is exempt from IHT if made within two years.[47] If he dies before he receives the legacy, his obligation can be enforced against his representatives.

**5.49** One may of course make an outright gift *inter vivos*. The major consideration here is IHT.[48]

**5.50** It may sometimes be difficult to distinguish between gifts and *mortis causa* donation: the test is whether the gift is irrevocable and unconditional, and evidence of the donor's intention is important.

**5.51** One may undertake a binding obligation, by unilateral promise or bilateral contract, to leave someone property on death. However, in terms of the Requirements of Writing (Scotland) Act 1995 the former, and the latter if it concerns land, must be constituted in writing.[48a]

Promises and wills may be difficult to distinguish: the test is whether the words imply an immediately binding obligation.[49] In

---

[45] (1884) 11 R. (H.L.) 10.

[46] Bankruptcy (Scotland) Act 1985, s.34. Antenuptial marriage contracts no longer get favourable treatment: Law Reform (Husband and Wife) (Scotland) Act 1984, s.5(1)(b).

[47] IHTA 1984, s.143.

[48] See paras 12.05 *et seq.*

[48a] ss.1(2)(a)(ii), 1(2)(b); in force August 1, 1995. Pre-Act obligations will require writing under the common law. *McEleveen v McQuillan's Exx*, 1997 S.L.T. (Sh. Ct) 46 discusses the problems of constitution and proof.

[49] See *Miller v. Milne's Trs* (1859) 21 D. 377.

*Trotter v. Trotter*,[50] where the "promise" was linked to revocation of
a legacy, it was deemed to be itself a legacy, and hence revocable.

One may create an *inter vivos* trust over property in favour of a **5.52**
beneficiary. But it is important whether or not the trust is
revocable. If it is the truster still has control over the property and
it is consequently available to his creditors for diligence or on
bankruptcy. In that case the trust has little point as a means of
inheritance: one might as well simply make a testamentary trust or
a will, both of which have effect only on death.

Revocability depends on the truster's intention, discovered from **5.53**
the trust deed and surrounding circumstances. Two factors are
crucial. Is the trust for the management of the grantor's affairs
during his lifetime? If so it is revocable even if its words say it is
irrevocable. Is the beneficiary given an immediate enforceable
right—a *jus quaesitum*—or a mere right to succeed on the grantor's
death? If a *jus quaesitum* the trust is irrevocable; otherwise not.[51]

### REARRANGEMENTS AFTER DEATH

If the beneficiaries agree they can vary the division of the estate in **5.54**
any way they wish. So they may, by a deed of arrangement, disclaim
a benefit under a will, intestacy or legal rights, or vary them and
take different ones.

> "When . . . every possible beneficiary desires and consents to a **5.55**
> particular course being adopted—all the beneficiaries being of
> full age and *sui juris*—and none of them being placed under
> any restraint or disability by the . . . deed itself—then no one
> has any right or interest to object."[52]

Note that, failing such agreement or a specific legacy, beneficiaries **5.56**
have a right only to cash and not specific assets. The executor
should then sell the assets and distribute the proceeds.

Deeds of arrangement may have tax advantages. **5.57**

(1) *Inheritance tax*. Normally a disclaimer or election is a **5.58**
disposal for IHT purposes: so IHT would be due twice, from the
deceased's estate on death and from the beneficiary on the
arrangement.[53] But the variation is treated as made by the
deceased, and so is exempt from IHT, if (i) it is made within two
years after death, by the beneficiaries in writing, with no consideration received in return; and (ii) they make written election to the

---

[50] 1916 1 S.L.T. 357.
[51] See Wilson & Duncan, 11.05–11.17.
[52] *Gray v. Gray's Trs* (1877) 4 R. 378 at 383, *per* Lord Gifford.
[53] Unless either disposal was IHT-exempt, *e.g.* to a spouse.

Capital Taxes Office within six months after variation. If the election means that more IHT is due from the estate—as may happen if a legacy to a spouse is redeployed to a child—the executor must also elect, and can refuse if he has insufficient estate to pay the tax. (ii) is unnecessary for simple disclaimers. Only one tax-exempt variation per item is allowed.[54]

**5.59**    (2) *Capital gains tax.* The same rule applies to CGT. Here election will not affect the estate (because CGT is not chargeable on death) but may benefit the beneficiary. One need not claim for both CGT and IHT—it may pay one not to—but if one does the deed must say so explicitly.[55]

There is a potential disadvantage under income tax. If a parent redeploys funds to his child he is treated as making a settlement. Until the child reaches age 18 his resulting income will be aggregated along with the parent's rather than being taxed in the child's hands. The tax bill will usually be much higher.[56]

**5.60**    Irrespective of tax, the deed must be valid under the general law. Three points are relevant. A child aged 16 or 17 now has capacity to be party to a deed of variation, though if he thereby gives up benefits he may subsequently before age 21 seek to set it aside as a prejudicial transaction. It will be wise at the outset for all the parties to have the court ratify the deed to avoid later challenge by the child.[57] Secondly, there may be potential unborn or underage beneficiaries with contingent rights which have not yet vested (because, for instance, they must outlive the end of a liferent). Their consent can be dispensed with by court petition,[58] and the rights can be actuarially valued and insured against. The problem can be minimised if the will provides for rights to vest at the testator's death: that also avoids the risk of partial intestacy arising if the beneficiary dies before vesting. Finally, it is no bar to variation that the beneficiary has already received or used the property—with one exception, an alimentary liferent.[59]

**5.61**    A testator may consciously consider the possibility of a post death rearrangement. Classically he leaves his wife the whole estate and relies on her and other beneficiaries to sort matters out most tax efficiently. But the risk is that beneficiaries may not agree, and that tax legislation may bar the procedure. Alternatively he can set up a discretionary trust by will: there is IHT on his death but no further charge if the trustees distribute the assets within the next two years.[60]

---

[54] IHTA 1984, s.142. For children under 18 see s.17; paras 4.67–4.68, above.
[55] Taxation of Chargeable Gains Act 1992, s.62(6).
[56] ICTA 1988, s.663(1).
[57] Age of Legal Capacity (Scotland) Act 1991, ss.1–4. See Barr & Edwards, 1992 S.L.T. (News) 77; paras 4.67–4.68, above.
[58] Trusts (Scotland) Act 1961, s.1.
[59] See Gloag & Henderson, 47.10.
[60] IHTA 1984, s.144.

In effect he achieves the flexibility of post-death rearrangement **5.62** without some of the defects.

**Further reading**

D.G. Antonio, "Mortis Causa or Inter Vivos Donation?", 1954 S.L.T. (News) 121.

A. Barr & L. Edwards, "Age of Legal Capacity: Further Pitfalls", 1992 S.L.T. (News) 77.

D. Brand, "Time for Special Destinations to Die?", 2000 S.L.T. (News) 203

Clive, *Husband and Wife* (4th ed., 1997), 4.109–4.123 (life assurance), Chap. 17 (marriage contracts).

Currie, *Confirmation* (8th ed.), 13.10–13.27.

A.M.C. Dalgleish, "Insurance Policies in Executries", 1988 Law Soc. Scot. P.Q.L.E. 83.

W.G., "Donation Mortis Causa", 1951 S.L.T. (News) 53.

G.L. Gretton, "Destinations" (1989) 34 J.L.S. 299.

G.L. Gretton, "Destinations and Leases", 1982 S.L.T. (News) 213.

G.L. Gretton, "Life Policies and the Law of Succession" (1988) 33 J.L.S. 141.

J.M. Halliday, "What Makes a Destination Special?" (1977) 22 J.L.S. 16.

McBryde, *Contract*, paras 2.14–2.27.

M. Morton, "Special Destinations as Testamentary Instructions", 1984 S.L.T. (News) 133.

D. Nichols, "Special Destinations in Scotland" (1990) 35 J.L.S. 189.

CHAPTER 6

# WILLS: FORMAL VALIDITY

**6.01** A will is a declaration of what a person—the testator—wishes to be done with his property after his death[1]. Thus defined, the term "will" has a wide scope. It is not a precise term of legal art; its meaning may vary according to the context. "Its proper and strictest legal sense is probably . . . the aggregate of the *mortis causa*[2] writings which together fulfil [the writer's] completed intentions."

**6.02** That said, "will" is often used in a narrower sense. Like other terms its precise meaning must be determined from the document in which it appears, supplemented where necessary with extrinsic[3] evidence of the writer's intention. Rarely it may comprise non-testamentary documents such as marriage contracts which deal with disposal of assets on death.[4] More commonly (and colloquially) it has a more restricted sense than "testamentary writings": in this sense it would not cover a lifetime letter which, *inter alia*, made provision for legacies on death. (This is particularly important where a testator proposes to revoke all previous legacies: he is best to refer to "testamentary writings".)[5] Finally, a will can be contrasted with a *codicil*, a secondary document which adds to or amends an earlier will.

**6.03** There is a further distinction, between a simple will and a *trust disposition and settlement*. Under an ordinary will the testator's estate is distributed by executors directly to beneficiaries. A trust disposition and settlement is used where the estate is to be retained after the executry in the hands of testamentary trustees and administered for some continuing purpose, such as a liferent or accumulation; the trustees act initially as executors and the document conveys the estate to them. In effect it is a sub-category of will which operates through the mechanism of a trust.

---

[1] Erskine Inst. III.ix.5.
[2] *i.e.* relating to death.
[3] *i.e.* from outwith the document: see paras 10.04–10.12.
[4] as in *Dunsmure v. Dunsmure* (1879) 7 R. 259.
[5] Thus in *Clark's Exr v. Clark*, 1943 S.C. 216 "all wills previously executed by me" did not revoke a bequest made in a letter. If a restricted sense is aimed at, it is safer to itemise the revoked documents explicitly to avoid doubt.

In most respects (bar procedure and terminology) all these **6.04** categories of document are legally similar. All are varieties of testamentary writing, effective only on the grantor's death; the same rules of formal and essential validity, vesting and interpretation apply.[6] In this book "will" applies to all unless otherwise stated.

Most legal systems require some formalities in making a will. **6.05** The reasons are obvious. They guard against fraud: a handwritten will is difficult to forge. They ensure that the testator is fully aware of the importance of his act, and that the document is a complete and seriously-meant declaration of his testamentary intention. These points have added weight with wills as opposed to lifetime contracts, since inevitably the testator has passed away by the time his will is questioned.

The problem is to balance the need for formalities with giving **6.06** effect to every serious expression of intention by the testator. On the whole Scots law takes a liberal view of formalities, by contrast at least with England where wills are normally invalid unless made before witnesses. Moreover, with the Wills Act 1963 and the admission of "international wills", the trend is towards easier recognition of wills made in countries whose formalities differ from ours.[7]

The Scots law was substantially reformed by the Requirements **6.06a** of Writing (Scotland) Act 1995. This applies only to documents executed on or after August 1, 1995; earlier ones remain governed by the pre-Act law. Moreover, its scheme can be understood only in the light of the old law to which it was a response. Finally, both legal regimes may be involved if a testator made wills (or a will and a later codicil) on either side of August 1, 1995.[7a] For those reasons knowledge of the pre-Act law will remain important for many years to come.

The main provisions of the Act are stated in more detail later.[7b] **6.06b** The most fundamental feature is to distinguish clearly between requirements for (a) validity (what minimum formalities must be followed for a will to be capable of being legally valid?) and (b) proof (what formalities must be followed for it to be presumed valid without further evidence?). In the latter case the will has been made in a way which makes it clear that it is genuine, so that extrinsic proof from witnesses can be dispensed with. For that reason the criteria for (b) are, understandably, more stringent than for (a).

---

[6] Special IHT rules govern certain types of trust, *e.g.* accumulation and maintenance trusts. See Norrie & Scobbie, pp. 29–30, 36.

[7] See paras 14.42–14.43.

[7a] If the date of a will cannot be proved, it is presumed to have been executed after the Act came into force: Requirements of Writing (Scotland) Act 1995, s.14(6).

[7b] See paras 6.58 *et seq.*

**6.06c**  In that lies the main difference from the pre-1995 law. The old law makes no clear consistent difference between the two functions of formalities. It imposes a high standard of formalities, which meet both tests (a) and (b): in summary, that the will be attested (witnessed) or holograph (in the grantor's own writing). Mere signature by the testator, with nothing more, meets neither test.[7c] Thus many informal documents might fail even though the testator clearly intended them as a will. By contrast, the 1995 Act substantially lessened the requirements for (a)—thus largely eradicating the last problem—while preserving a higher (though also somewhat reduced) threshold for (b).

**6.06d**  This chapter therefore initially sets out the "pre-1995 Act" rules. The main provisions of the Act follow.

INFORMAL WILLS

**6.07**  Few countries allow oral or "nuncupative" wills for property of any great value: the risk of fraud is too great. English law once allowed them for moveable property, but no longer.[8] In Scotland an oral legacy was until recently valid, but only up to £8.33 (£100 Scots).[9]

**6.08**  Roman law allowed a soldier to make an informal will, the *testamentum militare*. England has an analogous statutory rule for members of the armed forces on military service and seamen at sea,[10] where it is useful because (formalities apart) it allows a will to be made at age 16 rather than 18. That age limit is not a problem in Scotland. The rule is not part of Scots law, and it is unlikely that the *testamentum militare* is either. In the only relevant modern case, *Stuart v. Stuart*,[11] the point was immaterial because (irrespective of formalities) there was no concluded testamentary intent: nothing but instructions for a future will.

TYPES OF FORMALITY: WILLS MADE BEFORE AUGUST 1, 1995

**Formalities and probativity**

**6.09**  Scots law requires no particular form of words, so long as they clearly express the testator's intention. Any sort of writing—ink, typing or handwriting—will do. Even pencil writing is valid,[12]

---

[7b] See paras 6.58 *et seq.*

[8] Except for soldiers' wills: Wills Act 1837, s.9. See generally J.G. Miller, *The Machinery of Succession* (2nd ed., 1996), Chap. 8.

[9] Under the Requirements of Writing (Scotland) Act 1995, s.1(2)(c), all wills are required to be in writing.

[10] Wills Act 1837, s.11; Wills (Soldiers and Sailors) Act 1918.

[11] 1942 S.C. 510.

[12] *Tait's Trs v. Chiene*, 1911 S.C. 743.

though most unwise. The problem, apart from the risk of fraudulent alteration and fading, is that pencil alterations on an ink document are taken to be mere drafts for a revised new will and do not show concluded testamentary intent.[13]

Wills might be made in three ways. They might be attested **6.10** (executed before witnesses according to statutory formalities); holograph (in the testator's handwriting and signed by him); or adopted as holograph (those words being written by the testator, and signed). In addition a formally valid will may validate an informal document by adopting it, and minor defects in execution may be cured by court decree under section 39 of the Conveyancing (Scotland) Act 1874.

Attested wills have one great benefit: they are probative. A **6.11** probative document is one which is presumed to have been validly executed because it appears so. It proves both its own authenticity and the existence of the rights and obligations which it contains; no other evidence is necessary. Wills which are holograph or adopted as holograph are not automatically probative but "privileged": while formally valid although not attested, the grantor's handwriting and signature must be proved to be genuine. But once that initial hurdle is overcome, which occurs when the executor applies for confirmation, the distinction disappears and holograph wills then become probative.[14]

A probative will may be reduced—set aside—by an action in the **6.12** Court of Session. That is not easy: strong proof is needed to challenge its apparent validity, especially where the signatures are genuine and the challenge relates to some other irregularity. *McArthur v. McArthur's Trs*[15] illustrates this: someone who would benefit on intestacy tried to reduce a will because it was not properly witnessed. His action failed because the witnesses' evidence was contradictory and had no independent corroboration.

In *McLure v. McLure's Exx*,[15a] by contrast, delay barred the action. The pursuer, M, waited ten years to bring it: he knew he had a remedy but chose to wait; the executor consequently could no longer bring a counter-action for debts M owed the estate. In the circumstances it was no longer open to M to seek to reduce the will.

## Attestation

Several "authentication statutes" prescribe how attested deeds **6.13** must be executed. The main rules evolved before 1700, reaching their highpoint with the Subscription of Deeds Act 1681 and the

---

[13] *Munro's Exrs v. Munro* (1890) 18 R. 122.
[14] 1964 Act, s.32; before the Act confirmation had no effect on the formal validity of wills.
[15] 1931 S.L.T. 463.
[15a] 1997 S.L.T. 127

Deeds Act 1696 which form the framework for the modern law. More recently the trend has been to lessen the formalities.[16]

**6.14**    In essence there are four required formalities.

(a) The testator must have subscribed the will personally on each page; if he could not write, he could subscribe vicariously by notarial execution.[17]

(b) Two independent witnesses must have seen the testator sign or acknowledge his signature to them. Acknowledgement need not be in so many words—it may be tacit, by actions—provided it is clear and unambiguous.[18]

(c) The witnesses must have signed on the last page, at the very end of the will.

(d) The witnesses must be designed—described—after their signatures, or in the testing clause.

### Witnesses

*(a) Who may act as witness?*

**6.15**    One could not witness a will if one was blind, insane, less than 16 years old,[19] or could not write. One had to be "independent" and one had to "know" the testator, but both tests were very flexible. One might, as in *Simsons v. Simsons*,[20] be related to the testator and benefit under the will; the risk is that the will is set aside if circumvention or undue influence are inferred.[21] At the other extreme, the witness need not have known the testator beforehand—someone off the street is acceptable—provided they are properly introduced. As the witness's role is purely to speak to the validity of the testator's signature, he need not have known the contents of the will.

*(b) When should witnesses sign?*

**6.16**    They should have signed as quickly as possible, preferably (though not absolutely essentially) together and at once, and certainly before the testator dies. The classic authority is now *Walker v. Whitwell*[22] which in laying down that formulation cast

---

[16] Conveyancing (Scotland) Act 1874, ss.38, 39.

[17] See paras 6.45 *et seq.*

[18] *Cumming v. Skeoch's Trs* (1879) 6 R. 963, approved in *Lindsay v. Milne's Exr*, 1995 S.L.T. 487.

[19] Age of Legal Capacity (Scotland) Act 1991, s.9(g). Previously the minimum age was 14.

[20] (1883) 10 R. 1247.

[21] *cf.* England where the legacy fails: Wills Act 1837, s.15.

[22] 1914 S.C. 560, revd. 1916 S.C. (H.L.) 75.

doubt on earlier laxer decisions where a gap of some four months was accepted.[23] In *Walker* the testatrix dictated her will to her son, who saw her sign; a second witness signed before she died six days later, but he himself only signed afterwards. The Court of Session thought that acceptable, especially considering that the son knew the contents of the will. The House of Lords disagreed. Testator's and witnesses' signatures (they said) are essential formalities which form a continuous process; the witnesses sign with the testator's consent, which obviously lapses on death.

### Completing the testing clause

The testing clause is the last clause of an attested deed. It **6.17** narrates the circumstances of its execution and designs the witnesses (usually by their occupation and address). Place and date of execution, though not essential, should be stated. An attested will is dated when the testator acknowledges his signature rather than when he signed.[24] The date may be important where revocation by a later will is alleged, or where the testator was incapax when the will was made.[25]

The clause should describe any material—significant— **6.18** alterations made in the will before signature, such as words scored out or written on erasures. (Those should themselves be signed or initialled or they will be treated *pro non scripto* and ignored.) It also mentions differences between the testator or witnesses' names in the will and their actual signature. But it cannot itself alter the will. That is because it is left blank till after signature: it can be filled in, even after the testator's death, at any time before the will is registered for preservation or relied on in pleadings in a court action.[26] This point should be checked before sending a will to the Books of Council and Session for registration after the testator's death.

The witnesses' and testator's signatures come after the testing **6.19** clause, but should be on the same page as the last words of the body of the will. It is sensible to leave enough space to fit the clause in so that it does not spill over onto another page.

### Defects in execution

Section 39 of the Conveyancing (Scotland) Act 1874 may save a **6.20** will even if it is formally invalid: the will may be declared valid and the defect disregarded. The section only applies if the will was subscribed by the testator and "bear[s] to be attested by two

---

[23] *Stewart v. Burns* (1877) 4 R. 427.
[24] *Tait's Trs v. Chiene*, 1911 S.C. 743.
[25] *Waddell v. Waddell's Trs* (1845) 7 D. 605.
[26] Conveyancing (Scotland) Act 1874, s.38.

witnesses subscribing". Now thanks to the defect the will is improbative—its validity is not automatically presumed—so the person relying on the will has the onus of proving that it was in fact subscribed by the grantor and attested by the witnesses. He may do so in an application to the Court of Session or (more simply) the sheriff court in whose area the deceased was domiciled, or when applying to be confirmed as executor under the will.

**6.21** Some defects are so minor as not to need section 39; some are curable under it; some are too grave for that. It is a matter of degree. On the one hand section 39 was not needed where, in *Grieve's Trs v. Japp's Trs*,[27] a witness included her maiden name in her signature. On the other, it is useless where, as in *Walker v. Whitwell*, a witness signed after the testator died, or did not see the grantor sign.[28] But it can be used, say, where the will is not signed on every sheet,[29] or where it is too late to insert witnesses' designations in the testing clause under section 38 of the Act.[30]

HOLOGRAPH WILLS

**Definition**

**6.22** A will is holograph if all essential parts are in the testator's own handwriting and it is subscribed by him.[31] Alternatively a will prepared by someone else (or typed) could be "adopted as holograph" by the testator signing and *writing* those words, or similar words, at the end—preferably, but not essentially, above his signature. No witnesses were necessary.

**6.23** In rare cases typing may be valid on its own, with no writing apart from the signature. In *McBeath's Trs v. McBeath*[32] the testator typed a will and typed "accepted as holograph" above his handwritten signature. The will contained a statement that he typed it. Due to illness, typing was his invariable method of preparing documents. The Court of Session, by a four to three majority, upheld the will on this reasoning: the essence of holograph is that the granter writes the document personally; the law evolved before typewriting and should reflect its invention; so what is in fact typed by the grantor must be recognised as holograph. This logic suggests that a signature might itself be typed, and some of the court were

---

[27] 1917 1 S.L.T. 70.
[28] *Smyth v. Smyth* (1876) 3 R. 573; *Forrest v. Low's Trs*, 1907 S.C. 1240; 1909 S.C. (H.L.) 16. See also *Williamson v. Williamson*, 1997 S.L.T. 1044 where a witness, Wilson, mistakenly signed "Williamson"; this could not be cured under s.39.
[29] *Bisset, Petr*, 1961 S.L.T. (Sh. Ct) 19.
[30] *Thomson's Trs v. Easson* (1878) 6 R. 141: see paras 6.17–6.19, above.
[31] Erskine Inst., III.ii.22.
[32] 1935 S.C. 471; a seven judge court.

not prepared to rule it out. The main, often insuperable, hurdle would be the need to prove who typed the document and "signature".

In *Chisholm v. Chisholm*[33] there was no adoption as holograph **6.24** or statement that the will was typed by the testator. That second point allowed Lord Guthrie to distinguish *McBeath* on its facts and hold the will invalid. That was a dubious argument: such statements were insufficient evidence of holograph in contested applications for confirmation of executors.[34] At any rate the facts in *McBeath* were so special that it is rarely likely to be followed.

Suppose a testator attempted to make an attested will but failed. **6.25** Perhaps the supposed "witnesses" did not see the testator sign, or did not appear at all. The will can still be valid if it is holograph.[35]

## Proof

A holograph will is not probative: anyone seeking to rely on it **6.26** must prove that the writing and signature are genuine. A statement *in gremio*—in the body—of the will has no value, *pace Chisholm*. If the will can be forged, so can the statement.

An action of declarator is one option,[36] but the point usually **6.27** arises where an executor applies for confirmation of his appointment under a holograph will. Commissary practice at one time relaxed the strict law. If an *in gremio* statement was present confirmation was granted without further proof; if absent, it was not. Granting confirmation merely ratified the executor's title to deal with the estate; the will was not deemed probative and could still be challenged.

The 1964 Act made two changes. By section 21 confirmation **6.28** requires affidavits from at least two people that the handwriting and signature in the will are those of the testator. By section 32, once confirmation is granted the will is now deemed probative for all purposes, so challenge will be difficult. If the testator died before September 10, 1964 the old law applies; the Act is not retrospective.[37]

Questions of confirmation apart, a holograph will proves its own **6.29** date. In the absence of contrary evidence it is deemed made on the date it bears. That is not the case with *inter vivos* deeds.[38]

## Printed will forms

It is possible to buy printed forms on which to make a will. The **6.30** testator fills in the blanks relating to legacies, name of executor and the like. In principle that is not disastrous: the document will be a

---

[33] 1949 S.C. 434.
[34] *Cranston, Petr* (1890) 17 R. 410.
[35] *Lorimer's Exrs v. Hird*, 1959 S.L.T. (Notes) 8.
[36] See Macphail, *Sheriff Court Practice* (2nd ed., 1998), para. 20.19.
[37] This simplifies the old law: see Currie, 3.122; Meston pp. 88, 103.
[38] Conveyancing (Scotland) Act 1874, s.40.

perfectly valid will provided it is duly witnessed. The problem arises if the form follows English formalities or if two witnesses have not signed. If it is to be valid it must be as a holograph will.[38a]

**6.31** Scots law holds a document holograph if all the essential parts are in the grantor's handwriting. It must of course be possible to deduce testamentary intent from them. The questions then are: what parts are essential; and are the printed parts to be disregarded in deciding that?

**6.32** The modern law originated in *Macdonald v. Cuthbertson*.[39] A testator living in China made an unwitnessed will on a printed form. Read as a whole it made perfect sense, but the legacies and the words bequeathing them were printed; about the only holograph words were some names and addresses. Lord McLaren, dissenting, thought printing in this context was in effect holograph (this was later the basis for the decision in *McBeath's Trs*). But the court held that printed words must be formal and superfluous, adding nothing of any importance to the handwritten part. If that test is met (which it was not in *Macdonald*) the will receives effect.

**6.33** In *Carmichael's Exrs v. Carmichael*[40] that test was met. All vital words were holograph, except the words of bequest which were now felt inessential; "cutting out the [printed] words . . . there is still enough to make a perfectly good and intelligible will".

**6.34** Modern cases apply this rule flexibly. To decide if the will is holograph, the court reads the will as a whole to see if the sense of the document can be gathered from the holograph part. One cannot ignore the printed words. If they do not add to or contradict the holograph part the will receives effect. The "essential" holograph parts may be quite brief. So in *Bridgeford's Exr v. Bridgeford*[41] they identified the testator, legatee and executor, and legacies; that was enough (a printed clause revoking previous wills was ignored). By contrast, to stress that the will is read *in toto*, in *Tucker v. Canch's Tr.*[42] there was a holograph clause revoking previous wills but there were no holograph legacies; the revocation clause could not receive effect on its own.

SIGNATURE

**Method of signature**

**6.35** Both attested and privileged wills require the testator to have subscribed the will. Signature shows completed testamentary intention: the testator has finally made up his mind. The rule is rigorously adhered to:

---

[38a] This of course refers to "pre-1995 Act" wills. Under the Act the problem disappears as witnesses are no longer required.

[39] (1890) 18 R. 101.

[40] 1909 S.C. 1387 at 1389, *per* L.P. Dunedin.

[41] 1948 S.C. 416.

[42] 1953 S.C. 270.

"Subscription [is] the essential and only admissible evidence of a **6.36**
concluded expression of will on the part of a testator . . . the rule is
inflexible—no subscription, no will."[43]

So it must have been the testator's own act. To guide his hand— **6.37**
as opposed to merely supporting his arm above the wrist—is fatal.[44]
A "rubber stamp" signature is useless, as someone else might have
applied it.[45]

It must be completed, but what that means may vary according **6.38**
to circumstances. Did the testator try to write more and fail? If so,
the will also fails.[46] But a shortened or nickname may suffice—
"Connie" in *Draper v. Thomason*[47]—as may initials. The test should
be to prove that this was the testator's normal method of signature
in the circumstances, taking into account that this may be a family
letter rather than legal document. Exceptionally the courts ignore
that "usual practice" test, as in *Lowrie's J.F. v. Macmillan*[48] where
they wished to prevent the Crown defeating the writer's clear
intention and taking as *ultimus haeres*.

Such "pet" signatures are only likely in holograph wills. They are **6.39**
invalid in attested wills because, by requiring proof of surrounding
facts, they make the will improbative.[49] Merely omitting an initial
or using a maiden name can be rectified by a reference in the
testing clause.

**Place of signature**

The testator must have subscribed: signature must be at the end **6.40**
of the document. While the courts make a presumption against
intestacy so as to give effect to the testator's wishes if at all
possible, failure to subscribe is fatal. The reason is that signature
must show that the testator has a completed testamentary
intention—he has finally made up his mind—and signature
elsewhere cannot show that.

So the signature must not be at the top or in the margin.[50] If in **6.41**
the middle, bequests above are valid but those added below are
not.[51] It should be on the same page as the last operative provisions
of the will, or it may be impossible to infer a link between the two.
So if the will is on one side of a sheet and the signature on the

---

[43] *Foley v. Costello* (1904) 6 F. 365.
[44] *Noble v. Noble* (1875) 3 R. 74.
[45] *Stirling Stuart v. Stirling Crawfurd's Trs* (1885) 12 R. 610.
[46] *Donald v. McGregor*, 1926 S.L.T. 103.
[47] 1954 S.C. 136; also *Rhodes v. Peterson*, 1972 S.L.T. 98.
[48] 1972 S.L.T. 159.
[49] But the 1874 Act, s.39 may be used for initials on any but the last page: *Gardner v. Lucas* (1878) 5 R. (H.L.) 105.
[50] *Taylor's Exxs v. Thom*, 1914 S.C. 79; *Robbie v. Carr*, 1959 S.L.T. (Notes) 16.
[51] *McLay v. Farrell*, 1950 S.C. 149.

back, it fails. In *Baird's Trs v. Baird*[52] signature and testing clause were on the back: that failed. Had the testing clause run from one side to the other that might have been valid, but is not safe practice since it means the testator signing a blank sheet.

**6.42**    Similarly a link like "P.T.O." may suffice. Even if the only signature is on a separate sheet that may be enough provided there is a clear connection or some form of words which "adopts" the otherwise invalid will.[53]

**6.43**    The testator must also have signed an attested will on *every* page. Strictly speaking that is only true when there is more than one separate sheet (if one sheet is folded into pages only the last need be signed) but is always best since otherwise there may be no clear link between the various pages.[54] A holograph will, being less easily forged, need only have been signed on the last page.[55]

**6.44**    Section 39 of the 1874 Act *may* be available to cure defective subscription; but there must have been subscription of some sort. So it was allowed in *Bisset, Petr*,[56] where only the last page was signed, but failed in *Baird*.

NOTARIAL EXECUTION

**6.45**    A notary is, in modern speech, a solicitor, and a notary public is the equivalent of the English commissioner for oaths. Any solicitor can be appointed one. He has the power to administer oaths for affidavits: formal sworn legal declarations which are required, say, on bankruptcy or selling a matrimonial home.

**6.46**    A notary public, like various other officials, could also execute a will on behalf of someone who was blind or could not write for any reason. The procedure was (and its post-1995 equivalent remains) optional: a blind testator can if he chooses execute a will himself,[57] though there is a grave risk of fraud or circumvention.

**Who may act?**

**6.47**    Notarial execution might, despite its narrow name, be by a solicitor, notary public, justice of the peace, or Church of Scotland minister or his assistant in his own parish.

**6.48**    A notary had to be absolutely independent: he had to have no personal interest in the will he executed. That "is essential to the ends of justice, to the protection of the rights of parties and to the

---

[52] 1955 S.C. 286; *cf. Bogie's Exrs v. Bogie*, 1953 S.L.T. (Sh. Ct) 32.
[53] *e.g. Russell's Exr v. Duke*, 1946 S.L.T. 242.
[54] *Ferguson, Petr*, 1959 S.C. 56.
[55] *Cranston, Petr*, (1890) 17 R. 410.
[56] 1961 S.L.T. (Sh. Ct) 19.
[57] *Duff v. Earl of Fife* (1823) 1 Sh. App. 498.

securing of purity in a public office".[58] He was disqualified from acting if he was a legatee. Similarly if the will made him personally executor or trustee; but if it appointed someone else, disqualification required a connection between notary and trustee which gave the notary a likely benefit under the will. Now trustees and executors must always act gratis unless a will lets them charge for their work: so mere partnership between notary and trustee was not by itself enough.[59] Nor was a contract of employment[60]: an assistant solicitor might safely notarise though his employer was trustee. But if the will permitted the trustees to appoint their partners as solicitors to the trust, the notary might then get fees through the firm, and was at once disqualified.[61]

**6.49** The rule is strict. The need to make the will urgently is no excuse: after all, fraud may be easier then. Even where a will conferred a benefit and the notary made a later codicil, the codicil falls: it is treated as part of the will.[62]

**6.50** The effect is drastic. The whole will falls, disinheriting all the beneficiaries. Admittedly in *Irving v. Snow*[63] it was suggested that the provision in favour of the notary might alone be struck down, but that was a special case: the court could not invalidate the will because it was made under English law and was therefore valid in Scotland under the Wills Act 1963, but they were loath to see the clause giving a benefit to a Scottish notary.

## Procedure

**6.51** Section 18 of and Schedule I to the Conveyancing (Scotland) Act 1924 lay down the formalities. They must have been strictly observed and completed in one continuous uninterrupted act; all were vital and failure in any respect cannot be cured under section 39.[64]

**6.52** Testator, notary, and two witnesses gathered, and the will was read to the testator. He stated he was blind or could not write (as appropriate) and authorised the notary to sign. Immediately below the will the notary wrote a docquet to this effect and signed, stating his capacity, and the witnesses signed opposite his signature. The ordinary testing clause followed all this.

---

[58] *Ferrie v. Ferrie's Trs* (1863) 1 M. 291.
[59] *McIldowie v. Muller*, 1982 S.L.T. 154.
[60] *Hynd's Tr. v. Hynd's Trs*, 1955 S.C. (H.L.) 1 (assistant solicitor).
[61] *Finlay v. Finlay's Trs*, 1948 S.C. 16.
[62] *Crawford's Trs v. Glasgow Royal Infirmary*, 1955 S.C. 367.
[63] 1956 S.C. 257.
[64] *Hynd's Tr. v. Hynd's Trs*, 1955 S.C. (H.L.) 1, where the docquet was filled in back at the solicitor's office.

### INCORPORATION OF OTHER DOCUMENTS

**6.53**  A testator might find it convenient to make a legacy by an informal letter, say, to friends or family. He might, at the other extreme, attempt to make a formal will which ultimately turned out to be invalid. A printed will form was an obvious example. Such writings were not valid wills on their own, unless holograph in their own right, but could be validated by being adopted—ratified—by another document.

**6.54**  The logic behind this was that the adopting document incorporated the informal one. The latter was thus in effect a schedule to the former. The adopting document had itself to be formally valid, whether attested or holograph. In addition it is essential that it unequivocally identified the informal writing. It might do this by specific reference, or, more usually, by reference to a general class of writings: "writings signed by me" and the like.

**6.55**  Later writings might adopt earlier ones. One way, apart from a separate formal writing, was to append a formal note to the informal one. The best example was a docquet adopting as holograph. Alternatively it might be a codicil to a will. *Craik's Exx v. Samson*[65] illustrates this: a holograph codicil was written on a will form; it referred to the will by reducing the amount of a legacy in it; it thus ratified the will as a whole. In similar vein was *Macphail's Trs v. Macphail*,[66] where a codicil referred to an unsigned and undated list of legacies enclosed along with it in a sealed envelope addressed to the executors: given that the list was in fact a completed testamentary document rather than a draft, it was thus made valid insofar as it did not conflict with the codicil.

**6.56**  It was common for a will to state that future informal writings be treated as valid. Unsigned writings could be adopted, but that was unwise. The risk of fraud apart, signature has the advantage of clarity: it shows concluded testamentary intention. In its absence a note is more likely to have been a mere ineffective draft for a will: one cannot easily tell.

**6.57**  It was more usual to adopt writings "signed by me" or "under my hand". The limits of this device were firmly drawn in *Waterson's Trs v. St Giles Boys' Club*[67] to exclude writings which are not subscribed, unless it is clear from the language that "under my hand" is to have a wider meaning.

---

[65] 1929 S.L.T. 592.
[66] 1940 S.C. 560.
[67] 1943 S.C. 369.

FORMALITIES: WILLS MADE ON OR AFTER AUGUST 1, 1995

## Basic formalities

To be valid, the Requirements of Writing (Scotland) Act 1995 **6.58**
requires testamentary documents—"any will, testamentary trust
disposition and settlement or codicil"—to be made by way of a
"written document" (section 1(2)(c)). It must be subscribed by the
grantor (section 2(1)). Other legislation may prescribe laxer formalities (section 2(4)): in the context of informal wills made
through family correspondence, one should bear in mind that,
though "writing" currently envisages a tangible document,[68] the
Scottish Ministers have power under the Electronic Communications Act 2000[69] to modify legislation so as to encourage the use of
electronic communications.

Signature is (section 7(2)) much as under the old law: full name **6.59**
or surname plus forename/initials or another name, description,
initial, or mark. In the latter case, it must be proved that the name
(etc.) was the testator's usual method of signing that type of
document and that he intended it as his signature. Subscription
means (section 7(1)) signing at the end of the last page of the
deed.

The formalities for basic validity are thus liberalised. Witnessing, **6.60**
or signature on all pages, are no longer necessary; a typewritten
letter to a family member, signed by a pet name, would (for
example) suffice. Besides signature, it must of course still be clear
that the document was intended to have testamentary effect; but
that is a separate issue.

## Presumption of validity

If certain extra formalities are met, the document may be **6.61**
presumed valid without the need to prove this. They are a matter
of evidence rather than essentials for validity; in their absence, the
document is still in principle valid, but that must be proved: was it
genuinely signed by the purported testator? Section 3 of the 1995
Act sets out the extra formalities.

The first relates to the grantor's signature. The document must **6.62**
"bear"—appear on the face of it—to have been subscribed by him.
In addition, he must have signed (not necessarily subscribed) on
each separate sheet; so, strictly—as with the old law on
probativity—it is not essential to sign each page where the will
comprises only one piece of paper.

The other criteria relate mainly to witnesses. Witnessing, no **6.63**
longer a test for basic validity, is now central to the section 3

---

[68] Interpretation Act 1978, Sched. 1.
[69] s.8.

presumption. Only one is now needed. Otherwise the requirements are similar, though not strictly identical, to their "pre-Act" equivalents. The witness must know the testator, be 16 or over, and mentally capax. She must sign; subscription—signature at the end—may be wise but is not essential. The testator must have signed in her presence or acknowledge his signature to her. The whole process—of testator's and witness's actions—must be continuous. Finally, the deed must identify the witness by name and address (those details may be added at any time before the will is used in legal proceedings or registered in the Books of Council and Session or sheriff court books).

**6.64** If the will also states where and when it was subscribed, that is presumed to be correct (section 3(10)). This may be important in determining if the 1995 Act applies. Failing that, these details would need to be proved. If this cannot be done, the will is presumed to have been made after the Act came into force (section 14(6)).

**6.65** Finally, the section 3 presumption as to subscription will not apply if something in the will or testing clause indicates that, in fact, the testator did not subscribe it or it was not validly witnessed. A similar point applies to the presumption as to date and place of subscription (sections 3(1)(c), (10)).

### Proof of validity

**6.66** If the will was not signed by the testator, it is totally invalid; the 1995 Act gives the courts no general dispensing power to declare it valid on the basis of evidence that it was written by the testator.[70] If on the other hand it was signed but, for whatever reason, it could not be presumed valid by virtue of section 3, it is still in principle valid. One may under section 4 apply to the court to decide the matter; if the court is satisfied, it will endorse the will with a certificate accordingly (or, if it has already been registered, grant decree). The matter may be raised by separate court action or, more normally, incidentally to other proceedings (such as confirmation); evidence is normally by affidavit—from one person[71]—that the subscription is genuine.

**6.67** Confirmation can only be granted if the will is presumed valid or held valid (under sections 3 or 4 respectively).[72] The section 4 procedure is thus analogous to that for holograph wills under the old law.

---

[70] The Scottish Law Commission has separately proposed such a power: Report No. 124 (1990), paras 4.1–4.20.

[71] Act of Sederunt (Requirements of Writing) 1996 (S.I. 1996 No. 1534).

[72] Succession (Scotland) Act 1964, s.21A, inserted by Requirements of Writing (Scotland) Act 1995, Sched. 4, para. 39.

## Informal documents

The relaxed formalities under the 1995 Act mean that many **6.68** documents will be effective which would have failed under the old law: for instance, the printed will form which had no, or only one, witness; or the typed and signed letter. It will be less necessary to include a general power in a (valid) will to adopt other (invalid) documents as valid, as was previously common. This is just as well, as such a clause is not permitted under the 1995 Act: the Act refers only to validation of "annexations", which must be specifically identified in the adopting document (section 8(1)). However, the omission is not practically important: such clauses typically adopt only documents "under my hand", and under the Act those are now independently valid without any need for such adoption.

## Testators who are blind or cannot write

The old notarial execution is replaced by a similar procedure **6.69** (section 9). The main differences from the old law are that:

(a) The list of those entitled to act is amended, *e.g.* by omitting Church of Scotland ministers.

(b) If the will confers a benefit on the executing person, then it is no longer totally invalid (as happens under the old law) but only to the extent that that person, spouse, or child benefits.

NEGLIGENT PREPARATION OF WILL

Suppose a solicitor, instructed to prepare a will, does not do so **6.70** with due care. He fails (for instance) to ensure that it is properly witnessed, or to follow the correct procedures for notarial execution. The will is ineffective as a result; potential beneficiaries consequently do not inherit. (This could happen for other reasons than formal invalidity. The solicitor may (say), as in *Weir v. J.M. Hodge & Son*, ignore the existence of a special destination over the testator's property.)[73]

This is professional negligence. Has the disappointed beneficiary **6.71** a remedy against the solicitor? A number of Common Law jurisdictions, creatively extending the concept of delictual liability for economic loss caused by a professional adviser's negligent misstatements, have allowed the beneficiary to recover damages.[74] The

---

[73] 1990 S.L.T. 266.
[74] *Ross v. Caunters* [1980] Ch. 297, *White v. Jones* [1995] 2 A.C. 207 (England); *Gartside v. Sheffield, Young & Ellis* [1983] N.Z.L.R. 37 (New Zealand).

main Scots authority, *Robertson v. Fleming*,[75] denied the beneficiary a remedy. Modern judges till recently regarded it as outdated but (as a House of Lords decision) still binding precedent to be followed. A more recent (though unreported) decision[76] now follows *White v. Jones* and allows a remedy.

**6.72** In any event such claims, even though allowed in principle, can be difficult to establish in practice. In *Weir*—issues of legal doctrine apart—there was in the court's view insufficient evidence that the testatrix ever intended to leave her house to the pursuer. Even given negligence and a duty of care to the beneficiary, there was no proven causative link with the pursuer's loss. In the most recent case, *MacDougall v. MacDougall's Exrs*,[77] the pursuer clearly fell outwith the ambit of any possible duty of care. He was not a beneficiary under the invalid will, but merely a potential legatee of such a beneficiary.

**Further reading**

J. Blaikie, "Negligent Solicitors and Disappointed Beneficiaries", 1989 S.L.T. (News) 317.

Currie, *Confirmation*, Chaps 3, 4.

A.G.M. Duncan, "The Limits of Disqualifying Interest", 1979 S.L.T. (News) 173.

K.G.C. Reid, "What is a Probative Writ?" (1985) 30 J.L.S. 308.

Halliday, *Conveyancing* (2nd ed., 1996), Vol. 1, Chap. 3.

M.C. Meston & D. Cusine, "Execution of Deeds by a Mark" (1993) 38 J.L.S. 270.

K.G.C. Reid, "Execution of Deeds" (1987) 32 J.L.S. 148.

---

[75] (1861) 4 Macq. 167: it concerned a guarantee rather than a will.

[76] *Robertson v. Watt & Co.*, July 4, 1995, Inner House, noted by MacQueen, (1998) 3 S.L.P.Q. 145.

[77] 1994 S.L.T. 1178.

# REVOCATION OF WILLS

## REVOCABILITY

### General

A will is "ambulatory": that is, it operates from the testator's **7.01** death and is ineffective till then.[1] Even including a declaration of irrevocability in the will does not prevent revocation.

For the same reason wills are treated as an exception to the **7.02** normal rule that a deed is irrevocable once delivered by the grantor to the grantee or someone on the grantee's behalf. With *inter vivos* deeds the rationale is that the grantor, by his act of putting the deed out of his physical control, shows his intention to be bound by it; that logic does not apply to a will which by its nature cannot take effect till death.[2]

That said, a testator may incur a binding obligation to leave **7.03** property to someone on death. Revocation will need the recipient's consent, though he cannot stop the testator disposing of the asset to someone else while alive.

The simplest case involves an onerous contract between donor **7.04** and donee: both parties undertake obligations. So in *Paterson v. Paterson*[3] a mother agreed to make an irrevocable settlement of her property in her son's favour, while in return he lent her money and paid her rent; her later will broke the agreement, and so the court set it aside. Alternatively there may be a unilateral promise, binding immediately albeit only payable by the estate after the promisor's death. Yet again, a person may have a *jus quaesitum tertio*, an irrevocable third party right, under a contract between two other people: the classic example is a child under a marriage contract.[4] In all these cases the donee's right is a debt of the

---

[1] Erskine. Inst., III.ix. 5.
[2] *Clark's Exr v. Clark*, 1943 S.C. 216.
[3] (1893) 20 R. 484.
[4] *Fernie v. Colquhoun's Trs* (1854) 17 D. 233; *Carmichael v. Carmichael's Exx*, 1920 S.C. (H.L.) 195.

grantor's estate and hence payable ahead of mere legacies; again unlike a legacy, it will pass to the donee's heirs if he dies before the grantor.

### Mutual wills

**7.05**  Suppose X and Y make a will contained in one document, each leaving his or her property to the other and (perhaps) thereafter to their child or some stranger. That is a mutual will. Either can still dispose of his or her own assets while alive. The question is whether he can revoke the will, whether before or after the other dies.

**7.06**  In bare principle he can revoke: the "will" is treated as two wills in one document. But he cannot if it is contractual: an express or implicit agreement (and hence irrevocable) that each shall dispose of his or her property as stated in the will.

**7.07**  The issue can arise while both are alive, but usually when Y has died and the survivor X wishes to revoke a provision in favour of a child. The terms of the will are crucial. A clause governing the power to revoke is obviously important (though not conclusive): if the spouses must both jointly revoke, the survivor cannot do so by himself.[5] Reciprocity of legacies also points to contract. Beyond that, much depends on what right Y was given in X's property. Often he has a liferent and the child is given the fee: that suggests irrevocability. If he has the fee, revocability is usual[6]—but not always: the will may still expressly prevent revocation.[7]

**7.08**  The Scottish Law Commission decided against reform on the ground that mutual wills are so complicated already that few people make them.[8]

METHODS

### Destruction

*(a) Methods and requirements*

**7.09**  Destruction of a will must be *animo et facto*: there must be an intention to revoke, *animus revocandi*, and a physical act of destruction.

**7.10**  Apart from the obvious case of physical destruction of the original will by the testator, a special point arises. What constitutes destruction? In rare cases symbolic destruction is sufficient. In

---

[5] *Corrance's Trs v. Glen* (1903) 5 F. 777.
[6] *Hanlon's Exr v. Baird*, 1945 S.L.T. 304.
[7] *Duthie v. Keir's Exr*, 1930 S.C. 645.
[8] Report No. 124, para. 4.84.

*Nasmyth v. Hare's Trs*,[9] the testator cut off the seal attached to the end of the document. This was an effective revocation despite the fact that it was still a valid holograph document. The reason was that while sealing normally is irrelevant to formal validity, in this case the testator had chosen to include this extra solemnity of execution; so his action was taken as symbolic of revocation. Also unusual was *Thomson's Trs v. Bowhill Baptist Church*[10] where there was very clear evidence of intention to revoke certain clauses: they were scored out, then physically cut out, the testator had signed near the gap, and had signed a written explanation above and below them; while this was only a copy of the original will, in the circumstances the actions constituted destruction.

The act must be carried out by the testator himself or on his **7.11** authority. In *Cullen's Exr v. Elphinstone*[11] a widow instructed her solicitors to prepare a new will, which they executed notarially since she was blind; uninstructed, they destroyed the old will; their act was legally ineffective. But conversely, will mere authorisation of destruction suffice? *Bruce's J.F. v. Lord Advocate*[12] makes clear that merely instructing a new will to be made does not authorise destroying the old; on the other hand, it was suggested tentatively that if the solicitor there had been ordered to destroy but had failed to, that might be regarded as constructive cancellation.

Destruction by accident, in anger, or while drunk or insane does **7.12** not revoke. *Animus revocandi* is absent. The problem is proving intention or lack of it. For example, in *Laing v. Bruce*[13] the pursuers claimed that a will had been in the hands of the deceased before her death and was not found afterwards, and that at that time the deceased was insane. They could not prove her insanity; had they been able to they could have had the will "set up" again as unrevoked.

It may be known that the testator had a will in his possession at **7.13** the time of his death which cannot subsequently be found. There is then a legal presumption that he destroyed it *animo revocandi*, which can however be rebutted by evidence to the contrary.[14]

*(b) Accidental destruction: proving terms of will*

If a will has been lost or destroyed it may be arguable that it was **7.14** not thereby revoked and hence is still valid: *e.g.* if destroyed without the testator's instructions, or accidentally, or it merely

[9] (1821) 1 Sh. App. 65.
[10] 1956 S.L.T. 302.
[11] 1948 S.C. 662.
[12] 1969 S.C. 296.
[13] (1838) 1 D. 59.
[14] *Bonthrone v. Ireland* (1883) 10 R. 779; *Laing*, above; *Lauder v. Briggs*, 1999 S.C. 453 where Lord Penrose thought an argument against the existence of the presumption "persuasive" but considered that it was settled law until the Inner House decided otherwise.

cannot be found. The remedy is an action to "prove the tenor" to set it up again and prove its contents. The procedure is available for any legal document, such as an IOU.[15] The problem is one of evidence, both of the terms of the document and of the absence of *animus*. A draft or copy is the best proof of the terms. Oral evidence is however competent and may suffice; the courts seem particularly willing to accept it if the will had been maliciously destroyed, since insisting on written evidence would effectively unjustly disinherit the pursuer. But to succeed he will require witnesses' clear and consistent evidence as to at least the essentials of the will (legatees, identity and amount of legacies).[16]

**7.15**    To establish the *casus amissionis*—how the document went missing—requires very clear evidence in the case of a revocable document such as a will. "*Casus amissionis* means not only that the writing has actually been destroyed or lost, but that its destruction or loss took place in such a manner as implied no extinction of the right of which it was the evidence."[17] It is only natural, after all, that the testator may have changed his mind without telling anyone. So in *Clyde v. Clyde*,[18] the facts were insufficient to rebut the presumption of destruction *animo revocandi*: the testator had made a formal will in his nephew's favour; 12 years later, seven years before his death, he had his solicitors return it to him; there was no evidence of ill-feeling or intention to alter it, but no one else had access to where he kept it. Conversely in *Morrison v. Morrison*[19] there was adequate evidence of *casus amissionis* (document was burnt after testator's death) but insufficient proof of its terms or even that it was properly subscribed as a completed will.

**Deletions and alterations**

**7.16**    A will may have been altered before its formal execution or afterwards. Both situations are discussed here, but one should bear in mind that the guiding rules are different. If before, the question is purely one of authentication: did the changes take effect as part of the original deed? If later, it is one of revocation also.[20] The distinction mainly affects attested wills, and is less important in holograph ones.

*(a) Attested wills*

**7.17**    The ordinary rules for execution apply to alterations made at or before the time of execution. Unauthenticated alterations may invalidate the whole deed if they affect an essential part such as the

---

[15] *Borland v. Andrew's J.F.* (1901) 4 F. 129. Also see Walkers, *Evidence*, 20.4–20.7.
[16] *Leckie v. Leckie* (1884) 11 R. 1088; *Conner v. Brown*, 1989 G.W.D. 31–1401.
[17] *Winchester v. Smith* (1863) 1 M. 685.
[18] 1958 S.C. 343.
[19] 1992 G.W.D. 23–1350.
[20] But *cf. Syme's Exrs v. Cherrie*, 1986 S.L.T. 161 where this distinction was ignored. See Halliday, *Conveyancing*, Vol. I, 3.28–3.30; Reid, 1986 S.L.T. (News) 129.

names of legatees. However, section 39 of the Conveyancing
(Scotland) Act 1874 can be used to cure the informality of
execution: this was done for unauthenticated interlineations in
*Elliot's Exrs.*[21] In *Syme's Exrs v. Cherrie*[22] it was said that a
declaration in the testing clause might also work.

**7.18** Note, too, that the testing clause cannot alter the provisions in
the main body of the will in any way (for the obvious reason that it
is added after execution) and any such attempted additions are
ignored. Thus in *Smith v. Chambers' Trs*[23] the testing clause could
not declare legacies to be "alimentary".

**7.19** Subsequent alterations raise the question of *animus revocandi*.
The classic statement of the required authentication was made by
Lord McLaren in *Pattison's Trs v. University of Edinburgh*.[24] He
required four elements:

**7.20** "(1) If a will or codicil is found with the signature cancelled,
or with lines drawn through the dispositive or other essential
clause of the instrument, then, on proof that the cancellation
was done by the testator himself, or by his order, with the
intention of revoking the will, the will is to be held revoked;
otherwise it is to be treated as a subsisting will."

**7.21** Intention is crucial. In *Fotheringham's Trustee v. Reid*[25] it was
absent: a woman deleted her married name simply intending to
revert to her maiden name.

**7.22** "(2) If a will or codicil is found with one or more of the
legacies or particular provisions scored out . . . this raises no
case for inquiry as to the testator's intention to revoke the
instrument in whole, but [it does] as to the intention to revoke
the particular provision; . . . the provision [is not] revoked
unless [there is] evidence that the scoring was done by the
testator himself or by his direction with the intention of
revoking the clause. If the deletion were authenticated by the
testator's initials, recognisable as his handwriting, [that is]
sufficient proof that the deletion was the act of the testator,
the full signature being only necessary to an act of positive
disposition or bequest."

**7.23** "(3) If a will or codicil is found with marginal or interlineal
additions, apparently in the testator's handwriting . . . these
[are] not part of the instrument, except in so far as they are
authenticated by the signature or initials of the testator."

---

[21] 1939 S.L.T. 69.
[22] 1986 S.L.T. 161.
[23] (1878) 5 R. (H.L.) 151.
[24] (1888) 16 R. 73.
[25] 1936 S.C. 831.

**7.24** "(4) When the will or codicil contains words scored out and others inserted in their place,. . . the cancellation of the words in the original writing is conditional on the substituted words taking effect. Accordingly, if the substituted words are rejected on the ground that they are unsigned, the deletion is also to be rejected, and the will ought to be read in its original form."

*(b) Holograph wills*

**7.25** The authentication rules are much laxer because fraud is less likely. In *Robertson v. Ogilvie's Trs*[26] three out of seven trustees' names were written on erasures; provided the words were holograph of the testator (as was proved) the deed was valid. Even unauthenticated deletions may be given effect. In *Milne's Exr v. Waugh*[27] four holograph testamentary writings, all signed, were found after the testator's death in a sealed envelope; some bequests were scored out in ink. It could be inferred from the circumstances that the testator made the deletions *animo revocandi*. But the courts are rightly chary of this method and need very clear proof.[28]

**Revocation by later will**

**7.26** A will often expressly revokes all previous testamentary writings. The effect of such a provision depends on how the court construes it in an effort to discover the testator's intention. It may not always revoke all previous bequests. "Testamentary writings" has a wider meaning than "wills", and in *Clark's Exr v. Clark*[29] a revocation of "all wills previously executed by me" did not revoke a specific legacy of a stamp collection previously delivered to a legatee. In *Gordon's Exr v. McQueen*[30] a revocation of "two wills which are recorded in the Books of Council and Session in Edinburgh" was ineffective to revoke the testator's only previous will which did not meet that description. A revocation clause should either refer to "testamentary writings" or, if not a blanket revocation, accurately identify the will being revoked.

**7.27** Revoking a will also revokes any ancillary documents, such as a codicil or an informal writing which derived its validity from it.

**7.28** A will may also be revoked by implication. Again the point came up in *Clark's Exr* regarding the stamp collection. "As a general rule a later settlement of the *universitas* of the grantor's estate ['my whole estate' or some such wording] will be held impliedly to

---

[26] (1844) 7 D. 236.
[27] 1913 S.C. 203.
[28] *Allan's Exx v. Allan*, 1920 S.C. 732.
[29] 1943 S.C. 216.
[30] 1907 S.C. 373.

revoke the provisions of an earlier settlement on the ground that the two deeds are inconsistent and cannot stand together. But there is no presumption that a general disposition revokes a former bequest of a specific subject." Did the testator in reality mean to dispose of the whole estate in the later will? As always the court must, avoiding speculation, attempt to elicit his intention from the whole scheme of the will (read in conjunction with the previous wills).[31]

By way of example, the testator in *Duthie's Exrs v. Taylor*[32] **7.29** conveyed her whole means and estate to testamentary trustees. That by itself might point to a universal settlement; but the will then directed various legacies and did not dispose of the residue of the estate. Looking at the testator's whole scheme it was not a universal settlement, and legacies in an earlier stood except insofar as inconsistent with it. In *Clark's Exr*, too, the scheme of the will suggested that by "whole estate" the testator actually meant only his investments; and in the circumstances his delivering the stamp collection also suggested he meant the will not to affect it.

Universal settlements apart, the rule is that revocation by **7.30** implication occurs only where there is necessary inconsistency. Insofar as two wills are not inconsistent they are read together. For instance, in *Stewart v. MacLaren*[33] the testator had, in a third codicil to a will, confirmed various provisions in the will and first codicil but made no reference to the second codicil. The second codicil was held not to be revoked: "the words of revocation must be clear . . . you cannot speculate one way or the other". This principle was well stated in *Stoddart v. Grant*[34] where it was said that "it is a well-established principle of the law of Scotland that where a person deceased has left various writings, probative in themselves, for disposing of his or her property, they are to be understood as constituting one testamentary settlement in so far as they have not been revoked and are not inconsistent with each other".

Where implied revocation is alleged, the onus of proof is of **7.31** course on the person alleging it. Proof must be beyond reasonable doubt. This was stressed in *Mitchell's Administratrix v. Edinburgh Royal Infirmary*[35] where, in a codicil, one provision suggested revocation of certain legacies while the other was against it. The facts were neutral; the legacies stood. Given that in other wills the

---

[31] Using extrinsic evidence to resolve ambiguity in limited circumstances: see paras 10.04–10.12, below.
[32] 1986 S.L.T. 142.
[33] 1920 S.C. (H.L.) 148.
[34] (1852) 1 Macq. 163.
[35] 1928 S.C. 47 at 51–54, *per* L.J.-C. Alness; approved in *Duthie's Exrs v. Taylor*, 1986 S.L.T. 142.

testator generally used express revocation, and that they were prepared by a solicitor (whom one would expect to use precise legal language to achieve revocation), it was not possible to infer implied revocation in the particular will being disputed.

**The *conditio si testator sine liberis decesserit***

7.32    In Scots law, unlike English, a will is not revoked if the testator later gets married or divorced. However it may be revoked by the subsequent birth of a child to the testator if it is a universal settlement and it makes no provision for the child. This is the *conditio si testator sine liberis decesserit.*

7.33    The rule applies in favour of any child born after the date of the will. The basis of the doctrine is generally taken to be a (fictitious) equitable presumption that the testator would have provided for later-born children if he had thought about them. It therefore only applies if the will made no such provision, however small.

7.34    The presumption can be rebutted by proof that the omission was deliberate: the testator meant not to make provision for the child in the will. But rebuttal is not easy. Evidence of a conscious and positive decision by the testator is probably necessary. It is not rebutted by mere passage of time between the child's birth and the testator's death: in *Milligan's J.F. v. Milligan*[36] 10 years passed but that was not sufficient. One can contrast *Stuart-Gordon v. Stuart-Gordon*[37] where the testatrix died shortly after her daughter was born: it was proved that when considering her legacies in view of her bad health, and knowing the daughter was well provided for anyway, she had decided to omit her.

7.35    The *conditio* is not automatic. Only the child itself can invoke it and bring an action to reduce the will; he need not if he so chooses. If he dies his representatives cannot raise the action in his place for the benefit of his estate; nor can another disappointed legatee. Even so a practical problem can occur: an executor appointed under that will may be refused confirmation unless he rebuts the *conditio*, on the grounds that the will is presumed invalid.[38]

7.36    Unlike a simple legitim claim, the *conditio* revokes the will entirely. Intestacy may result[39] and the child can then claim legitim. But the widow's prior rights take precedence: they may exhaust the whole estate if it is small, leaving nothing for the child. The child may be better off simply to claim legitim in opposition to the will, because then intestacy is avoided and thus prior rights cannot arise.[40]

---

[36] 1910 S.C. 58.
[37] (1899) 1 F. 1005.
[38] Currie, 3.170–3.174.
[39] Unless the legacy contains a destination-over, or its lapse causes an earlier will to "revive" in its place: see paras 7.38 *et seq.*
[40] The Commission proposes to abolish the *conditio*: Report no. 124, paras 4.46–4.49.

## Conditional revocation

English law clearly recognises the doctrine of *dependent relative*  **7.37**
*revocation* that, when a revocation is linked to a new will or legacy,
it is dependent on the legacy taking effect. Very few Scots cases
admit to its existence, and then without referring to it by name.
*Gemmell's Exr v. Stirling*,[41] for instance, stressed that the test is that
the revocation is coupled with the legacy in some way; they are
interdependent. Lord McLaren in *Pattison's Trs*[42] regarded deletions as invalid unless the new substituted words took effect.[43]

## Revival of the revoking will

On one view revocation does not bury a will: it puts it in  **7.38**
suspended animation. It can in some cases be revived. Suppose a
testator makes a will, will no. 2, which revokes an earlier will, will
no. 1. At a later date will no. 2 is itself revoked. The testator dies
without a further valid will. Does will no. 1 revive by virtue of
revocation of the will which revoked it?

In some cases there is no problem. Often will no. 2 is revoked by  **7.39**
a method which also ensures will no. 1 remains dead. That may be
the *conditio si testator*, or an express revocation of all previous wills.
The problem arises when the final revocation is specific to will no.
2. For instance, will no. 1 contains provision for future children
while will no. 2 does not: a child is then born. In that case the
*conditio* revokes will no. 2 but has no effect on will no. 1.

The case law is inconsistent. In *Elder's Trs v. Elder*[44] will no. 1  **7.40**
was expressly revoked by will no. 2, which was itself revoked by the
operation of the conditio. The court held that will no. 1 did not
revive: while the law presumes that a will which makes no provision
for future children is revoked on the birth of a child, there is no
presumption that a prior will which has been expressly revoked by
the later will is restored (even if it makes provision for them). By
contrast, in *Nicolson v. Nicolson's Tutrix*[45] will no. 1 was merely
impliedly revoked because will no. 2 was a universal settlement; on
that ground the court refused to follow *Elder* and held that will no.
1 revived.

The most recent case, *Scott's J.F. v. Johnston*,[46] also upheld will  **7.41**
no. 1. The court appears to have taken the rule as settled, whereas

---

[41] 1923 S.L.T. 384.
[42] (1888) 16 R. 73 at 77.
[43] *MacRorie's Exrs v. McLaren*, 1982 S.L.T. 295 (the Outer House judgement
reversed on appeal at 1984 S.L.T. 271 on other grounds) took a similar line on
implied revocation. The Commission (despite earlier misgivings) considers the
existing rule satisfactory: Report No. 124, para. 4.77.
[44] (1895) 22 R. 505.
[45] 1922 S.L.T. 473. But *cf. Bruce's J.F. v. Lord Advocate*, 1969 S.C. 296.
[46] 1971 S.L.T. (Notes) 41.

it is still open to doubt. The practical advice given in *Scott* is to make certain that when will no. 2 is made, the testator is asked to ensure that will no. 1 is physically destroyed—either by him or his solicitor acting on his instructions. That way one can be certain that it will not revive.[47]

**Further reading**

M.C. Meston, "Dependent Relative Revocation in Scots Law", 1977 S.L.T. (News) 77.

M.C. Meston, "Revival by Revocation of the Revoking Will", 1974 S.L.T. (News) 153.

M.C. Meston, "The Conditiones Si Sine Liberis" (1981) 26 J.L.S. (Workshop) 203.

"Wills and the Testator's Animus Revocandi", 1984 S.L.G. 90.

K.G.C. Reid, "Execution or Revocation?" 1986 S.L.T. (News) 129.

---

[47] For the Commission's proposals see Report No. 124, paras 4.67–4.76.

# CHAPTER 8

# WILLS: ESSENTIAL VALIDITY

The term "will" is self-explanatory. A will is a declaration of what a **8.01** person wills to be done with his or her estate after his or her death.[1] So, as with any legal act, he must know what he is doing. Legal capacity to undertake an act requires the ability to understand its nature and effects.[2] If that is absent, the person cannot make a will. Similarly, he must actually have made up his mind to make a will. Mere jottings for a possible future will are not enough. In legal terminology, the testator must have both testamentary capacity and concluded testamentary intent.

The underlying concept is not unique to wills. It is basic to the **8.02** whole law of contract. Contracts can, in principle, be set aside if consent is defective or non-existent. But by the nature of things the emphasis is different with wills. A contract gives rise to immediately enforceable legal obligations: consequently the rules of capacity aim to protect the maker from the consequences of his actions. Error is thus an important concept. After his death the need is to protect his relations' expectations to inherit. Someone may have taken advantage of the testator's declining mental strength. So the stress is on circumvention and related doctrines.

## CAPACITY TO MAKE A WILL

Scots law traditionally regarded pupils, boys under 14 and girls **8.03** under 12 years of age, as not having the "use of reason". Consequently they could not make wills. Minors, children between 12 or 14 and 18, had before 1964 no power to make a will of heritable property, but were then given unrestricted testamentary capacity.[3] The age limit has now been harmonised at 12 for both sexes by the Age of Legal Capacity (Scotland) Act 1991.[4] English

---

[1] Erskine, Inst., III.ix.5.
[2] See Stair, Inst., III.viii.37.
[3] Succession (Scotland) Act 1964, s.28.
[4] s.2(2). The Act applies to testamentary documents executed on or after September 25, 1991.

law is much more restrictive: one must be 18 in order to make a will, unless one is on active military service or a seaman, when the age limit is 16.[5]

**8.04**    In practice the power of testation is of little real use till at least age 16, at which point one can take employment and get married. For anyone younger the rules of intestate succession will cover most eventualities.

**8.05**    Unlike children, women have always been allowed to make a will. Their right to own property during a marriage was until this century quite restricted, but a will only takes effect after the marriage is ended by death and those restrictions were absent.

### Insanity

*(a)  The present law*

**8.06**    An insane person lacks the power of rational thought, and so cannot test. The law presumes a person to be sane, so the onus is on whoever challenges a will to prove insanity. If a testator was the subject of an order under the Mental Health Acts, one can presume his insanity: but the presumption can be rebutted. The question is always whether, at the time of the will, the testator understood the nature and effect of his will. The will is valid if, as in *Nisbet's Trs v. Nisbet*,[6] it can be shown that he had a lucid interval at the time he made it. Expert medical evidence is important.[7] So too is the language of the will itself: if on its face it appears perfectly rational, that goes some way towards showing sanity.

**8.07**    The testator may only be partially insane: he may suffer from insane delusions. Perhaps he thinks his family is persecuting him. Many people may occasionally have such delusions but are quite capable of disposing of their estate rationally. There is every incentive for relatives offended by a will to allege delusions: how could any sane person not have left them better provided for? The courts look askance at such claims. The rules of insanity are not to protect relations against disinheritance; that is the function of legal rights.[8]

**8.08**    So delusions need not invalidate a will. The basic rule is:

**8.09**    "The question whether there is such unsoundness of mind as renders it impossible in law to make a testamentary disposi-

---

[5] Wills (Soldiers and Sailors) Act 1918. Note that the lower age limit for nominations is 16 in both England and Scotland: see paras 5.28–5.32, above.

[6] (1871) 9 M. 937.

[7] See *e.g. Truesdale v. Downie*, 1989 G.W.D. 7–318, *Rennie v. Stephen*, 1991 G.W.D. 26–1559, and *Brogan v. Rennie*, 1991 G.W.D. 31–1885 (in none of which was insanity proved).

[8] See paras 4.34 *et seq.*, 9.01–9.07.

tion is one of degree . . . if his act is the outcome of a delusion so irrational that it is not to be taken as that of one having appreciated what he was doing sufficiently to make his action . . . that of a mind sane upon the question, the will cannot stand. If the testator is not generally insane, the will must be shown to have been the outcome of the special delusion . . . The delusion must be shown to have been an actual and compelling influence."[9]

Thus even suicidal depression may be disregarded if it did not **8.10** affect the will.[10]

*Morrison v. Maclean's Trs*[11] shows the limits of the rule. The **8.11** testator was given to obscene and rambling conversation. He spoke of having "no relations". He said he had been fed when young from an eagle's nest (indeed it seems he had). The court, reluctant to judge its fellow man, stressed two points. First, delusions must be baseless, such as no sane person could possibly believe. Second, "no amount of moral depravity will afford any direct evidence of impaired intellect". His will might be objectionable to some, but it was rational. So it was valid.

On the same logic, someone who is so intoxicated or drugged as **8.12** to lose the power of rational thought cannot make a will.[12]

## *(b) Law reform*

In England, unlike Scotland, the courts have traditionally had **8.13** wide protective powers over people who cannot look after their own affairs. For instance, disputes as to parental rights may be resolved by making a child a ward of court. Similarly the Court of Protection has power to make an *inter vivos* settlement or a will for someone of unsound mind.[13] This allows a legacy to be made to, say, children or housekeepers, and for tax-avoidance schemes.

Analogous ideas have been much argued in Scotland. Some say **8.14** the incapax's *curator bonis*, the person appointed by the court to administer his affairs, should be able to ask it to make a will. The Commission, which initially had no firm view, ultimately rejected the introduction of such a power.[14]

The problem really resolves into one of principle and practice. It **8.15** is a basic doctrine that a will reflects the testator's own personal intention. He cannot in theory delegate his will-making power to

---

[9] *Sivewright v. Sivewright's Trs*, 1920 S.C. (H.L.) 63.
[10] *Smith v. Smith's Trs*, 1972 S.L.T. (Notes) 81; *Ballantyne v. Evans* (1886) 13 R. 652.
[11] (1862) 24 D. 625.
[12] *Laidlaw v. Laidlaw* (1870) 8 M. 882.
[13] Administration of Justice Act 1969, s.17.
[14] Memorandum No. 70 (1986), paras 4.1–4.5; Report No. 124 (1990), paras 4.78–4.80.

anyone else, though he can instruct his trustees to select a beneficiary from a class clearly identified by him in his will. To allow such delegation if he is insane conflicts with that principle. Moreover the rule has its logic. The *curator bonis* will be caught in the crossfire of pressure from self-seeking relatives. How can he know what the incapax would want?

That said, courts will now sometimes permit a *curator bonis* to dispose of an incapax's assets because that reduces IHT on his estate. The Adults With Incapacity (Scotland) Act 2000 will allow similar steps on the principle of ensuring "benefit" to the incapax.[14a]

**8.16** The tax aspect, minimal under capital transfer tax, is again important now that IHT covers only gifts made within seven years of death. Otherwise Scots law solves the problem better than English law. In many cases the family's legal rights will give them adequate protection. They need not rely on a will, and they can inherit despite it if it cuts them out.

### Facility and circumvention

**8.17** An old person may suffer a degree of mental deterioration which, without amounting to insanity, leaves him easily imposed on by others. Someone may—maliciously or not—take advantage of this to persuade him to make a will in their favour. That is the essence of facility and circumvention.

**8.18** Three elements are necessary: facility, the weakened mental state; circumvention, "getting round" the testator; and lesion, harm to his interests. The question to be asked is:

> "whether . . . the pursuer was weak and facile in mind, and easily imposed on; and whether the defender . . . taking advantage of the pursuer's facility and weakness did, by fraud or circumvention, procure the deed . . . to the lesion of the pursuer?"[15]

**8.19** The three elements are inseparable, interrelated, and counter balance each other. Plainly the more facile the testator, the easier it is to manipulate him. So the greater the evidence of facility, the less evidence that need be brought of circumvention. In effect the concept is a sliding scale, merging at one end into insanity (where the mental element is everything) and at the other[16] undue influence (where only pressure on the testator is needed).

---

[14a] ss.1, 66 and commentary by A.D. Ward in Annotated Statutes; *D's C.B.*, 1998 S.L.T. 2. *Curators bonis* will be termed "guardians". The relevant provisions are not yet in force.

[15] See McBryde, *Contract*, para. 11.09 and cases cited.

[16] *Munro v. Strain* (1874) 1 R. 1039.

## (a) Facility

Facility is a clear enough concept: a weakening of faculties which **8.20**
does not amount to insanity but leaves the testator open to
persuasion. Defining it is less simple. There is a large grey area
where it borders at one extreme on insanity and at the other on
undue influence, and a given situation may raise any or all these
issues. Many cases are on the borderline.

Take *Gibson's Exr v. Anderson*.[17] A will was made in the **8.21**
defender's favour. The evidence could suggest either facility or
insanity. They differed only in degree: "if the evidence might have
warranted the conclusion that the mind of the deceased was
completely incapacitated, it seems the shortest and easiest step
from that to the conclusion that the deceased was facile in
disposition". On the other hand facility differed from mere
pliancy—lack of mental fibre, one might say. "Pliancy falls far
shorter of facility in its legal sense than facility itself does of
idiocy." The testator was "senile, silly and illiterate . . . of mental
incapacity so marked as to disqualify him from framing the
simplest of documents".

Facility may take different forms. "A man may be weak and **8.22**
facile from want of judgment or reason . . . [or] from mere
nervousness and incapacity to resist solicitation . . . and therefore
. . . you must endeavour to see whether there is any correspondence between the kind of facility that is proved and the kind of
arts employed against him."[18] But susceptibility to persuasion is
vital. One must not confuse that with mere lack of intellect or
stupidity: one can be stupid but obstinate. The question is "the
state of the mind morally and constitutionally": openness to
machination, not simple lack of understanding.[19]

## (b) Circumvention

This is essential, and can take many forms. Perhaps, as in **8.23**
*Wheelans v. Wheelans*,[20] one takes the facile person to a solicitor's
office and produces a document to sign at once. The case law
speaks of *fraud* and circumvention, but that means a sort of moral
fraud wider than, say, in contract law: "improper practices and
solicitation by interested parties" was the definition in Morrison.
"It is not necessary that there should be deceit. It is enough that

---

[17] 1925 S.C. 774, *per* Lord Blackburn.
[18] *Morrison v. Maclean's Trs*, n. 11.
[19] *Cairns v. Marianski* (1850) 12 D. 1286. Thus the mental deterioration seen in
dementia, if it falls short of insanity, may well not constitute facility: see cases at
n. 7.
[20] 1986 S.L.T. 164.

there should be solicitation, pressure, importunity, even in some cases, suggestion."[21]

**8.24**　If facility and lesion are present, only slight evidence of circumvention is needed.[22] But it can often be virtually impossible to prove specific instances of circumventing conduct. So the law has traditionally not required that: inference from the surrounding facts as a whole will do if coupled with evidence of facility.[23] In non-will cases the courts may insist on detailed averments of deceit or dishonesty,[24] but even there that is not always required if the grantor is now dead or incapax.[25]

### Undue influence

**8.25**　Suppose that a solicitor prepares a will for a client. It contains a legacy in his favour. The client is not encouraged to obtain independent legal advice. Here there is a relationship of trust between testator and adviser; there must be a suspicion that the solicitor took advantage of his position to secure a benefit under the will. That is the essence of undue influence. If proved, the will is voidable: it can be set aside.

**8.26**　This is merely an aspect of a wider theory that the courts should protect people from manipulation by others in a dominating position, such as banks. It occurs also in contract law. There the English courts have suggested that the underlying doctrine is inequality of bargaining power, and that undue influence can be presumed where a transaction is manifestly disadvantageous to the weaker person.[26] Scots law does not go quite so far in that context.

**8.27**　Undue influence may co-exist with facility and circumvention. This happened in *Ross v. Gosselin's Exrs*.[27] A lady died aged 90. Her will left the residue of her estate to her two nephews equally. She revised it when aged 74 and left nearly everything to one nephew, who was her solicitor. The other nephew alleged that she was eccentric and had delusions, that the solicitor looked after her affairs and induced her to give him large gifts, and that he told her the other was spendthrift. The case for circumvention was slim; delusions and eccentricity do not constitute facility (the lady may have been obstinate rather than easily-imposed on). Undue influ-

---

[21] Lord Kyllachy in *Parnie v. Maclean*, unreported, approved in *Gibson v. Anderson*, 1925 S.L.T. 517 at 526, *per* Lord Blackburn; *Anderson v. The Beacon Fellowship*, 1992 S.L.T. 111.

[22] Erskine, Inst., IV.i.27.

[23] *West's Trs v. West*, 1980 S.L.T. 6; *Pascoe-Watson v. Brock's Exr*, 1998 S.L.T. 40 which discussed the three elements of the doctrine and how to prove them.

[24] *McDougal v. McDougal's Trs*, 1931 S.C. 102.

[25] *Mackay v. Campbell*, 1967 S.C. (H.L.) 53.

[26] *National Westminster Bank v. Morgan* [1985] 1 All E.R. 821 (H.L.). The literature on the subject is vast.

[27] 1926 S.C. 325.

ence was more likely. Lord President Clyde distinguished the doctrines:

> "The essence of undue influence is that a person, who has **8.28** assumed or undertaken a position of quasi-fiduciary responsibility in relation to the affairs of another, allows his own self interest to deflect the advice or guidance he gives, in his own favour. On the other hand, the essence of circumvention and facility is that a person practises on the debility of another whose individuality is impaired by infirmity or age, and moulds the inclinations of the latter, to his own profit."

Three questions arise where undue influence is alleged. To what **8.29** relationships does it apply? What actions constitute it? Finally, how must it be proved?

One cannot exhaustively define the categories of relationship in **8.30** which undue influence may occur. The test has been widely phrased as a "fiduciary or quasi-fiduciary position"[28] or, more recently in *Honeyman's Exr v. Sharp*,[29] as "where a person, in pursuance of his profession or calling, undertakes the giving of advice to another and where, as a result, there develops a relationship between the adviser and the advised in which . . . the latter places trust and confidence in the former." That was a case of a fine art dealer. Other cases have included people in official positions—clergymen, doctors and lawyers—and parents and children. But a friend or, more intimately, a mistress[30] may be excluded. The list is not closed.

What sorts of behaviour amount to undue influence? Cases of **8.31** wills have used a narrow test: there must be coercion or fraud, "coercion or compulsion overbearing the will of the testator and destroying free agency".[31] In *Weir v. Grace*[32] the judge cited conduct which excites terror, or a wife who prejudices her husband against his relations and stops him meeting them. In lifetime transactions the test is wider: abuse of the position of trust. The distinction has little logic. It was doubted in *Honeyman*, where the dealer gave biased advice to obtain a gift from a terminally ill lady and also helped prepare her will. It is worth noting that precisely the same debate has occurred in relation to duress in contract, delict, and criminal law, where the theory of the "overborne will" is now discredited.[33]

---

[28] *Forbes v. Forbes' Trs*, 1957 S.C. 325.
[29] 1978 S.C. 223, *sub nom. Rodgers v. Sharp*, 1978 S.L.T. 977; see also *Gray v. Binny* (1879) 7 R. 332, *MacGilvary v. Gilmartin*, 1986 S.L.T. 89.
[30] *McKechnie v. McKechnie's Trs*, 1908 S.C. 93; and see *Anderson v. The Beacon Fellowship*, above at n. 21 (representative of religious organisation which owed the pursuer money.)
[31] W.H.D. Winder, 1939 S.L.T. (News) 165.
[32] (1899) 2 F. (H.L.) 30.
[33] See (1982) 98 L.Q.R. 556.

**8.32** With undue influence, like facility and circumvention, the actions complained of may be those of some third person. An outsider may "get at" one, not directly, but through one's spouse. Outwith the context of wills, this may happen when a bank wants the couple to grant a guarantee or mortgage: it only deals with one of them but may unduly influence the other.[34]

**8.33** Normally the person alleging undue influence must prove it. But evidence of precise acts of coercion may be hard to come by. Nevertheless some situations are exceptionally suspicious: the surrounding facts may allow an inference of undue influence which demands that the trusted person provide an innocent explanation. The classic example is the solicitor who prepares a will under which he is given some benefit: in that case (besides breaching professional ethics) the onus of proof shifts to him to give an explanation of his conduct.[35] Solicitors are particularly severely judged: in other relationships the onus of proof may remain on the pursuer.[36]

### The effect of incapacity on the will

**8.34** If a will entirely lacks consent (as with insanity or nonage) or the testator's consent is defective by virtue of facility and circumvention or undue influence, the remedy is to have it reduced, *i.e.* set aside, by an action in the Court of Session.

**8.35** If the action is successful the will normally falls completely. That is perhaps unjust in the sense that innocent beneficiaries suffer through one person's act of circumvention, but the rule seems clear. However, in one case partial reduction was in effect allowed. In *Horsburgh v. Thomson's Trs*[37] a will was perfectly valid, but a later codicil was challenged for undue influence. The codicil was reduced but not the will, despite the fact that as a rule a codicil and will are treated as forming one composite document. The decision was sensible but unusual.

Intention to Test

### Completed intention

**8.36** A will requires no set form of words, but it must show a completed testamentary intention. The testator must intend that document to be a valid will. If he is still at the stage of deliberation,

---

[34] *Kingsnorth Trust v. Bell* [1986] 1 All E.R. 423.

[35] Given an innocent explanation the legacy will stand: *Read v. Cattanach*, 1990 G.W.D. 31–1839.

[36] *Tiarks v. Paterson*, 1992 G.W.D. 23–1328 (relative prepared codicil in her own favour; undue influence not proved).

[37] (1912) 1 S.L.T. 73.

and intends it merely as jottings or instructions for a will to be made at some future time, it is ineffective. The governing test is the testator's intention.

It may be obvious that a document is a draft rather than a will. It may be headed "rough".[38] More often it is ambiguous and can be interpreted either way. In that case the court will accept extrinsic—external—evidence to supply an answer. Take *Rhodes v. Peterson*[39]: a woman wrote to her daughter telling her that she was going to make a formal will, but "I want you to have house and contents"; "just in case anything happens to me in the meantime this letter will establish your rightful claim". That was taken to be an immediate will and not just a reference to a future one. **8.37**

The problem frequently arises where someone sends an apparently valid will to a solicitor, signed and so formally valid, with a covering note to the effect that "I want a will made in this form." The letter casts doubt on the "will". Usually, as in *Munro v. Coutts*,[40] that is taken as a mere instruction for a will. Rarely it may be treated as valid. In *Maclaren's Trs v. Mitchell and Brattan*[41] the decisive factor was that it was subscribed and attested. **8.38**

Similarly a mere list of names or items will fail as a will unless something identifies them as legatees and legacies and the document shows completed testamentary intent; otherwise it is treated as mere jottings. Take the case of a deposit receipt with an attached list of names and amounts: a receipt itself can never be a testamentary document without some evidence that it is meant as a will. In *Cameron's Trs v. Mackenzie*[42] that was lacking: "£150 to Y" was not clear enough, despite being signed. Use of legal terminology, or reference to "my last will", are helpful. But the word "will" is not always conclusive if the other factors suggest a draft, as *Colvin v. Hutchison*[43] shows. The list did not come to the right total: that itself was not fatal (since in a true will the sums would simply abate pro rata to match the correct amount of the estate) but given that it was hardly comprehensible, was signed at the side, and showed no other evidence of being meant as a will, it was invalid. **8.39**

### Error

*(a) General principles*

Error plays a major role in the law of contract. Contracts rest on consent; apparent consent is nullified if it arose from "essential error" as to some fact central to the contract, such as the identity **8.40**

---

[38] *Sprot's Trs v. Sprot*, 1909 S.C. 272.
[39] 1971 S.C. 56: and see *Jamieson's Exrs*, 1982 S.C. 1.
[40] (1813) 1 Dow 437.
[41] 1959 S.C. 183.
[42] 1915 S.C. 313. *cf. Ayrshire Hospice, Petrs*, 1992 G.W.D. 39–2372 (list referred to "remainder" and in envelope marked "will": held to be valid will).
[43] (1885) 12 R. 947.

of subject-matter or parties. On the other hand error is easy to allege as an afterthought, and the law today is reluctant to recognise it unless it was caused by fraud or false representations.

**8.41** In theory a will can be set aside for essential error on the grounds that the testator was unaware of its nature, effect, or contents. In practice that is hardly ever necessary. Proof is difficult. There must also be fraud or circumvention: bare error is not enough. One illustration was *Munro v. Strain*[44] where a priest persuaded a terminally ill old man to leave money to the church, and had the will prepared for him. Facility apart, the will could be reduced for essential error. This was inferred from the surrounding circumstances: the will was not read over to the testator and he was known to have vigorously refused to make a will on those lines previously.

### (b) Error in drafting

**8.42** A solicitor preparing a will may have made a clerical error, and the testator may omit to check it; so the signed will, unknown to him, does not reflect his intentions. Such a will could perhaps fail for essential error.[45] In practice the courts will correct such errors, but only if they are obvious in the deed.[46]

**8.43** In England such an error can now be corrected if the drafter made a clerical error or did not understand the testator's instructions.[47] In Scotland that can be done for *inter vivos* documents under section 8 of the Law Reform (Miscellaneous Provisions) (Scotland) Act 1985. The Commission suggest a rule for wills on the English model, but wider, to cover deliberate disobedience by the drafter.[48]

### (c) Rules of interpretation[49]

**8.44** Apart from the validity of the will as a whole, there may be questions as to a particular legacy. The courts may, by using the normal rules for interpreting wills, often correct or ignore the mistake. Where the mistake concerned a fact which was the reason for the legacy—*falsa causa*—that does not invalidate the legacy unless the legacy was conditional on the fact being correct.[50] Where a legatee or class of legatees is misdescribed—*falsa demonstratio*—the legacy still has effect if one can ascertain the legatee. If the will

---

[44] (1874) 1 R. 1039.
[45] *Yeatman v. Proctors* (1877) 5 R. 179.
[46] *Reid's Trs v. Bucher*, 1929 S.C. 615.
[47] Administration of Justice Act 1982, s.20.
[48] Memorandum No. 70, paras 3.1–3.6; Report No. 124, paras 4.21–4.28.
[49] McLaren, Vol. 1, pp. 367, 385.
[50] *Currie's Exrs v. Currie's Trs*, 1911 S.C. 999; *cf. Grant v. Grant* (1846) 8 D. 1077.

is ambiguous, extrinsic evidence is allowed to explain it. So the court tries to give effect to the testator's intention as contained in the will: they will not go behind it to contradict it. If ultimately these rules of construction do not identify the legacy or legatee, the legacy falls through uncertainty.

## Further reading

McBryde, *Contract*, Chap. 11.

R.A. McCall Smith, "The Deluded Testator", 1973 S.L.T. (News) 61.

D.J. McNeil, "Making a Will for an Incapax" (1979) 24 J.L.S. 415.

W.H.D. Winder, "Mistakes as to Legatees", 1953 S.L.T. (News) 149.

W.H.D. Winder, "Undue Influence in Scots and English Law", 1939 S.L.T. (News) 165.

"Here's a How-de-doo", 1970 S.L.T. (News) 90.

"Reduction of Wills", 1963 S.L.T. (News) 53.

"Undue Influence", 1980 S.L.T. (News) 65.

# CHAPTER 9

# RESTRAINTS ON TESTAMENTARY FREEDOM

**Evasion of legal rights**

**9.01**    Legal rights operate as a control on testation. They cannot be defeated by any testamentary disposition. Hence the testator's spouse and offspring are protected against disinheritance: they can, if not satisfied with the provision for them in the will, claim legal rights instead. They can of course choose to accept the testamentary provisions.

**9.02**    The will is not automatically invalid. If legal rights are claimed the will is not thereby struck down. There are two main results: the legacies in it are abated—reduced—pro rata to allow for the legal rights to be paid; and the person claiming legal rights forfeits all benefit under the will.

**9.03**    Having said that, legal rights can be evaded in four ways.

**9.04**    (1) They can be defeated by a genuine *inter vivos* transfer of moveable assets to a third party. The tactic succeeded in the early case of *Agnew v. Agnew*[1]: a father made a deed of assignation in favour of his eldest son; it reserved a liferent to himself and excluded the younger son's right to claim legitim; it was irrevocable. The court held that the father was the unlimited proprietor of his estate and so could dispose of it by deeds *inter vivos*; and the transaction was not fraudulent despite its effect.[2]

Apparently the transfer need not even be irrevocable, as long as it is not a sham and has not actually been revoked.[3] In theory the donor is allowed to reserve some benefit from the property (such as its use or income from it): but that is inadvisable because the item remains part of his estate for IHT purposes. In practice a major reason for making lifetime gifts is to minimise IHT on death, and the reservation of benefit defeats that object.[4]

---

[1] (1775) Mor. 8210.
[2] See also *Lashley v. Hog* (1804) 4 Pat. App. 581.
[3] *Hutton's Trs v. Hutton's Trs*, 1916 S.C. 860.
[4] See paras 12.19–12.21.

(2) One can die intestate. If the estate is sufficiently small prior **9.05** rights will exhaust it and leave nothing for legal rights to operate on: the effect is to benefit one's spouse at the children's expense. Alternatively one can leave the estate to one's spouse: if she disclaims the legacy and the will names no alternative legatee in that event, artificial intestacy results (again allowing prior rights).[5]

(3) One can maximise the amount of heritable property in one's **9.06** estate. In this connection note that a security over land (a standard security) is a heritable asset for the creditor. The testator may *constructively convert* moveables to heritage if he directs his executors to sell them, buy heritage, and give that to a beneficiary: but that is not foolproof because the beneficiary can reconvert by opting for the moveables instead.[6]

(4) One can ensure that the asset is not part of one's estate at all. **9.07** Assets held in trust are an example. In particular take pension or life assurance proceeds: if payable to the testator or his executors they fall into the estate, but if to his widow or someone else they do not. Again this can benefit the widow at the children's expense, or vice versa.[7] It also avoids IHT on the proceeds, which are treated as belonging to the recipient rather than the deceased (if— as is common under pension schemes—the trustees have discretion whom to pay, there are special IHT rules but again the proceeds are not part of the deceased's estate).[8]

### Approbate and reprobate

The identical English term "election" succinctly describes the **9.08** purpose of approbate and reprobate. One cannot accept and reject the same legal document: one cannot take a benefit under it and at the same time insist on some independent benefit which clashes with its provisions. One must make a clear and free choice.

The idea has many applications. *Crum Ewing's Trs v. Bayly's Trs*[9] **9.09** was not a case of legal rights. A man's will made his daughter his executrix and also gave her power of appointment over part of his estate: *i.e.* power to decide to whom it would pass.[10] Her children accepted sums which she gave them in exercising that power; they could not then challenge her appointment as executrix under the father's will. Accepting one part of a deed was inconsistent with rejecting another part.

---

[5] As in *Kerr, Petr*, 1968 S.L.T. (Sh. Ct) 61. See paras 4.12–4.17.
[6] See Gloag & Henderson, para. 46.3.
[7] *Beveridge v. Beveridge's Exx*, 1938 S.C. 160; see Clive, 30.044.
[8] The testator's pension contributions or policy premiums, though in theory liable to IHT when paid, would normally be exempt as made out of normal income: IHTA 1984, s.21.
[9] 1911 S.C. (H.L.) 18.
[10] See paras 10.89 *et seq.*

**9.10**  A valid election needs four conditions.

**9.11**  (1) It must be a free choice. If made in ignorance of alternative courses of action it can be set aside. That happened in *Walker v. Orr's Trs*[11]: the electing children had insufficient knowledge of material facts; in particular they were not shown a copy of the will, not told the amount of the estate, and not urged to get independent advice; even 13 years later they could revoke the election. The deceased's executor should thus ensure that potential claimants are aware of their legal rights and what options they have. The force and limits of this rule were stressed in *Donaldson v. Tainsh's Trs*[12]:

> "I do not say that independent legal advice is absolutely essential, but it is the duty of trustees to see and insist that a widow, before she makes up her mind to an election which will be injurious to her pecuniary interests, is acting not from a mere emotional feeling as to what she may suppose to have been her husband's wishes, but after full information and deliberation."

**9.12**  (2) The elector must have legal capacity to elect. A child under 16 cannot make a binding election, but if aged 16 or 17 can elect but potentially challenge the election (until age 21) as a "prejudicial transaction".[13] A *curator bonis*[13a] when looking after an insane person's affairs should not exercise the power of election unless there are urgent reasons to do so, and he needs the court's approval.[14]

**9.13**  (3) The will which requires the election must itself be valid and enforceable.

**9.14**  (4) The legatee must be able, by election, to give effect to the legacy. Contrast *Brown's Trs v. Gregson*[15] where the will made an invalid bequest of property situated in Argentina.

**9.15**  Election may be explicit: for the executor's protection it is best in writing. At the other extreme mere silence or delay scarcely ever constitutes election[16] (though after 20 years legal rights prescribe anyway). The test is conduct which shows a clear intention to accept or reject the legacy. Taking a pension shows nothing: it is consistent with either. Nor does becoming executor under the will:

---

[11] 1958 S.L.T. 220.

[12] (1886) 13 R. 967 at 971 *per* L.J.–C. Moncrieff, approved in *Harvie's Exrs v. Harvie's Trs*, 1981 S.L.T. (Notes) 126 where an unadvised election was nonetheless valid.

[13] Age of Legal Capacity (Scotland) Act 1991, ss.1, 3; see paras 4.67–4.68.

[13a] To be termed "guardian" under Adults with Incapacity (Scotland) Act 2000, Sched. 4 (not yet in force).

[14] *Allan's Exrs v. Allan's Trs*, 1975 S.L.T. 227.

[15] 1920 S.C. (H.L.) 87.

[16] But *cf. Pringle's Exxs v. Pringle* (1870) 8 M. 622.

but to do so and then claim legal rights against it is a clear conflict of interest to be avoided.[17]

**9.16** The effect of an election depends on the method used. An express discharge of legal rights covers the whole estate, testate or not, unless the elector reserves the right to claim from current or future assets which fall into intestacy.[18]

**9.17** If discharge is implied from conduct it extends only so far as the will and legal rights conflict, so in principle legal rights are still claimable from the intestate estate. In practice the will often deals with election by a "forfeiture" or "full satisfaction" clause.

### Forfeiture and equitable compensation

**9.18** Election usually arises as a choice between legacies under a will and legal rights. At the very least one cannot take both where the two conflict. Two related problems complicate matters. What is the precise effect of a clause in the will that the legacies are in "full and final satisfaction of legal rights" or, conversely, an express forfeiture of the legacies if one claims legal rights? What then happens to the forfeited legacy? That is the question of equitable compensation.

*(a) When is there forfeiture?*

**9.19** The answer depends on the terms of the will and the effect of section 13 of the 1964 Act. Several situations can be distinguished.

**9.20** (1) Before 1964 if there were no "full satisfaction" clause the legatee need only elect to the extent that the will and legal rights were inconsistent. So, as in *White v. Finlay*,[19] if the will only dealt with part of the estate one could claim legal rights out of the rest.

**9.21** (2) A "full satisfaction" clause was common. Its scope was always a question of the testator's intention as expressed in the will. In principle it meant (and still means) that by accepting a legacy one lost one's legal rights in the whole testate estate, and vice versa on claiming legal rights.[20]

**9.22** (3) Suppose the will gave a liferent income, and the legatee elected for legal rights as a capital sum. Clearly the estate had to find extra cash in hand at once: other legatees suffered a pro rata reduction as a result. So *equitable compensation* occurred: the sum in the legacy went to them to compensate them. This might mean accumulating income over some time to pay them. That was the position in *Macfarlane's Trs v. Oliver*[21]; the court held that once

---

[17] *Smart v. Smart*, 1926 S.C. 392.
[18] As in *Petrie's Trs v. Mander's Trs*, 1954 S.C. 430.
[19] (1861) 24 D. 38.
[20] *Naismith v. Boyes* (1899) 1 F. (H.L.) 79.
[21] (1882) 9 R. 1138.

they had been compensated, the legatee's rights revived: he could claim the liferent income again. Equitable compensation did not automatically mean permanent forfeiture of rights under the will.

**9.23**    (4) If the will expressly forfeited the legacy in the event of the legatee claiming legal rights, that was permanent. There was still equitable compensation, but the legacy did not then revive; *Macfarlane* did not apply. If there was a "full satisfaction" clause, that was taken to imply forfeiture[22] and had the same effect.

**9.24**    (5) Section 13 of the 1964 Act now implies "full satisfaction", and hence forfeiture, into almost every will made after September 9, 1964. The old law still governs older wills. Section 13 provides:

> "Every testamentary disposition executed after [that date] by which provision is made in favour of the spouse or of any issue of the testator and which does not contain a declaration that the provision is made in full and final satisfaction of the right to any share in the testator's estate to which the spouse or the issue, as the case may be, is entitled by virtue of *jus relicti, jus relictae* or legitim shall (unless the disposition contains an express provision to the contrary) have effect as if it contained such a declaration."

Unfortunately the Act does not abolish equitable compensation. It merely applies to all wills the old law on "full satisfaction" clauses, so stopping legal rights reviving after equitable compensation. This was made clear in *Munro's Trs, Petrs*[23]: a husband and two sons were left a liferent under a post-Act will; they claimed legal rights. That meant complete forfeiture of the liferent, and the income had to be accumulated for the benefit of a grandchild who took the fee under the will. This caused lawyers much consternation, since till then they thought they had seen the last of this horrendous doctrine. If the Commission's proposals are enacted it will finally disappear.[24]

*(b) What is the effect of forfeiture?*

**9.25**    Three related issues cause problems.

**9.26**    (1) *Whom does forfeiture affect?* Suppose there is a legacy to the elector and another related one to his children: such as liferent to one and fee to the other. The elector, taking legal rights, loses his legacy; do the children also lose theirs? That depends on the words of the will. If it says they forfeit, they do. If nothing is said expressly about them, the test is: are the two gifts interconnected or

---

[22] *Rose's Trs v. Rose*, 1916 S.C. 827.
[23] 1971 S.C. 280.
[24] Report No. 124, paras 3.45–3.48.

independent? If the latter, there is no forfeiture.[25] If the elector's own original forfeiture was not express but inferred (as under section 13) the children will certainly not be affected.[26]

(2) *What property is affected?* Despite the wide terms of forfei- **9.27** ture and full satisfaction clauses, the elector may not lose all legal rights. It may be that the will does not dispose of the whole estate. Or, as in *Naismith v. Boyes*,[27] some event after the testator's death makes it impossible to give effect to all the legacies. There a beneficiary entitled to the fee of the estate died and the fee fell into intestacy. In such cases the elector may claim legal rights out of the intestate estate. The rationale was explained in *Campbell's Trs v. Campbell's Trs*,[28] where there was an express forfeiture clause:

> "The forfeiture provisions were intended to protect the settlement as a whole and play no part when part of the estate falls into intestacy."

(3) *What happens to the forfeited legacy?* We have seen that **9.28** equitable compensation takes effect. But that only goes on till the other beneficiaries are compensated; moreover, the accumulation may become illegal under the Trusts (Scotland) Act 1961.

What happens then depends on the will. The sum may be redirected to another person by a "destination-over" ("to X, failing whom to Y") or by accretion.[29] It may go to the residue or, failing that, fall into intestacy. If intestacy, the ironical result may be to send it back to the elector if he happens also to be the person entitled to succeed the deceased on intestacy.[30] But the courts understandably sometimes jib at such a result. In *Macnaughton v. Macnaughton's Trs*[31] there was a forfeiture clause covering the elector and his children, and a destination-over: ultimately all the beneficiaries chose legal rights so intestacy resulted. That should have given the elector the property; but the court ignored the strict rules and gave it to the children—"anyone but the elector" was the apparent rationale.

---

[25] *Ballantyne's Trs v. Ballantyne*, 1952 S.C. 458, and (on the same will) *Ballantyne's Trs v. Ballantyne*, 1993 S.L.T. 1237.
[26] *Nicolson's Trs v. Nicolson*, 1960 S.C. 186.
[27] (1899) 1 F. (H.L.) 79.
[28] 1950 S.C. 48.
[29] See paras 10.35–10.38, 10.50–10.58, 11.31–11.34.
[30] *Tindall's Trs v. Tindall*, 1933 S.C. 419.
[31] 1954 S.C. 312.

RESTRAINTS ON TIME: ACCUMULATIONS[32]

## Background

**9.29**　A testator may set up a testamentary trust to administer his estate after his death and carry out the instructions contained in the will. Among other things he may want property to be held in trust and the income accumulated in the fund for distribution to beneficiaries when, say, they reach adulthood. That is unobjectionable. At the other extreme one may try to have the income accumulated for ever and never paid out to beneficiaries. Or one may need to accumulate income for an indefinite period to permit equitable compensation. The law will not allow that: it limits the duration of accumulation.

**9.30**　English law frowns on perpetual trusts of any sort, except charitable trusts. In principle Scots law does not, and provided the purposes are sufficiently certain and are not contrary to public policy they are quite permissible. Trusts for hospitals, orphans, or dogs' homes would be valid. The only constraints are purely statutory.

**9.31**　The limits were originally laid down by the Accumulations Act 1800, known as the Thellusson Act after the testator whose ingenious trust inspired it. Thellusson was a wealthy English merchant who, in his will, directed that the residue of his estate was to be invested in land; the income was to be accumulated during the lifetime of his sons and grandsons; when the last one died the fund would be split among the family. Despite much litigation the trust was valid[33] and ultimately lasted some 60 years. What was striking was merely the sum involved (£600,000 at 1798 prices) and for that reason the Act ensued to prevent any repetition. Its direct successor is the Trusts (Scotland) Act 1961, s.5 and, extending the rules, the Law Reform (Miscellaneous Provisions) (Scotland) Act 1966, s.6.

## The statutory rules

**9.32**　The two Acts lay down six possible maximum periods for accumulation, affecting both lifetime and testamentary trusts. The truster's intention is irrelevant: the rules apply whether he expressly directed accumulation or merely gave trustees discretion which had that result. The rules must be strictly observed. Accumulation must fall within one of the periods, which are alternatives, and one cannot add one period to another to extend it. Not surprisingly one cannot contract out of the rules:

---

[32] See Norrie & Scobbie, pp. 84–88.
[33] *Thellusson v. Woodford* (1799) 4 Ves. 227; (1805) 11 Ves. 112.

"No private arrangement or consent to defeat the provisions **9.33** of the . . . Act, which . . . was dictated by public policy . . . can be given effect to by the Court. Were it otherwise . . . the Act might, without much difficulty, be so entirely defeated as to render it of no more effect than if it had been repealed."[34]

Note that, of periods (a) to (f), (e) and (f) affect only deeds which **9.34** took effect after August 3, 1966. In principle (a) *ends* at the grantor's death; (b) and (c) *start* then; (d) (e) and (f) can "straddle" it, and (d) alone can start long after it.

*(a) The lifetime of the grantor (1961 Act, section 5(2)(a))*

This applies to a direction in an *inter vivos* deed to accumulate **9.35** during the grantor's lifetime. The accumulation may also relate to the joint lives of the grantor and someone else. Formerly such accumulations had to end at the grantor's death. Under the 1961 Act that is unnecessary provided the deed also "directs" accumulation under (d), (e) or (f): any of those periods can be used as an alternative, but (b) and (c) are not permissible (because they would here provide an additional period). *McIver's Trs v. Inland Revenue* illustrates the operation of that rule: the deed directed accumulation till the grantor's son was 22; that was too wide to come under (d) and so the accumulation lapsed when the grantor died.[35]

*(b) Twenty-one years after the grantor's death (section 5(2)(b))*

This only applies where the date of death is the starting-point. If **9.36** the period starts before or afterwards one of the other rules must be invoked. It is a maximum period, so that if for part of it the income is used for some other purpose and not accumulated, that does not extend the termination date.

*(c) The minorities of persons living or in utero at the grantor's death (section 5(2)(c)).*

This may be any person, not necessarily the grantor's family. **9.37** While it refers to person(s), the maximum period will be about 21 years 9 months on the assumption of a posthumous child. "Minority" here means until age 21 rather than, as for most other purposes, 16 or 18.[36]

---

[34] *Maxwell's Trs v. Maxwell* (1877) 5 R. 248.

[35] 1974 S.L.T. 202.

[36] Trusts (Scotland) Act 1961, s.5(6). But when used in a trust deed it does mean 18: Age of Majority (Scotland) Act 1969, s. 1(2)(b). The Age of Legal Capacity (Scotland) Act 1991 does not affect the meaning of such terms.

*(d) The minorities of persons who would, under the terms of the will or deed directing accumulation, be entitled if of full age to the accumulated income (section 5(2)(d))*

**9.38**    This has no reference to the date of the testator's death: for instance, in *Re Cattell*[37] it applied to the minorities of persons born after his death. Furthermore it may permit accumulation during successive minorities as different beneficiaries are born and grow up. But it does require that they are actually entitled to the income at age 21 (and not later): they must be actual and not contingent—possible—beneficiaries, and so not dependent on trustees' discretion. The income available for accumulation will gradually reduce because as each child reaches majority he will get the right to the income arising, after that date, from his proportionate share of the trust funds.

*(e) Twenty-one years from the making of the deed (1966 Act, section 6(1))*

*(f) The minorities of persons living or* in utero *at the date of the deed (1966 Act, section 6(1))*

### The effect of illegal accumulation

*(a) The general principle*

**9.39**    Illegal accumulation does not invalidate the trust itself. That continues after the end of the permitted period except for its accumulation provisions: "the deed is to be read as if it had expressly declared that the accumulation directed should stop at the end of [the period]; and for the rest the deed is to be read and receive effect exactly as it stands".[38] Indeed the accumulation clauses may be referred to in order to interpret the rest of the deed, rather (on one view) like a revoked clause in a will.

*(b) Disposal of income*

**9.40**    The income which can no longer be accumulated must "go to and be received by the person[s] who would have been entitled thereto if such accumulation had not been directed".[39] What that means in practice depends on the terms of the will: the income may go to a beneficiary, go to residue, or fall into intestacy.

**9.41**    The test is whether the will makes a "present gift" to the beneficiary of the fund from which the income has been accumu-

---

[37] [1914] 1 Ch. 177.
[38] *Elder's Trs v. Treasurer of Free Church of Scotland* (1892) 20 R. 2, *per* Lord Kyllachy.
[39] Trusts (Scotland) Act 1961, s.5(3).

lated, rather than a right which takes effect at some future date.[40] If there is such a gift he gets the now unaccumulated income, but not otherwise. The Act does not operate to accelerate future rights. In that second case the income goes in the meantime to the residuary legatees if they are left a present gift of the residue. If they are not, it goes to the heirs on intestacy: the deed has made no provision for the event.

Contrast, then, *Landale's Trs v. Oversea Missionary Fellowship*[41] **9.42** and *Smith v. Glasgow Royal Infirmary*.[42] In *Landale* the residue was expressed to pass on the testator's death, and though the trustees could hold back enough to pay various annuities, they could make interim payments to the residuary beneficiaries, who therefore got the income. In *Smith* nothing was due to the legatees till the annuitants died; the income fell into intestacy. In neither case was the capital of the fund paid over, because it was still required for annuities; it was different in *Dowden's Trs*[43] where there were no trust purposes which required the fund to be retained.

The beneficiaries on intestacy are ascertained as at the testator's **9.43** death, despite the fact that the accumulated fund may emerge years later.

### (c) Legal rights

It is disputed whether legal rights can be claimed out of **9.44** accumulated income which falls into intestacy. The counter argument is based on the point that legal rights are fixed and valued at the testator's death whereas the accumulated funds emerged later; but the case law is inconsistent.[44]

### Successive liferents

A right of fee in an asset allows the *fiar* to use it, draw income **9.45** from it, and dispose of it in life or on death as outright owner. A liferent gives no right of disposal and lapses when the liferenter dies. The two commonly coexist through the mechanism of a testamentary trust: the fiar inherits a vested right immediately the testator dies but cannot use the property till after the liferenter's death.

A variety of liferent over land, the *entail* or *tailzie*, was for **9.46** centuries an important means of ensuring that family estates were kept intact and not sold. Modern commercial society opposes such controls and restricts the maximum duration of liferents. Before

---

[40] See *Vesting*, paras 11.08–11.09.
[41] 1982 S.L.T. 158.
[42] 1909 S.C. 1231.
[43] *Dowden's Trs, Petrs*, 1965 S.L.T. 88; 1965 S.C. 56.
[44] *Moon's Trs v. Moon* (1899) 2 F. 201; *cf. Lindsay's Trs v. Lindsay*, 1931 S.C. 586.

1968 the Entail Amendment Act 1848, s.48 applied to heritage, and the Trusts (Scotland) Act 1921, s.9 to moveables. They still govern deeds executed before November 25, 1968.[45]

**9.47**    For later deeds the Law Reform (Miscellaneous Provisions) (Scotland) Act 1968 applies to both heritage and moveables. Under section 18 it is not possible to create a liferent in favour of someone who is not alive or *in utero* at the date of the creator's death. The section has the effect that the liferent property belongs absolutely to the liferenter at the date when he becomes entitled to the liferent or (if he is under 18 then) when he becomes 18.[46] If the property is held by trustees they must make over the property to him at his expense. But none of this affects the rights of feudal superiors and holders of securities or other rights over the property.

RESTRAINTS ON PURPOSE: PUBLIC POLICY[47]

### Illegality, immorality, and impossibility

**9.48**    If a legacy is illegal, immoral, or impossible, it is void. If on the other hand the legacy is subject to a condition which is illegal, immoral or impossible, the condition is treated as *pro non scripto* (as if unwritten) and ignored: the legacy is fully effective.

**9.49**    Impossibility is defined strictly; it is something more than mere improbability. Where "if you marry X" is the condition, that is not impossible just because one is at the time married to Y. In *Barker v. Watson's Trs*[48] the testator's daughter was undergoing addiction treatment in a hospital at the time he wrote his will; the condition attached to the legacy was that she and her husband were "reconciled" at the date of his death. That was valid: it was possible, though of course nothing could be done about it by the time the will was known. In any case it was not really a condition in the sense "if you do this you will get the legacy": "words descriptive of the place or mode of life of a person at the date of death of the testator do not, properly speaking, create a condition".

**9.50**    In *Barker* the court, rightly, dismissed the idea of an immoral condition. More such examples occur where the beneficiary is required not to live with someone related. In *Fraser v. Rose*[49] a father left his daughter a legacy which was conditional on her not

---

[45] Meston (at p. 104) points out that about 1000 entails still exist.
[46] "Full age" in terms of Age of Majority (Scotland) Act 1969, unaffected by Age of Legal Capacity (Scotland) Act 1991.
[47] The purpose must also be certain, *i.e.* clear: para. 10.26.
[48] 1919 S.C. 109 at 120–121 *per* Lord Dundas.
[49] (1849) 11 D. 1466.

living with her mother—moreover the executors were to throw her out of the house; the legacy was held to be payable unconditionally. By contrast, in *Balfour's Trs v. Johnston*[50] the daughter had been taking an interest in an orphan; her father disapproved and made her legacy conditional on her not seeing the child—that was not contrary to public policy.

## Public policy

The courts have evolved a concept of public policy as a ground **9.51** on which to strike down provisions in a will. The basis of the doctrine is the testator's abuse of the power of testation; its scope is undefined and it rests on excessive self-glorification by the testator without any benefit resulting to anyone. "The testator's act may be regarded as going beyond the right of *testamenti factio* . . . [his] directions reach a certain pitch of grotesqueness, of extravagance, of wastefulness or of futility."[51]

It is recognised as a dangerous doctrine which risks arbitrariness, **9.52** and for that reason will not be invoked except in particularly outrageous cases. The court will wish to be convinced that the defects of the testator's scheme greatly outweigh any public benefit.

The idea first came to the fore in the *McCaig* cases. McCaig, **9.53** who built the famous Folly at Oban while alive, directed his testamentary trustees to use the revenue from his estate in perpetuity for the purpose of erecting artistic towers and statues of himself and his family on his estate. This would supposedly encourage young Scots artists. The court struck the legacies down. Formally they did so on the ground that he could not disinherit the heirs on intestacy unless he created beneficial rights in favour of others. He did not: the artists would receive no prizes and the public got no benefit. Some *obiter* remarks show the judges' attitude:

> "if it is not unlawful, it ought to be unlawful, to dedicate by **9.54** testamentary disposition . . . the whole income of a large estate to objects of no utility, private or public, objects which benefit nobody, and which have no other purpose or use than that of perpetuating at great cost, and in an absurd manner, the idiosyncracies of an eccentric testator."[52]

In a subsequent case the court struck down provisions in McCaig's **9.55** sister's will along rather similar lines.[53] Again no beneficial interest

---

[50] 1936 S.C. 137.
[51] *Mackintosh's J.F. v. Lord Advocate*, 1935 S.C. 406 at 410, *per* Lord President Clyde.
[52] *McCaig v. University of Glasgow*, 1907 S.C. 231 at 242, *per* Lord Kyllachy.
[53] *McCaig's Trs v. Lismore Kirk Session*, 1915 S.C. 426.

was conferred on anyone. The judges expressed the opinion that the directions were invalid as contrary to public policy: it was dangerous to permit a bequest which could only benefit the vanity of a testator who had no claim to be immortalised. One innocuous provision in the will was allowed to stand.

**9.56** Later cases have been more clearly decided on the grounds of public policy as such. In *Aitken's Trs v. Aitken*[54] the testator wanted part of Musselburgh High Street demolished and a massive bronze statue of himself erected. The object itself was reasonable: "interest in one's ancestors and . . . in their respectability if not their distinction, is a typical, and in some respects a not unlaudable, trait of the Scottish character". The manner of pursuing it was utterly fantastic. As a rule "the court is not to make itself the judge of what is for the public benefit. It is enough that the object is one, not immoral or contrary to public order, which a certain section of public opinion may regard as of public benefit". Here even that test was not met—quite the contrary; the provisions failed as "an irrational, futile and self-destructive scheme to carry out not unreasonable purposes".

**9.57** *Mackintosh's J.F. v. Lord Advocate*[55] concerned a testatrix's direction to spend her entire estate on erecting a mausoleum for her and to re-inter two close friends there. They were not relations; indeed she was illegitimate so (at that time) they could not be.[56] Now relations have a "right approaching in character to a right of custody" over graves, allowing them to apply for exhumation; she lacked that right. On that ground alone the court struck down the direction. That apart, it is clear that a reasonable provision for a tombstone or mausoleum is acceptable[57]; the court in *Mackintosh* were split as to whether the case was so unreasonable as to contravene public policy.

**9.58** In a similar way a legacy to put flowers on a grave in perpetuity may be both too indefinite and unreasonable to be valid.[58]

**9.59** Provided there is some public benefit, public policy is satisfied. So a provision to establish a fund for an army regiment, though large, is acceptable.[59]

**Further reading**

M.C. Meston, "Accumulations" (1981) 26 J.L.S. (Workshop) 218.

---

[54] 1927 S.C. 374 at 379–383, *per* Lord Sands.

[55] 1935 S.C. 406.

[56] Not the law now: the status of illegitimacy has virtually disappeared. Law Reform (Parent & Child) (Scotland) Act 1986, s.1.

[57] See *Death and Debt*, paras, 3.09–3.12.

[58] *Lindsay's Exr v. Forsyth*, 1940 S.C. 568.

[59] *Campbell Smith's Trs v. Scott*, 1944 S.L.T. 198.

M.C. Meston, "The Power of the Will", 1982 J.R. 172.
Wilson & Duncan, Chaps. 8, 9.
J. Murray, "Some of the Problems of Equitable Compensation", 1995 S.L.T. (News) 59

# Chapter 10

# INTERPRETATION OF WILLS

### General principles of interpretation

**10.01**    In interpreting the words of a will the fundamental principle is to give effect to the intention of the testator as expressed in the will. The testator's meaning must be deduced from the words he used.

**10.02**    The court must read the will as a whole, along with any codicils—additional ancillary testamentary writings which alter it. Where provisions conflict it tries to reconcile them; if that fails the most recent receives effect. If at all possible the will is construed in a sense that avoids intestacy: it is assumed that the testator meant something by it. Words are presumed to have their ordinary, primary meaning; terms which have a recognised technical legal meaning, such as "heirs", will have their ordinary technical sense.[1]

**10.03**    Consequently one is normally not permitted to contradict the terms of the will by using extrinsic evidence to show that the testator actually meant something else. The reasons are obvious: there would be unlimited scope for inconclusive conjecture as to the testator's real intention; evidence might easily be concocted. That may be *direct* evidence of the testator's intention—oral and written statements made by him—or *indirect* evidence of surrounding facts and circumstances which he knew about at the time when he made the will: both are excluded. Revoked clauses in the will may perhaps be considered in order to show what the rest of the will means, but even that is doubtful.[2]

### The use of extrinsic evidence[3]

**10.04**    Extrinsic evidence is however allowed if the will is unclear and the ordinary rules of interpretation provide no solution. In using it the court aims to put itself in the position of the testator at the

---

[1] *Macdonald's Trs v. Macdonald*, 1974 S.L.T. 87.
[2] *Devlin's Trs v. Breen*, 1945 S.C. (H.L.) 27; *cf. Currie's Trs v. Collier*, 1939 S.C. 247.
[3] See Walker and Walker, *Evidence*, 27.21; Macphail, paras 15.20 *et seq.*

time he made the will.[4] The aim is to explain the will, not to contradict it:

> "we must find the intention of the testatrix within the four **10.05** corners of the deed which she has legally executed. We are, undoubtedly, to look at the whole deed; and . . . if there be any doubt in the terms, we are to take into consideration the circumstances under which the deed was executed . . . [But] it is only if the terms of the deed appear to be in themselves doubtful in their import or legal construction, that it is either necessary or legitimate to affect or explain them by extraneous circumstances."[5]

Extrinsic evidence is admitted for six overlapping purposes.     **10.06**

(1) To enable a will to be read. If it is in code it has to be **10.07** deciphered; if it is in a foreign language it must be translated. The translation must be certified by an expert in the language.

(2) To establish whether a document is the testator's will. It may **10.08** never have been meant as a will in the first place, the writer having lacked concluded testamentary intent; it may have been destroyed *animo revocandi*. In either event the writer's intention may not be plain from the document. So, for instance, in the case of a draft will one must consider the terms of any covering letter. Such evidence is essential where a will is said to have been revoked by the *conditio si testator*.

(3) To construe words in an unusual, secondary sense where **10.09** their primary sense is ineffective. "A testator may give his own meaning to the words which he uses. His will becomes the dictionary from which the meaning of the terms used in it is to be ascertained."[6] In this way the provision can be implemented. Otherwise it would fail and intestacy would result.

Common examples at one time concerned the meaning of "child". Its primary sense was a legitimate, genetic child: adopted and illegitimate offspring were excluded. But external factors might point to the wider meaning: "a bequest by a testator, who is a bachelor . . . to his children may infer a gift to his illegitimate children surviving him, if he dies a bachelor, because the bequest would otherwise be inept".[7] That problem is now minimal: "children" now includes an adopted or illegitimate child unless the will says the opposite.[8]

---

[4] *Hay v. Duthie's Trs*, 1956 S.C. 511 at 528 *per* Lord Carmont.

[5] *Blair v. Blair* (1849) 12 D. 97.

[6] *Borthwick's Trs v. Borthwick*, 1955 S.C. 277 at 230, *per* L.J.–C. Thomson.

[7] *Scott's Trs v. Smart*, 1954 S.C. 12. For adoption see *Hay v. Duthie's Trs*, 1956 S.C. 511.

[8] But not for wills executed before September 10, 1964 (adoption) or November 25, 1968 (illegitimacy): 1964 Act, s.23(2); Law Reform (Miscellaneous Provisions) (Scotland) Act 1968, s.5.

**10.10**    (4) To prove what the testator knew about facts material to the construction of his will. For instance, in *Dunsmure v. Dunsmure*[9] the testator made a legacy of "any money I am entitled to under my late father's will". But he was also due money under his parents' marriage contract, and he knew it; in the circumstances the words covered both will and marriage contract. As this was a holograph will without professional advice the court felt particularly well-disposed to allow this extended meaning.

Similarly in *Livingstone v. Livingstone*[10] the testator referred in a codicil to "the sum of £6,000". The same sum occurred in the original will. Did the codicil give a fresh legacy or just repeat the old one? The value of the estate, insofar as the testator knew it, was a relevant factor suggesting the latter.

This rule applies particularly to a *legatum rei alienae*, a bequest of property the testator did not own. The law presumes that he made a mistake, and the legacy fails. If it is proved that he made the legacy deliberately, knowing the facts, the executors must try to implement his wishes and acquire the object for the legatee or, failing that, pay him the cash value instead.

**10.11**    (5) Two identical legacies in the same will are taken to be a mistake and only one is payable. Extrinsic evidence can rebut this presumption against double provisions.

**10.12**    (6) To identify the subject or the object of a legacy, if the will is ambiguous as to the property bequeathed or the beneficiary or purposes. Ambiguity can be *patent* (it is plain on a first reading) or *latent* (doubt arises only when the will is applied to the external facts).

It is sometimes said that only latent ambiguity permits extrinsic evidence. If a patent ambiguity cannot be solved by reading the will, the affected legacy is uncertain and lapses.[11] In fact the case law is not consistent and it is difficult to separate the categories. But (supposing latent ambiguity) only indirect evidence is normally allowed. The exception is where the will is meant to refer to one legatee but two or more people actually match the description: if the context gives no clues the testator's correspondence or oral statements are admissible evidence as to who was meant.[12]

If there is no ambiguity at all, the terms of the will stand or fall on their own. Extrinsic evidence cannot alter them. So in *Fortunato's J.F. v. Fortunato*[13] a clearly worded legacy of a public house could not include an adjoining flat: in reaching this interpretation it

---

[9] (1879) 7 R. 261.
[10] (1864) 3 M. 20.
[11] See *Yule's Trs*, 1981 S.L.T. 250 where "child" was read as a clear error for "grandchild".
[12] See Walker and Walker, *Evidence*, 27.24.
[13] 1981 S.L.T. 277.

was permissible to refer to other clauses in the will, but not to the circumstances in which it was made or the way in which the property was managed.

Despite applying the rules of interpretation and extrinsic evidence, a legacy may still be too uncertain to receive effect. It lapses and intestacy may result.

### SUBJECTS AND OBJECTS OF LEGACIES

**Types of subject and object**

A legacy is a bequest of specified property to a specified **10.13** recipient or for a specified purpose. The item is the subject, the recipient is the object.

The subject of the legacy is usually straightforward, though—as **10.14** in *Dunsmure*—ambiguity may need to be resolved. Before 1868 it was not possible to leave heritage by will, but only by an immediate—*de praesenti*—conveyance taking effect on death and using the word "dispone"; there is now no restriction, and the only question is whether the testator intended a particular term to include heritage and, generally, what it meant.

The object is frequently a class of relation. Most of these terms **10.15** have acquired a legal meaning which will apply unless the testator is proved to have used them in a different sense. "Child" we have seen. "Issue" refers to children, grandchildren, and other descendants: but only those descendants who have no surviving relative between them and the deceased testator, and who therefore inherit in place of—not along with—the intervening generation. (If the testator (say) leaves a son who has a grandson, only the son can inherit as "issue"; the grandson can inherit only if the son died first.) But a legacy to "dependants" will fail for uncertainty as the term has no precise meaning.[14]

"Next-of-kin" usually means the relations entitled to inherit if **10.16** one dies intestate; in *Nelson's Trs v. Nelson's Curator Bonis*[15] that was a daughter, but the term was taken to mean a nephew: this was decided in the light of the will having been altered in other respects to exclude the daughter from benefiting. The same point applies to "heirs".[16]

A legacy to "wife" or "husband" needs great care. Divorce does **10.17** not necessarily revoke it; it remains valid if "wife" was added simply to identify a named legatee, as in *Couper's J.F. v. Valentine*.[17]

---

[14] *Robertson's J.F. v. Robertson*, 1968 S.L.T. 32.
[15] 1979 S.L.T. 98; also *Borthwick's Trs v. Borthwick*, 1955 S.C. 227.
[16] For date at which heirs identified see paras 10.18 *et seq.* and 11.72 *et seq.*
[17] 1976 S.L.T. 83.

If however it is a family provision, for the recipient in the character of wife—as when the legatee is not named—the legacy either falls or goes to whoever is the wife when the legacy is payable. That happened in *Burns' Trs*[18]: when the testator made his will and when he died, his nephew was married; when (32 years later) the legacy became payable to the nephew's wife, he was remarried; the new wife took the legacy. In the same way a legacy to a "fiancé(e)" is not conditional on marriage unless it says so.[19]

**10.18** Most of these classes, by their nature, change their membership through time. More children will be born or die. At what point in time is their meaning to be interpreted: when the will is made; when the testator dies; or when the legacy vests or is paid?

**10.19** It is often said that a will "speaks from the date of the testator's death". That is true to the extent that before then it is revocable and has no effect. But its meaning is not necessarily fixed at that date. There are two closely related issues.

**10.20** (a) *Identifying the members of the class*. Subject to the will indicating some other date, the tendency is for the class if possible to be identified (and for the legacy to vest in its members) when the testator dies.[20] Examples would be a legacy to "my children", "my heirs", or "issue of X". If the legacy is payable at some later date, and the class enlarges in the interval, the new members will be included as well. However if the class must be identified by reference to a date later than the testator's death, that is the date when its membership is fixed (and, as a rule, when vesting and payment occur). Thus with a legacy to "heirs of X" the heirs can only be ascertained when X dies. The heirs may even, surprisingly, have to be identified at some specified point after the death of the person whose heirs they are. Typical examples would be:

> (i) a legacy to Y coupled with a destination-over "failing Y . . . to the heirs of X". The heirs' entitlement may arise at a point later than X's death, such as Y's dying before attaining a specified age.

> (ii) a legacy payable at a specified point later than the testator's death to "my heirs then surviving"—such as the end of a liferent.

**10.21** (b) *Changes in the law*. The relevant law may change, *e.g.* by redefining the scope of illegitimacy, "issue", and "heirs". At what point is the legal meaning of the class (as opposed to the factual

---

[18] 1961 S.C. 17.

[19] *Ormiston's Exr v. Laws*, 1966 S.L.T. 110.

[20] *Gregory's Trs v. Alison* (1889) 16 R. (H.L.) 10 at 14, *per* Lord Watson. See further (on vesting) paras 11.72 *et seq.*, below. See Henderson, *Vesting*, pp. 225–229.

identity of its members) fixed? The House of Lords recently decided in *Wright's Trs v. Callender*[21] that, in general, the law applied is that in force when the testator died. The logic is said to be that the testator is deemed to envisage it possibly changing in the interval between making his will and dying (and he could change his will in response if he chose to), but not in the period between his death and the date (if later) when the legacy vests or is payable. Thus in *Wright's Trs* a legacy payable in 1989 to "issue" (*i.e.* lawful issue) could not include someone who could not have been legitimate under the law when the testator died in 1917 but was legitimated by an Act in 1959. But again it seems that a legacy to "heirs of X" is an exception to the rule: the relevant law is (as in (a) above) that in force when the legacy vests in the heirs, since only then can his heirs possibly be known for certain.

Despite the above rules, some law reforms apply expressly only to deeds executed after they come into force; the law used to interpret an earlier deed thus remains that in force when the deed was made. Two important examples are:

(i) interpreting legacies to "issue" or "children" (do they include illegitimate and adopted children?)[22] and

(ii) references to "minority" or "full age" (age 21 or 18?).[23]

## Uncertainty

### (a) General rule

We have already seen that a will, or a legacy, may be ambiguous. **10.22** That occurs whenever there is no item matching the subject or no person matching the object. The maxim is that *falsa demonstratio non nocet*: *dummodo constet de re* (or, as appropriate, *de persona*): mere misdescription does not invalidate the bequest if the ambiguity can be cured by extrinsic evidence. If it cannot the legacy fails; it is void for uncertainty.

A classic example concerning the object was *Cathcart's Trs v.* **10.23** *Bruce*.[24] The legacy was to "General Alexander Fairlie Bruce".

---

[21] 1993 S.L.T. 556, 1993 S.C.L.R. 415, following *Cockburn's Trs v. Dundas* (1864) 2 M. 1185 (a case on change in meaning of "heirs"). See Meston's comments at 1993 S.C.L.R. 426–427.

[22] Law Reform (Miscellaneous Provisions) (Scotland) Act 1968, s.5; Law Reform (Parent & Child) (Scotland) Act 1986, s.1(4)(c) (applying to wills executed on or after November 25, 1968 and December 8, 1986 respectively); Succession (Scotland) Act 1964, s.23(4) (wills executed on or after September 10, 1964).

[23] Age of Majority (Scotland) Act 1969, s.1(2)(b) (deeds executed on or after January 1, 1970, unless exercising a special power of appointment created by a deed before that date).

[24] 1923 S.L.T. 722; and *Keiller v. Thomson's Trs* (1824) 3 S. 279.

There was in fact a General Alexander J., and a Mr Alexander F. From extrinsic evidence—letters—referring to the "General's" children as young men, it was clear that the real General was meant. There the description fitted neither possible beneficiary. It is a finer point if one is described accurately but not the other, as in *Nasmyth's Trs v. N.S.P.C.C.*[25] where the legatee was the N.S.P.C.C. but the S.S.P.C.C. claimed it was meant. On the face of it there is no ambiguity: the court in *Nasmyth* said that "positive evidence" is needed to disregard the description and choose the inaccurately-named person, but it gave no guidance as to what exactly that meant.

**10.24**   The subject causes fewer problems. In *Magistrates of Dundee v. Morris*[26] trustees were directed to set up the Morgan Academy, but no cash legacy was itemised. That would not raise latent ambiguity. But it was not void for uncertainty: the will specified the size of the school, and thus allowed the legacy to be ascertained—as a sum sufficient to pay for the school.

**10.25**   If the uncertainty relates to something integral to the legacy, the legacy fails. So in *Wood v. Wood's Exx*[26a] an instruction to the executrix "to share out as she knows I would wish it" failed, there being nothing to show that she did know what the testator wished. But if, by contrast, it is some ancillary matter, it can be possible to disregard that and give effect to the legacy. Thus in *McGinn's Exx v. McGinn*[27] a house was bequeathed to children with a request, if it were sold, that each receive an (unspecified and unquantifiable) "proportion": the request was treated as a mere suggestion and the legacy stood. As usual the court tried to discover a meaning which upheld the will and avoided intestacy.

### (b) Class gifts; selection of objects by trustees

**10.26**   A legacy may be left to a defined class of people. If sufficiently certain, it is effective. But "if there can be a reasonable doubt as to who is comprehended within the so-called description, the courts will treat the bequest as void". So in *Salvesen's Trs v. Wye* a bequest to "any poor relations, friends, or acquaintances of mine" was invalid.[28]

**10.27**   One problem is whether to read such lists "disjunctively" (*i.e.* as separate provisions) or "conjunctively" (as one provision, with several criteria all of which must be met in each case). In *Salvesen's Trs* the list was construed disjunctively, hence widely; "poor relations" would be acceptable but "friends" was not, so the whole

[25] 1914 S.C. (H.L.) 76 at 83, *per* Lord Dunedin.
[26] (1858) 3 Macq. 134 (H.L.)
[26a] 1995 S.L.T. 563
[27] 1994 S.L.T. 2.
[28] *Salvesen's Trs v. Wye*, 1954 S.C. 440. See Wilson and Duncan, 14.100–14.119.

list fell for uncertainty. Note that as a general tendency (though with exceptions) "and" is interpreted conjunctively and "or" disjunctively.

One may occasionally have to consider whether a gift is to **10.28** individuals or a class, as in *Millar's Trs v. Rattray*[29]: a legacy to "the children of [X], of whom there are ten" was taken to be a class which included three children born after the date of the will; the number simply identified the class without limiting it.

It is a fundamental principle that a testator cannot delegate to **10.29** someone else the power to make a will—that, after all, is why a will cannot be made for an incapax. But he can by his own will appoint testamentary trustees and instruct them to choose beneficiaries from within a class defined by himself:

> "A party may, in the disposition of his property, select **10.30** particular classes of individuals and objects, and then give to some particular individual a power, after his death, of appropriating the property, or applying any part of his property, to any particular individuals among that class whom that person may select and describe in his will."[30]

That class must itself be sufficiently certain: if trustees are given **10.31** total discretion to distribute property as they think fit, with no guidance from the testator, that is void from uncertainty.[31] Subject to that constraint, instructions will be given effect.

Where the bequest is to "charities", the law is more generous. **10.32** Admittedly the testator must create some mechanism for the charities to be selected: if, as in *Angus's Exx v. Batchan's Trs*,[32] he appoints no trustees or executors for that purpose, the bequest is ineffective. On the other hand the omission is not fatal if the legacy is sufficiently precise not to rely on trustees' discretion: as in *Ballingall's J.F. v. Hamilton*[33] where it was to "heart diseases and cancer research".

Subject to trustees or executors being appointed, the bequest to **10.33** charities is effective. "Charitable purposes" are a class in their own right and need no further definition in the will. But note that they have different senses in England and Scotland. In England their meaning is precise: "trusts for the relief of poverty; trusts for the advancement of education; trusts for the advancement of religion; and trusts for other purposes beneficial to the community".[34] In

---

[29] (1891) 18 R. 989.
[30] *Crichton v. Grierson* (1828) 3 W. & S. 329 at 338, *per* Lord Lyndhurst L.C.
[31] *Sutherland's Trs v. Sutherland's Trs* (1893) 20 R. 925.
[32] 1949 S.C. 335. See Wilson and Duncan, 14.21–14.34.
[33] 1973 S.L.T. 236.
[34] *Commissioners of Income Tax v. Pemsel* [1891] A.C. 531.

Scotland that test only applies for tax purposes.[35] Otherwise the term has a loose commonsense meaning.

**10.34** "Charity" is exceptional: other similar terms are ineffective. "Public purposes", for instance, is void for uncertainty[36]: it might include political donations. The problem occurs where the testator, unwilling to use one word, combines "charity" with a term which on its own would be uncertain. The test then is whether the two words are read disjunctively, referring to separate objects, or to take the other merely to explain and further define "charity". If the first, the whole clause is void; if the second, it is valid. So in *McPhee's Trs v. McPhee*[37] "religious and charitable" was valid, while in *Rintoul's Trs v. Rintoul*[38] "charitable or social institutions" was uncertain. But it depends how the court interprets the particular will: in *Wink's Exrs v. Tallent*[39] "benevolent or charitable" was upheld. Word order, punctuation, and the general scheme of the will all influence the interpretation chosen.[40]

## MULTIPLE LEGACIES AND LEGATEES

### Destinations-over[41]

**10.35** A destination-over is a provision in the will in the form "to A, whom failing to B" or "to A or B". It names the original legatee or "institute" (A) and then a further legatee B to whom the property may pass in A's place.

**10.36** B may be either a conditional institute or a substitute. A conditional institute is an alternative legatee; a substitute is a second successive legatee. Now if A for some reason never inherits from the testator (perhaps he dies before him), in either case B inherits in his place. The difference arises if A does inherit. If there is conditional institution, B's right immediately lapses altogether. If there is substitution, B can potentially still take the property after A dies, but A can defeat B's right by disposing of the property before he (A) dies or by his will.

**10.37** The rule is clear; the problem is to decide if an ambiguously worded clause creates a substitute or a conditional institute. That depends on whether heritage or moveables are at issue. If heritage, substitution is presumed; if moveables (or a mixture of both), conditional institution. Each item of property is looked at sepa-

---

[35] *Inland Revenue v. Glasgow Police Athletic Association*, 1953 S.C. (H.L.) 13.
[36] *Blair v. Duncan* (1901) 4 F. (H.L.) 1.
[37] 1912 S.C. 75.
[38] 1949 S.C. 297.
[39] 1947 S.C. 470.
[40] See Wilson & Duncan, 14.108.
[41] See Henderson, *Vesting*, pp. 49–55.

rately, so that both presumptions may occur in the one will. But while the presumptions are strong, the terms of the will may rebut them.

In *Watson v. Giffen*[42] spouses jointly owned a house. The wife **10.38** left her half-share "to my said son . . . whom failing, to my own heirs in fee". The son survived her but died intestate before her heir (her brother). This was treated as substitution: the share went to the brother, despite the existence of the same words for moveables elsewhere in the will. By contrast, in *Crumpton's J.F. v. Barnardo's Homes*[43] cash was left to charities "in case [X] dies without issue". He did, but not before outliving the testatrix: by his survivance the charities' right lapsed.

## Cumulative and substitutional legacies

Testamentary writings may leave more than one legacy to the **10.39** same person. The legacies may be cumulative or substitutional: if cumulative, both are payable; if substitutional, only one is.

The testator's intention may be clear upon reading the writings so as to reconcile their provisions and find out the testator's overall scheme. There may in fact not be two effective legacies: the later may have revoked the earlier. Failing that one must rely on legal presumptions.

(1) If one deed contains identical legacies, these are presumed to **10.40** be substitutional. The testator is taken to have repeated one legacy through forgetfulness. Where the amounts differ, the legacies are cumulative. On the other hand, in *Gillies v. Glasgow Royal Infirmary*[44] there were two identical quarter-shares of residue: the court treated these as cumulative on the strained reasoning that these were not legacies as such.

(2) If the legacies are in different deeds—and both are **10.41** operative—they are cumulative whether identical or not. (This assumes that the later deed has not revoked the earlier, in which case plainly only the later is effective.) The principle was laid down in *Arres' Trs v. Mather*[45]:

"When a testator by one or several instruments gives two or **10.42** more legacies to the same individual, he presumably intends that they shall all have effect, and in the absence of any expression or other indication of intentions to the contrary [the law accepts this]. Nor will a mere speculative conjecture or plausible doubt be allowed to affect the legal presumption

---

[42] (1884) 11 R. 444.
[43] 1917 S.C. 713.
[44] 1960 S.C. 438.
[45] (1881) 9 R. 107. See also *Edinburgh Royal Infirmary v. Muir's Trs* (1881) 9 R. 352.

for cumulation, which is generally in accord with the real intention, and is the prima facie legal presumption precisely because it is so, for the aim . . . of the law is to ascertain and carry into effect the testator's intention. The presumption may . . . be overcome, not only by distinct expression that the later bequest was intended to be substitutional, but by anything which satisfies the court that it was so intended."

**10.43**    In reaching a conclusion the court may look not only at the scheme of the deeds but also at extrinsic evidence. In *McLachlan v. Seton's Trs*[46] the history of the wills was crucial. The first was made under duress, and consequently the testatrix later made a new will: in it she deliberately repeated some (but not all) of her earlier legacies. On these facts the legacies were therefore not cumulative but substitutional.

### Division per capita and *per stirpes*[47]

**10.44**    We have seen this distinction in intestate succession.[48] Per capita division allows all the legatees to share equally. By contrast, *per stirpes* division is initially made at the level of the *stirps*,[49] the branch of the family tree indicated by the will as appropriate; thereafter members of the *stirps* usually subdivide the amount equally per capita. Take a legacy jointly to A's son B and C's sons D and E: if they take per capita each gets one-third; if *per stirpes* (with the head of each *stirps* being A and C respectively) B gets one-half while D and E each take one-quarter.

**10.45**    When a bequest is left to a number of individuals, it is presumed unless the will indicates otherwise that all who survive the testator take equally per capita. If, however, the legatees are described as members of a group or class (such as "the issue of X") *per stirpes* division is a possibility. If they have the same degree of relationship to the deceased (*e.g.* all are grandchildren) per capita division is preferred[50]; if different degrees (one is a child, the others are grandchildren), *per stirpes* at the degree nearer the deceased.

**10.46**    But general rules do not fully answer the problem, which is always one of interpreting the particular will. Even if it (unusually) uses the term *per stirpes*, that just begs the underlying question: who is the head of the *stirps*? At what point in the family tree did the testator want the legacy to be divided? *Per stirpes* division occurs if "the children of X" does not merely identify who they are,

---

[46] 1937 S.C. 206.
[47] See Henderson, *Vesting*, pp. 218–224.
[48] At paras 4.48–4.51.
[49] *Stirpes* is the plural of *stirps*; per capita means "per head".
[50] *Campbell's Trs v. Welsh*, 1952 S.C. 343.

but also what their share is: they inherit essentially in a representative capacity in place of X, X's share goes to them in aggregate, so division is *per stirpes* at the level of X.[51]

*Per stirpes* division is thus a two-stage process. First one identifies **10.47** the various *stirpes* and divides the estate among them. Having ascertained what share each *stirps* gets, one divides that among its members. This second stage is in principle, but not always, per capita.

*Cobban's Exrs v. Cobban*[52] and *Laing's Trs v. Samson*[53] illustrate **10.48** the concept. In *Cobban* the estate was to be "divided equally between X and his children and my brother Y and his children". Division was per capita among all the legatees because the children inherited along with X and Y rather than—more normally—in their place if they died. "X failing whom. . .." would by contrast have suggested an equal *per stirpes* split between X's and Y's families. In *Laing's Trs* division was among "my surviving brothers and sisters and the lawful issue of those who may be deceased": the issue got what their parent would have got, so division was *per stirpes* at the level of the brothers and sisters. For the same reason, a legacy to "X and Y in liferent and their children in fee" will be divided *per stirpes* so that the children (in aggregate) get the same assets as their respective parents.[54]

In *Laing* division within the *stirps* was per capita because all the **10.49** "issue" were of one generation (children). By contrast in *Boyd's Tr. v. Shaw*[55] there were also grandchildren; subdivision at the level of the children was again *per stirpes*, to ensure that grandchildren got the same as their parent (a predeceasing child) would have received if alive.

### Accretion

A legacy may be to several legatees, such as "A, B and C". If all **10.50** the legatees survive and acquire a vested right, the position is simple: each takes a proportionate share of the legacy, and if one of them later dies before receiving actual payment his right then passes to his heirs as part of his own estate. The problem arises if one dies before his right vests: does his share fall into intestacy[56] (or residue) or does it accrue to the other legatees? In the second case there is accretion.

The solution depends on whether the legacy is treated as **10.51** "several" or "joint". If several, each share passes separately and

---

[51] *Thomson v. Cumberland*, November 16, 1814 F.C.
[52] 1915 S.C. 82.
[53] (1879) 7 R. 244. See *Boyd's Tr. v. Shaw*, 1958 S.C. 115.
[54] *Home's Trs v. Ramsay* (1884) 12 R. 314. See also McLaren, Vol. II, p. 1420.
[55] 1958 S.C. 115. On this problem see Robertson, 1979 S.L.T. (News) 133. The case law is not consistent.
[56] Including a destination-over will avoid intestacy.

*(several) in Scotland*

there is no accretion. If joint, the legacy remains undivided and the share accresces to the survivors. The underlying issue is whether the testator intended one aggregate legacy to the beneficiaries en bloc or separate legacies merely payable out of one total fund.

**10.52**     In the simple case—"A and B" with nothing further said—the legacy is joint and there is accretion to the survivor. But if there are "words of severance" that points to the testator intending separate legacies; consequently accretion is excluded and intestacy results. *Paxton's Trs v. Cowie*[57] explains what is meant:

**10.53**     "When a legacy is given to a plurality of persons named or sufficiently described for identification 'equally among them', or 'in equal shares', or 'share and share alike', or in any other language of the same import, each is entitled to his own share and no more, and there is no room for accretion in the event of the predecease of one or more of the legatees. The rule is applicable whether the gift is in liferent or in fee to the whole equally, and whether the subject of the bequest be residue or a sum of a fixed amount or corporeal moveables. The application of this rule may, of course, be controlled or avoided by the use of other expressions by the testator importing an intention that there shall be accretion in the event of the predecease of one or more of the legatees."

**10.54** However, words of severance will not always bar accretion. They are simply strong evidence of the testator's intention, and that may still point to a collective legacy and thus accretion. Two common types of provision achieve this result:

**10.55**     (1) Words of survivorship: "equally among X, Y, and Z, and the survivor". If X fails to survive his share accresces to the others.

**10.56**     (2) A class gift: where beneficiaries are selected not essentially as individuals (out of the testator's regard for them personally) but as members of an identified group, normally relations.

Numerous cases discuss class gifts. "Equally among the children of [X]" is one instance.[58] Similarly a "one-third share", normally a clear sign of severance, would not prevent accretion where the will as a whole made clear that the legatee inherited merely as one of three sons.[59]

If the will names the beneficiaries individually, that makes a class gift unlikely. The fact that the legatees happen to form a class is not enough unless they explicitly inherit *as a class*. Adding their names suggests that their individual identity is more important than their membership of the class: for instance "A, B, C, and D,

---

[57] (1886) 13 R. 1191 at 1197, *per* L.P. Inglis.
[58] *Muir's Trs v. Muir* (1889) 16 R. 954.
[59] *Roberts' Trs v. Roberts* (1903) 5 F. 541.

the children of my late sister".[60] But names are not always fatal: the testator's apparent intention is always central. The names may be mere subsidiary identification—"my children (who are X and Y)"; more important, there may be words of survivorship. Both features allowed accretion in *Menzies' Factor v. Menzies*.[61]

**10.57** *Mitchell's Trs v. Aspin*[62] indicates what care is necessary in drafting such clauses. Residue was to go in equal shares to children in liferent, and to their issue in fee; "failure" of any issue would divide that person's share equally *per stirpes* among the other children and issue. Perhaps the testator intended accretion: but he had not provided for the event of issue never existing at all, and (despite strong dissenting judgments) the Court of Session and House of Lords both ignored accretion and held that the share fell into intestacy.

**10.58** Accretion is not limited to the death of a legatee; it can occur whenever a legacy fails for any reason. In *Fraser's Trs v. Fraser*[63] a legacy was to A and B but the testator revoked B's share. Had there not been words of severance, it would have accresced to A; as it was, B's share fell into intestacy.

### Conditio si institutus sine liberis decesserit

**10.59** Normally if a legatee dies without acquiring a vested right his legacy lapses. Unless there is accretion (as a joint legacy) or a destination-over (naming an alternative legatee), the bequest falls into residue or intestacy. The *conditio si institutus sine liberis decesserit* is an equitable exception to that rule: it implies into the will a conditional institution of the legatee's children to inherit in his place if he fails to survive. They inherit in preference to a substitute named in the will, a residuary legatee, an heir on intestacy, or anyone to whom the legacy would otherwise accresce. The theoretical rationale is that the testator overlooked the possible death of the institute and would have inserted a conditional institution to children if he had thought of it.[64]

**10.60** The doctrine depends on the institute—the original legatee— being closely related to the testator. The courts have arbitrarily limited the relationships to which it applies. It covers the testator's children, grandchildren, and other descendants (but not step-children). It does not apply to brothers or other collaterals, with one exception: nephews and nieces are included if the testator was in *loco parentis* to them.[65] But in practice the *loco parentis* test is

---

[60] *White's Trs, Petrs*, 1957 S.C. 322.

[61] (1898) 1 F. 128; similarly *Young's Trs v. Young*, 1927 S.C. (H.L.) 6.

[62] 1971 S.L.T. 29; 1971 S.L.T. 166 (H.L.).

[63] 1980 S.L.T. 211.

[64] English law has a similar rule: Wills Act 1837, s.33(1). For the Commission's proposals see Report No. 124, paras 4.50–4.65.

[65] *Hall v. Hall* (1891) 18 R. 690.

meaningless. How the testator viewed the nephew during his lifetime is unimportant; what matters is simply that he "has placed himself in a position like that of a parent towards the legatees— that is to say he has made a settlement in their favour similar to what a parent might have been presumed to make".[66]

**10.61** In effect the *conditio* is presumed automatically from the relationship. The presumption may be displaced, but the onus of proof is on those who oppose its application and not those who assert it. Three factors will assist rebuttal:

**10.62** (1) Express exclusion of the *conditio*. Even so, a simple survivorship clause—"to my children surviving at my death"—will not by itself defeat it. The *conditio* overrides accretion: if a child predeceased, his descendants get his share; only if he had none does it go to the surviving children.

**10.63** (2) A bequest made from personal regard for the legatee rather than in view simply of his relationship. It is not essential for the *conditio* that the beneficiaries form a class, all of whom are instituted, but it makes it easier to displace it if the beneficiaries are selected members named individually.[67]

**10.64** (3) The testator did not overlook the existence of the institute's children. An example is *McNab v. Brown's Trs*[68]: the testatrix left property in liferent, and then in fee to her two sons equally and the survivor of them and "the issue of either of them who predeceases me". One son died after the testatrix but before the liferent expired: he had not predeceased her, so his children could not invoke the *conditio*.

**10.65** The original potential legatee must have been validly instituted in the first place. Conditional institution under a destination-over will suffice. So the *conditio* is excluded if he had died before the date of the will,[69] or before any codicil which affected his legacy.[70] Probably the *conditio* applies if he survives the testator but dies before acquiring a vested right.[71] It applies whether the legacy is of a capital sum or a right to income, *e.g.* a liferent.[72] Indeed, where the legacy is of income the courts have sometimes applied it if the legatee actually drew the income: on his death the income would pass in turn to his offspring under the *conditio* rather than lapse into intestacy for want of an alternative legatee.[73]

---

[66] *Bogie's Trs v. Christie* (1882) 9 R. 453, *per* L.P. Inglis.
[67] *Knox's Exr v. Knox*, 1941 S.C. 532.
[68] 1926 S.C. 389.
[69] *Travers's Trs v. Macintyre*, 1934 S.C. 520.
[70] *Miller's Trs v. Miller*, 1958 S.C. 125 (where the codicil did not concern the legacy, so the *conditio* applied.)
[71] *McGregor's Trs v. Gray*, 1969 S.L.T. 355; *cf. Mitchell's Exx v. Gordon's Factor*, 1953 S.L.T. 134.
[72] *Renwick's Trs v. Russell*, 1938 S.C. 855.
[73] *Reid's Trs v. Reid*, 1969 S.L.T. (Notes) 4.

Suppose the institute would have inherited a further legacy by **10.66** accretion. In principle the *conditio* does not apply to the additional accresced provision: only to the institute's original share. In practice the will often introduces complications:

(1) It may give the institute's children the benefit of accretion, **10.67** stating that they are to take "such share, original and accrued, as their parent would have taken if he had survived".

(2) It may also contain words of survivorship. These override (1): **10.68** the accrescing share goes to the survivors. Take a legacy to "A, B, and C, and the survivors": A dies leaving children; B dies with none; C survives. A's original (one-third) share goes to his children; B's accresces to C, and A's children get none of it.[74]

(3) Suppose that in (2) C had also not survived. Applying (2) **10.69** would cause intestacy in respect of B's and C's shares. In that case, reversing the normal rule, if (1) is also present it is given full effect: A's children get everything.[75]

Legacies: Classification and Payment

## Classification

How a legacy is classified is important for two reasons. First, it **10.70** determines exactly what rights the legatee has in respect of the property bequeathed. Second, it dictates the order of priority in which legacies are paid, and thus in which they lapse or are reduced if the estate is too small to pay them all: that raises the issues of ademption and abatement.

(1) *Specific (or special) legacies.* These are legacies of a specified **10.71** item, like a house or the right to receive a debt, or an identified investment: "my 1,000 shares in X Company Ltd". The legacy is confined to that item, and lapses if the testator no longer owns it when he dies: it is "adeemed". The item is regarded as assigned on death to the legatee, who can bring an action for its delivery not just from the executor but from anyone in possession of it.[76]

(2) *Demonstrative legacies.* These, like special legacies, refer to a **10.72** particular item, but state the source or funds from which the testator wishes it to be provided or paid. The question is then what happens if the source is insufficient for the legacy. A special legacy would lapse to the extent that the fund is insufficient. A demonstrative legacy, by contrast, gives the legatee a claim against the residue of the estate for the excess.

---

[74] *Miller's Trs v. Brown*, 1933 S.C. 669. See Murray, pp. 168–173; Henderson, pp. 102–109.

[75] *Beveridge's Trs v. Beveridge*, 1930 S.C. 578.

[76] In that case the executor is also nominally a defender.

**10.73** (3) *General legacies*. These are generic, "bequeathed indefinitely without any character distinguishing [them] from others of the same kind belonging to the deceased"[77]; "a legacy not of a special article or debt, but of a certain quantity or value which may be measured in money (as is usual) or in goods of a specified description".[78] The legatee has a right to sue the executor to enforce its payment or delivery.

**10.74** (4) *Residue*. This covers the whole of the testator's estate (heritable and moveable) which remains after paying the testator's debts and carrying out the antecedent purposes—such as legacies—of his will or wills. It includes property not disposed of by the will and legacies which fail initially or (perhaps because they are conditional on some event which does not occur) lapse after the testator's death. Residuary legatees have no right to insist on particular assets from the estate, unless they all agree on a division. The executors have discretion whether to transfer the assets in specie, *i.e.* physically, or to sell and distribute the proceeds. (They will consider the value of the asset (has it risen or fallen since the death?) and the tax effect on the estate. If they *sell* rather than transfer in specie, there may be IHT reliefs for losses[79] or, conversely (if values have risen), CGT on gains.)

A will should dispose of residue: otherwise that property devolves under the rules of intestacy. In that case the heirs on intestacy are those as at the testator's death, not those at the later date when a legacy lapses and the intestacy becomes known.[80]

### Ademption of specific legacies

**10.75** A specific legacy is adeemed if it no longer belongs to the testator when he dies. The testator may have destroyed or disposed of the asset. The legacy lapses entirely: the legatee gets nothing. The test is twofold: was the legacy specific, and was the item part of the estate at death? That is purely factual: in modern law the testator's intention in disposing of the asset (was it deliberate?) is irrelevant.

**10.76** The problem is usually whether the legacy still survived at the date of death. *Ogilvie-Forbes' Trs v. Ogilvie-Forbes*[81] summarised it: "the question is whether a testator has at the time of death the same thing existing, it may be in a different shape—yet substantially the same thing". There a legacy of a house was adeemed by its transfer to a limited company, albeit a company controlled by the testator. Similarly, in *Ballantyne's Trs v. Ballantyne's Trs*[82] there

---

[77] Erskine, Inst., III.ix.11.
[78] McLaren, Vol. 1, p. 575.
[79] See paras 12.35–12.38, 12.75–12.76 below.
[80] *Lord v. Colvin* (1865) 3 M. 1083.
[81] 1955 S.C. 405 at 411, *per* L.P. Clyde.
[82] 1941 S.C. 35.

was ademption where the bequeathed sums, identified as being in a bank account at Glasgow, were uplifted and re-deposited by the testator in a new account at Hawick.

There is no ademption if the item was not yet finally disposed of. **10.77** In *McArthur's Exrs v. Guild*[83] a hotel sale was conditional on the licence being transferred to the buyer; that happened after the testator died; ademption had not occurred. Much the same happened in *Tennants' Trs v. Tennants*[84] where shares had been transferred but not yet registered with the company. (Note that, even if ademption is absent, the legatee might hold those shares subject to a constructive trust in the buyer's favour, requiring him to complete the transfer and to forward any dividends received in the meantime.[85])

The risk of ademption can be minimised by wording legacies to **10.78** refer to assets owned at death. "Any car I may own at the date of my death" is an example.

## Abatement of legacies

The testator's debts, including executry expenses and IHT, must **10.79** be paid or provided for before any legacies. So must legal rights, if claimed. The estate may then not be large enough to pay all the legacies. They must abate—be reduced. The will may itself state how, but failing that the order is as follows:

    (a) Residuary legacies abate first.

    (b) General legacies next abate *pari passu* (equally).

    (c) Demonstrative legacies do not abate until the specified fund is exhausted, but then abate like general legacies.

    (d) Specific legacies are payable though no assets remain for general legacies.

Legacies' order of priority does not depend on their mere numbering in the will unless the will says so. Other factors may point to a different order.[86]

## *Legatum rei alienae*

This is a legacy of an item which did not belong to the testator **10.80** when he made the will. The law presumes that he made the legacy by mistake (and it lapses) unless it is proved to have been

---

[83] 1908 S.C. 743.
[84] 1946 S.C. 420.
[85] See R. Burgess, "The Unconstructive Trust?" 1977 J.R. 200.
[86] *McConnel v. McConnel's Trs*, 1931 S.N. 31 (H.L.).

deliberate. In that second case the executor must try to purchase the item to give to the legatee; if he cannot the legatee receives the cash value instead. But, as was pointed out in *Meeres v. Dowell's Exr*,[87] it is not enough to show that the testator ought to have known the facts; he must actually have done so.

### Precatory bequests

**10.81**　Instead of the testator instructing his executors what legacies to pay, he may use words like "I would prefer that. . .". Normally this is taken as a polite form of instruction which the executors must follow.[88]

**10.82**　Sometimes the request is outwith the executors' power to fulfil. In *Milne v. Smith*[89] the testator left a legacy to his son and hoped that his partnership would be carried on. This was a precatory condition attached to the legacy; it could not be enforced (neither the son nor the other partner might be willing), so the legacy was payable unconditionally.

**10.83**　Alternatively the testator may request a legatee to dispose of the legacy in some way. To the extent that this attempts to restrict the legatee's right of ownership, it is unenforceable under the doctrine of *repugnancy*.[90] The most it can do is to create a destination over the property, which the legatee can evacuate by disposing of it as he wishes while alive.

### Interest on legacies

**10.84**　In principle legacies are payable with interest from the testator's death to the date of payment. There is no fixed "legal rate": the rate is what the estate earned or should have earned if properly administered.[91] But circumstances may waive interest: for instance, the estate may have been insolvent for part of the period.[92] In any event the will often makes legacies payable interest-free.

CONDITIONAL LEGACIES

**10.85**　A legacy may be payable subject to conditions. These may be suspensive (payment is postponed till the condition is fulfilled) or resolutive (the legacy lapses if a specified event occurs, such as remarriage). The condition may be ineffective for several reasons,

---

[87] 1923 S.L.T. 184.
[88] *Reid's Trs v. Dawson*, 1915 S.C. (H.L.) 47.
[89] 1982 S.L.T. 129.
[90] See Murray, pp. 39–44.
[91] *Kearon v. Thomson's Trs*, 1949 S.C. 287.
[92] *Waddell's Trs v. Crawford*, 1926 S.C. 654.

and it is then disregarded and the legacy takes effect unconditionally. It may be impossible. It may be *contra bonos mores*,
contravening public policy: the normal example is a restraint on
cohabitation or marriage. It may be uncertain: in this respect
England requires a tougher test for resolutive than suspensive
conditions (because they defeat a right already given to the
legatee) but Scots law does not, "it [being] only necessary in order
to allow of the condition being enforced that it be expressed in
terms sufficiently determinate to advertise the beneficiary and the
court of the general course of conduct which has been enjoined".[93]

Conditions may be *potestative*, depending for fulfilment on action **10.86**
by the legatee; on the "approbate and reprobate" principle[94] they
bind the legatee if he accepts the legacy. They may be *casual*,
depending on some external event such as a liferenter's death; or
they may be *mixed*, combining both elements. A potestative
condition may be taken as fulfilled when the legatee has done all
he or she can to fulfil it. So in *Miller & Anr, Petrs*[95] she was willing
to look after the testatrix as required in the will; only the testatrix's
confinement to hospital prevented her doing so. She was entitled to
the legacy. Similarly in *Simpson v. Roberts*[96] a legacy was conditional on staying in a particular job. The legatee was willing to
work but was dismissed; she got the legacy because it was not her
fault she could not fulfil the condition.

The conditions may be inconsistent with the bequest: if so they **10.87**
are disregarded. This is another example of the doctrine of
repugnancy which resolves conflicts between mutually-
contradictory provisions. The classic instance occurs where property is left in fee—outright ownership—and conditions are
attached which are appropriate to a lesser right such as a liferent.
In particular, the beneficiary's right of fee may be subject to the
trustees not making payment till a specified age such as 25. Then,
as in the leading case of *Miller's Trs v. Miller*,[97] the beneficiary can
insist on payment unless he is legally incapax (*e.g.* under 18) or
payment is being withheld in order to safeguard some other
purpose of the trust. Withholding property purely to manage it for
the owner is not consistent with full ownership.

## Powers of Appointment

In principle a testator cannot delegate his power of testation. **10.88**
However, when making a legacy he may create a power of
appointment in respect of the property in question: a power to

---

[93] *Balfour's Trs v. Johnston*, 1936 S.C. 137 *per* Lord Moncrieff.
[94] See paras 9.08–9.17.
[95] 1977 S.L.T. (Sh. Ct) 67. See Wilson & Duncan, 7.20.
[96] 1931 S.C. 259.
[97] (1890) 18 R. 301.

select to whom the property will subsequently pass. He either reserves the power to himself or grants it to the legatee or some third party; the recipient of the power cannot himself delegate it to someone else.

**10.89**    Powers of appointment are *special* or *general*. Under a special power beneficiaries are chosen from a defined class. A general power gives an unlimited choice. That is in effect as wide a power of disposal as any owner can have: so if the testator purports to give a legatee a liferent plus a general power, he in fact makes the legatee unrestricted owner. The power is incompatible with the liferent, which on its own would allow assets to be used but not disposed of. The one exception, where the liferent remains in force, is an alimentary liferent, which (unlike other liferents) cannot be brought to an end by the liferenter acquiring the fee: in this case he has no right of disposal.

**10.90**    Someone exercising a power must have legal capacity: the rules are the same as for wills. He must exercise it according to the terms laid down by the grantor. Failure to adhere to the terms may invalidate the appointment as being:

**10.91**    (1) by an unauthorised method. Exercise may have to be (say) by will rather than lifetime deed. However, the will need not expressly refer to the power: a legacy of the testator's property generally (rather than specific items) may also by implication include the property subject to the power.[98]

**10.92**    (2) ultra vires (outwith the power). The appointer cannot impose restrictions on how the beneficiary is to use the property, or (if the power is special) choose a beneficiary from outwith the stipulated class.

**10.93**    (3) a fraud on the power, in the sense not of deceit but an unwarranted abuse of rights.[99] He cannot use the power to benefit himself, *e.g.* by allocating the property to himself, or to someone else but in return for a bribe.

**10.94**    Any unauthorised exercise can be challenged by anyone who is rightfully entitled to benefit under the power. But the appointment can still be effective provided that the invalidity is only partial and can be "severed" from the rest of the exercise. Thus (say) it may be possible to disregard conditions imposed on the beneficiary.

**Further reading**

Henderson, *Vesting*, Chaps. 7, 15, 17.
M.C. Meston, "Bequests to Heirs", 1974 S.L.T. (News) 109.

---

[98] *Hyslop v. Maxwell's Trs* (1834) 12 S. 413.
[99] Similarly "fraud on the minority" in company law. See *Callander v. Callander's Exr*, 1976 S.L.T. 10. See Gloag & Henderson, para. 44.29; Murray, Chap. 17.

M.C. Meston, "Per capita and *per stirpes* division; The *conditio si institutus*; Accretion" (1981) 26 J.L.S. (Workshop) 195, 203, 212.

Murray, *Law of Wills*.

G. Robertson, "*Per Stirpes* Division", 1979 S.L.T. (News) 133.

J.R. Scott, "The *Conditio si Institutus*", 1958 S.L.T. (News) 229.

W.H.D. Winder, "Ademption of Legacies", 1957 S.L.T. (News) 185.

"Fraud on a Power", 1976 S.L.T. (News) 157.

# CHAPTER 11

# VESTING

GENERAL RULES

**The concept of vesting**

**11.01**    Property is said to "vest" in someone when he acquires an indefeasible right to it. In the context of succession that has two practically important aspects.

*(a) Vesting in the executor*

**11.02**    Under the old law a deceased person's heritable property passed directly to his heir on his death. By contrast the moveables vested in the executor for the purpose of administration when he obtained confirmation of his title: he was then empowered to ingather it and distribute it to the beneficiaries under intestacy or the deceased's will. Any dealings by the executor with the property before confirmation constituted unauthorised "vitious intromission" which laid him open to liability for all the deceased's debts.

**11.03**    Under the Succession (Scotland) Act 1964[1] all the deceased's property—heritable and moveable—now vests in the executor upon confirmation. There is one important exception. Heritable property subject to a special destination vests purely to allow the executor to convey it to the next-entitled person, if that is necessary. So in a destination of form "A, then B", on A's death his executor's role is to transfer ownership to B. In the more usual survivorship destination, "A and B and survivor", B is already joint owner, automatically becomes full owner, and the property does not need to vest in the executor at all.[2]

*(b) Vesting in beneficiaries*

**11.04**    While a testator still lives, his legatees have a mere *spes successionis*, the chance to inherit on his death. He can normally revoke his will at any time, so they cannot have an indefeasible

---

[1] s.14(1).
[2] s.18(2). See Meston, pp. 82–83; (1965) 10 J.L.S. 73.

vested right. That arises on his death at the earliest; the will may itself postpone vesting till some later date. Legal rights and rights on intestacy vest on the death of the spouse, parent or intestate respectively.

Precisely what right does vesting give the beneficiary? It has **11.05** been called a "right of property".[3] But it is not outright ownership of the items involved. He may be unable to recover them from a third party who acquires them from the executor for value and in good faith[4]; if they include a house, he cannot mortgage that (because he has as yet no recorded title to it); and he cannot necessarily demand possession of them, because the will may postpone payment or transfer till a later time.

What the beneficiary has, rather, is a personal right against the **11.06** executor to compel him to pay over or deliver the vested estate in terms of the will or intestacy. Legal ownership at this stage rests with the executor: it passes to the beneficiary only when transferred by delivery (in the case of moveables) or recorded written disposition or notice of title (for heritage).

The beneficiary can dispose of his vested right by *inter vivos* **11.07** assignation: outright, or in security for a loan. It forms part of his estate on his death, so may be subject to IHT. Most important, it does not lapse in that event but passes to his heirs in their turn under his own will or intestacy.

### Vesting and payment

*(a) General principles*

Vesting is quite distinct from receiving possession or payment **11.08** under a legacy or intestacy. Possession is immaterial to vesting. The two may coincide, but need not. For debts must be paid before any legacy: that alone can delay payment for up to 12 months after death.[5] Moreover, a will may provide that a legacy vests on the testator's death but is not payable until some specified future event: usually the end of a liferent[6] or the legatee reaching 18 or some other age.

In that case, if the beneficiary survives the date of vesting but **11.09** dies before receiving payment, his legacy goes to his heirs. If he had no vested right (because he died before the testator, or because the will instead postponed vesting until the date of payment), the legacy passes instead by destination-over or with residue under the testator's will, or by the *conditio si institutus*[7] or the rules of intestacy.

---

[3] *Haldane's Trs v. Murphy* (1881) 9 R. 269 at 295, *per* Lord Young; *cf.* (1986) 31 J.L.S. 148, 396; (1987) 32 J.L.S. 218. See paras 10.70–10.74, above and 13.99.

[4] Succession (Scotland) Act 1964, s.17.

[5] McLaren Vol. II, p. 1164.

[6] See Gloag & Henderson, 47.1.

[7] See paras 10.59 *et seq.*

*(b) Vesting, minority and taxation*

**11.10** Questions of vesting may thus involve disputes between claimants for the legacy. But they also have important tax ramifications. In particular, in a testamentary trust it is crucial for IHT whether a beneficiary has an "interest in possession" in trust assets: a "present right of present enjoyment".[8] If he does, he is treated as owning the assets (so they are part of his estate for IHT), and the trust is denied the advantageous status of an accumulation and maintenance settlement.[9] *Stenhouse's Trs v. Lord Advocate*[10] illustrates the concept: a will gave trustees power to allocate funds to the testator's daughters once aged 22; they did so; the daughters took a vested right and, being adult, could insist on immediate payment. Combining those factors, they had an interest in possession in the funds.

**11.11** The problem often concerns bequests to minors. The testator wishes to delay payment till they are adult, with trustees administering the funds and the income arising from them until then. He has several choices:

**11.12** (1) The bequest may vest on his death, the trustees having power to accumulate the income rather than pay it out. That has three effects. The income cannot be accumulated beyond age 21.[11] If this is a "bare trust", with no other purposes to fulfil (such as a liferent), under the doctrine of repugnancy all the funds must be paid over at age 18.[12] For purposes of IHT the legatee owns the funds, and has an interest in possession despite the mere fact of accumulation; similarly he pays income tax on the income.

**11.13** (2) Vesting may be postponed to a specified age, say 21 or 25. This allows the funds to be withheld beyond age 18, though the will may also give the trustees discretion to pay them over at an earlier age. Again the child must get the income from age 21. He may be given a liferent (and so a right to the income) prior to that age: if so, IHT and income tax are treated as in (1). If not, they fall not on him but on the trust as a separate entity.

**11.14** (3) The trust may be an accumulation and maintenance settlement. Tax law restricts the duration (25 years) and beneficiaries (the testator's grandchildren and other defined relations); all the unaccumulated income must be used for the beneficiary's maintenance, education or benefit; and the beneficiary must initially have no interest in possession but will get one before (at latest) age 25. In practice the child usually gets the income from age 21, with the

---

[8] *Pearson v. I.R.C.* [1980] 2 W.L.R. 872; IHTA 1984, ss.5(1), 49(1), 59. For IHT see para. 12.24.
[9] IHTA 1984, s.71.
[10] 1986 S.L.T. 73.
[11] See paras 9.32 *et seq.*
[12] See para. 10.87.

funds vesting at age 25. In that case income tax and IHT fall on the trust, not the child, till those ages respectively.

### Rules of interpretation

The date of vesting may range from the testator's death to the **11.15** date of payment; earlier and later times are not possible. The date chosen depends on "the intentions of the testator, in so far as they can be discovered or reasonably inferred from the deed taken as a whole, and from the circumstances, legitimately collected, under which the deed was made . . . It is a *quaestio voluntatis*. That is the cardinal rule and guide."[13]

That dictum stresses a salient aspect of the law of vesting. The **11.16** words of the will are crucial. No two wills are identical; each case must be decided on its own facts. The courts have developed numerous rules to ascertain when vesting occurs (some of them arbitrary rather than logical), but ultimately these are merely guidelines, presumptions which must yield to the clearly expressed words of the will. Unfortunately the will is often unclear. The court may have a gut feeling what the testator really meant, but if he did not say so clearly, they have little choice but to apply those rules even if that gives a different outcome. As is often said, "the court will not make a testator's will for him".

All the usual rules for interpreting wills apply. In particular, the **11.17** scheme of the will and any codicils is read as a whole, while the family circumstances in which the testator made the will are relevant. There is a presumption against putting a construction on the will which results in partial or total intestacy, as the testator is taken not to have intended that: if he had, would he have made the will in the first place? The will may expressly declare when vesting is to take place. That is some help, but is not decisive; the declaration has to be read in the light of the rules of interpretation. The courts will accept it (perhaps reluctantly) if it makes the testator's intentions clear, but if it conflicts with the scheme of the will it simply obscures matters and may be disregarded.[14]

One presumption is especially important in the absence of some **11.18** contrary indication of the testator's intention: that in favour of vesting at the earliest possible date. This means vesting *a morte testatoris*, on the testator's death. Given two reasonably possible interpretations of the will, the courts prefer the one which allows that. But if that is impossible, they go to the other extreme:

"If the term of vesting is not the date of the death of the **11.19** testator, it is difficult to find any other period of vesting except

---

[13] *Carleton v. Thomson* (1867) 5 M. (H.L.) 151 at 153, *per* Lord Colonsay.
[14] *Carruthers' Trs v. Carruthers' Trs*, 1949 S.C. 530.

the period of distribution . . . except some special cases where the testator has either expressly or by implication assigned a term of vesting other than the period of distribution . . . Where no other period is suggested the term of vesting is either (1) the death of the testator, or (2) the period of distribution."[15]

CONDITIONAL LEGACIES

### Types of condition

*(a) Payment*

**11.20**   A legacy may be made payable on condition of a specified event occurring. This only postpones vesting if the condition is attached to the legacy itself. If the legacy is unqualified, and the condition relates merely to payment, vesting occurs in principle on the testator's death.[16]

*(b) Certain and uncertain events*

**11.21**   Some types of event are, by the nature of things, inevitable; some are not. The first is a *dies certus*: it must occur, though the exact date may be unpredictable; the legacy is taken as unconditional. The second is a *dies incertus*[17]: it may or may not occur, and there is a true condition. The first does not suspend vesting, the second may.

**11.22**   Suppose, then, property goes to X in liferent and Y in fee. The liferenter's death is *dies certus*. Though payment to Y is postponed until then, his right vests in him on the testator's death: so if he dies during the liferent his heirs get his legacy. To delay vesting would require an additional factor, such as words in the will or a destination-over whereby another legatee took in Y's place as conditional institute on his death.

**11.23**   Conversely, marriage or survival to a specified age are both *dies incertus*. So in *Mackintosh v. Wood*[18] a testatrix left her son one legacy due on her daughter's marriage, and another due on the daughter's death; on the son dying earlier the first legacy lapsed, but the second did not because, depending on a *dies certus*, it had already vested.

---

[15] L.P. Inglis in *Marshall v. King* (1888) 16 R. 40 at 43.
[16] *Alves' Trs v. Grant* (1874) 1 R. 969.
[17] Certain and uncertain day, respectively.
[18] (1872) 10 M. 933.

### (c) Suspensive and resolutive conditions

Even if the condition relates to a *dies incertus*, it will not **11.24** necessarily postpone vesting. That depends on whether the condition is suspensive or resolutive. The first suspends vesting until the condition is fulfilled and the legatee's right thus completed. The second allows vesting subject to defeasance[19]: the legacy vests immediately but falls if the relevant event occurs.

The type of event determines the type of condition. A suspensive **11.25** condition involves a factor personal to the legatee, such as his survival or marriage. The legacy only vests on the event. A resolutive condition is extraneous to him: say, the birth of children to someone else. The birth, and only that, defeats his already-vested legacy.

## Survivorship clauses and destinations-over

These are two common clauses by which a testator recognises **11.26** the possibility of a legatee dying before the date of payment and regulates what then happens to the legacy. Both are taken to fix vesting at the date of payment (be that at the testator's death or postponed till later) unless the will selects some other date.

### (a) Survivorship clauses

A survivorship clause is usually in the form "to X, Y and Z and **11.27** the survivors or survivor", or words to similar effect. The survivors are identified at the date of payment; predeceasing legatees have no vested right and their shares pass to the survivors by accretion[20] or (if words of severance exclude that) fall into intestacy.

The classic exposition of the rule came in *Young v. Robertson*[21] **11.28** where a clause in this form instructed a gift of fee to be paid at the expiry of a liferent. The House of Lords held that the fee vested in those alive at that date. Lord Westbury's dictum has since been taken to apply, not just to cases involving liferents, but all words referring to survivorship:

> "I apprehend it to be a settled rule of construction, that words **11.29** of survivorship occurring in a . . . will . . . should be referred to the period appointed by [it] for the payment or distribution of the subject-matter of the gift . . . The application of that rule would lead to this determination in two cases. [i] If a testator gives a sum of money or the residue of his estate to be paid or distributed among a number of persons, and refers to

---

[19] See paras 11.38 *et seq.*
[20] Or to their children, if the *conditio si institutus* applies: paras 10.59 *et seq.*
[21] (1862) 4 Macq. 314.

the contingency of any one or more of them dying, and then gives the estate or the money to the survivor, in that simple form of gift which is to take effect immediately on the death of the testator, the period of distribution is the period of death, and accordingly the contingency of death is to be referred to the interval of time between the date of the will and the death of the testator. In such a case, the words are construed to provide for the event of the death of any one of the legatees during the lifetime of the testator. [ii] . . . if a testator gives a life estate in [his property], and at the expiration of that life estate directs [it] to be divided among a number of objects, and then refers to the possibility of some one or more of those persons dying, without specifying the time, and directs in that event the . . . distribution to be made among the survivors, it is understood by the law that he means the contingency to extend over the whole period of time that must elapse before the . . . distribution takes place. [Therefore] the survivors are to be ascertained in like manner by a reference to the period of distribution, namely, the expiration of the life estate."

*un/rel?*

**11.30**  *Young v. Robertson* thus allows for two alternatives, failing indication to the contrary in the will: vesting *a morte testatoris* or, if later, at the date of payment.

*(b) Destinations-over*

**11.31**  A destination-over states who is to inherit in the event of a beneficiary's failure to live till the date of vesting. It provides an alternative beneficiary. The basic form is *"to A, whom failing to B"*.[22] A is the institute, the first potential beneficiary; B is the conditional institute, his right arising only in the event of A's death prior to the date of vesting. The legacy vests at the date of payment (following *Young*) and the destination-over takes effect then unless the will says otherwise.

**11.32**  Contrast conditional institution and substitution. The conditional institute inherits only if the institute fails; so vesting has to be postponed to find out if the institute survives the date of payment. A substitute beneficiary inherits after, rather than instead of, the institute: "to A, then B" is the sense. B can inherit as substitute whether or not A survives the date of payment. Consequently there is no need to postpone vesting, and *Young v. Robertson* does not apply. The legacy vests in the institute A on the testator's death, and then in B on A's death unless A has evacuated—revoked—the destination by will or in his lifetime.[23]

---

[22] Since "failing" is judged at the date of vesting, contrast its sense where immediate defeasible vesting occurs. See paras 11.35–11.37, 11.79 *et seq.*

[23] See paras 10.35 *et seq.*

So care is needed in wording a destination-over. Is substitution **11.33**
or conditional institution wanted? The drafter can ask two
questions:

(1) What sort of property is at issue? Substitution is strongly **11.34**
presumed with heritage, conditional institution with moveables
or—as is usual—a mixed estate of heritage and moveables. (2) Do
the words themselves override the presumption and point to one or
the other? "Whom failing" is neutral on its own. Stating (expressly
or by implication) that the destination depends on the institute
dying before vesting suggests conditional institution.[24]

The moral is to specify the date to which the institute and
conditional institute must respectively survive to obtain a vested
right. This is essential if vesting and payment are not to be
simultaneous. "To A if in life at the date of distribution, whom
failing to B if then in life" illustrates one solution.[25]

Note, too, that the form "*to A and B*" is unwise for any
destination-over. It can in rare cases imply that A and B have
successive rights, as with "A and his heirs" (his heirs' rights would
not arise before his death unless the will clearly said so). But in
general it suggests concurrent rights.[26]

*(c) Destinations-over to relations*

A destination-over to named beneficiaries causes no problem. **11.35**
But it may instead refer to a class of relations: "*to A failing whom
his heirs*", "*issue*", or "*children*". There the destination is "deriva-
tive": the conditional institute is not named as such but described
only in terms of his relationship to the institute.

The law treats a destination-over to "*heirs*" in the same way as **11.36**
one to a named legatee. It suspends vesting until the date of
payment. The problem here is simply who the heirs are. In this
case one identifies them at the date of vesting unless the will selects
a different time.[27]

A destination-over to "*A failing whom A's issue*" or "*children*" is **11.37**
treated differently. It does not, *by itself*, suspend vesting.[28] There is
immediate "vesting subject to defeasance" in A: his right vests *a
morte testatoris* but, if he predeceases the date of payment leaving
issue or children, it lapses and they inherit instead.[29]

---

[24] See Henderson, Vesting at pp. 49 *et seq.*
[25] Elder, *Forms of Wills*, no. 142, p. 116.
[26] *Cobban's Exrs v. Cobban*, 1915 S.C. 82; *Black's Trs v. Nixon*, 1931 S.C. 590.
[27] *Wylie's Trs v. Bruce*, 1919 S.C. 211. For destinations in title deeds *cf. Baillie's Trs v.
Whiting*, 1910 S.C. 891, *Macdonald's Trs v. Macdonald*, 1974 S.C. 23. See paras
10.20, 11.72 *et seq.*
[28] The will may contain other words which do suspend vesting: *e.g.* a survivorship
clause.
[29] *Wylie's Trs*, above at n. 27; *Allans Trs v. Allan*, 1918 S.C. 164.

**Vesting subject to defeasance**

*(a) The scope of the doctrine*

**11.38**    Unlike a suspensive condition, a resolutive condition allows a legacy to vest unless and until a specified event occurs. Vesting is defeasible by the event. If the event must occur before a set date (normally that of payment), and it does not, vesting at that point becomes absolute and indefeasible.

**11.39**    The classic case of defeasible vesting requires the birth of children or issue (to the legatee or someone else) before the legacy becomes payable at the end of a liferent. The scope and rationale of the doctrine have been explained thus:

**11.40**        "When a gift is made in such terms that it would take effect absolutely at the death of the testator but for the single contingency of the possible birth of issue to a particular person, that is a possibility which interferes so little for practical purposes with the primary legatee treating the legacy as his own, subject to his being divested by the single event, that it must be presumed that the testator intended that he should so treat it. . . . it is for the benefit of the [legatee] that he should be able to deal with his expectant interests as if they were vested in him . . . rather than that he should be prevented from dealing with them at all on the ground that they are kept in suspense."[30]

**11.41**    In this form the concept is relatively new,[31] and the courts have never been over-fond of it. Logic would apply it to other resolutive conditions, but that rarely happens. It occurs with simple legacies to a class—"the children of X" and the like.[32] Other isolated examples are a legacy made conditional on a named person remaining unmarried[33] or insane.[34] The problem there is: how to ensure the legacy is repaid if the event occurs? That practically limits the rule to "prepayment" defeasance occurring during liferents. The courts are very reluctant to extend the doctrine beyond three well-defined situations, all involving the birth of issue.

*(b) Types of defeasible vesting*

**11.42**    (1) A bequest to *A in liferent and A's issue in fee, whom failing to B in fee*. If any issue are alive when the testator dies the fee vests in them at once. If there are none the fee vests in B, but as soon as

---

[30] *Johnston's Trs v. Dewar*, 1911 S.C. 722, *per* Lord Kinnear.
[31] Emerging in *Taylor v. Gilbert's Trs* (1878) 5 R. (H.L.) 217.
[32] But only partially: see paras 11.74–11.78.
[33] *Smith's Trs v. Smith* (1883) 10 R. 1144.
[34] *Yule's Trs v. Deans*, 1919 S.C. 570.

any issue are born during the liferent B's right lapses and the fee vests in them.[35] (The fee will not later revert to B if they die before the liferenter.) If no issue are born by the end of the liferent—the date of payment—B's right then becomes indefeasible.[36]

With the style just cited, the *birth* of issue is the defeating event. **11.43** That is the effect of *"failing issue"*, which only requires issue to exist at some point after the testator's death, however briefly.[37] The will may specify a different event. It may require the issue to outlive the liferenter (*"leaving issue"*), or, as in *Taylor*,[38] to reach the age of majority. In either case B's right is not defeated if they die earlier.

(2) A bequest to A, followed by a direction to trustees *to hold for* **11.44** *A in liferent and his issue in fee*. The initial bequest must give A the fee outright, and not merely a liferent. The effect of the direction is to impose an additional trust purpose; if it lapses A's legacy becomes absolute.[39] So the fee vests immediately in A: if he dies leaving issue, it transfers to them; if not, it remains part of A's own estate on death. Under this formula the issue must actually outlive A; there is no defeasance if they predecease him.[40]

(3) A bequest *to A in liferent and B in fee, whom failing to B's* **11.45** *issue*. A destination-over usually suspends vesting till the date of payment. Destinations to "issue" or to "children" are the exception: the legacy vests *a morte testatoris* in B, subject to defeasance if he dies before payment *and* leaves issue who survive him.[41]

### (c) Suspensive conditions and double contingencies

There is no defeasible vesting unless the possible birth of issue **11.46** (or other such event) is the *only* thing to stop the legatee taking an immediate absolute vested right at the testator's death. It is excluded if the will in some other way suspends vesting.

For instance, a legacy cannot vest until the legatee (whether an **11.47** individual or class) exists and is identified. "The fee will not vest until the occurrence of the event which will determine who are the persons called, or the individuals composing the class are ascertained."[42]

---

[35] Also defeasibly, to allow issue born later in the liferent to share in the legacy. See paras 11.74–11.78.

[36] *Taylor v. Gilbert's Trs*, above at n. 31.

[37] *Carleton v. Thomson* (1867) 5 M. (H.L.) 151. Henderson, *Vesting*, discusses styles of wording at pp. 138 *et seq.*, 207 *et seq.*

[38] See n. 31.

[39] *Tweeddale's Trs v. Tweeddale* (1905) 8 F. 264; *Scott's Trs v. De Moyse-Bucknall's Trs*, 1978 S.C. 62.

[40] *Lindsay's Trs v. Lindsay* (1880) 8 R. 281.

[41] *Allan's Trs v. Allan*, 1918 S.C. 164.

[42] *Steel's Trs v. Steel* (1888) 16 R. 204 at 208, *per* L.P. Inglis. But the class may be enlarged after that as new members are born: see paras 11.74–11.78.

**11.48**   There may also be suspensive conditions. The legatee may have to reach adulthood: if that happens during the liferent, his right then vests but is still defeated if issue are born before payment.[43] With a survivorship clause there is simply vesting outright at date of payment, and thus no place for defeasible vesting before then.

**11.49**   Again there may be more than one destination-over: a "double contingency". Take *"To A in liferent and his issue in fee, whom failing to B, whom failing to C"* or *"whom failing to B or his issue."* The last-named legatee (C in one case, B in the second) may find his right defeated in two quite different ways. Vesting is suspended to the date of payment.[44]

**11.50**   The "double contingency" rule has two rather arbitrary limits which allow defeasible vesting. Firstly, the contingencies may not be successive but alternatives. Thus in *Coulson's Trs v. Coulson's Trs*[45] they were the legatee leaving issue or leaving a widow. Secondly, they may both simply involve the birth of issue to previously-named liferenters: *"to A in liferent and his issue in fee, whom failing to B in liferent and his issue in fee, whom failing to C."* The courts treat that as one contingency in duplicate; there is defeasible vesting in C.[46]

INTERMEDIATE AND ACCELERATED VESTING

**11.51** As we have seen the date of vesting is as a rule either the date of the testator's death *or*, if later, the date of payment. *Young v. Robertson* illustrates that. There is no half-way house. No-one, neither institute nor conditional institute, obtains a vested right before then.

**11.52**   However, there are exceptions. The testator's intention, seen in the will, is paramount. He may select some other intermediate date and displace the rule in *Young*. If an unforeseen event occurs, such as a legatee's early death, another legatee cannot obtain accelerated vesting or payment if that would frustrate the intention and defeat the purpose of the will. There are four distinct problems.

**Double events**[47]

**11.53**   A legacy may depend on the legatee surviving two events: a certain age (typically 18) and the expiry of a liferent. It cannot be paid till both have occurred; but it may vest at that age even if the liferent has not expired.

---

[43] As in *Taylor*, above at n. 31.
[44] *Lees' Trs v. Lees*, 1927 S.C. 886.
[45] 1911 S.C. 881.
[46] *Moss's Tr. v. Moss's Trs*, 1958 S.C. 501.
[47] See Henderson, *Vesting*, pp. 263–267; Elder, *Forms*, p. 131.

Reaching majority is a *dies incertus*[48]: if it is a condition of the    **11.54**
legacy (and not merely identifying the time of its payment) it
suspends vesting till then. The end of the liferent is *dies certus*, and
does not suspend vesting. So in principle the legacy vests at age 18,
whether that is before or after the liferent expires.

However, there may in addition be a destination-over. Its    **11.55**
wording is crucial. Normally it can be read as referring to failure to
survive the date of payment: so vesting occurs then or at majority,
whichever is later. But if it expressly applies to the date of majority,
that (whenever it is) is the vesting date.[49]

## Survivorship clauses[50]

If a legacy is payable to "*A, B, C and the survivor*", in principle it    **11.56**
vests at the date of payment. If A fails to survive that date, it vests
then in B and C. But suppose A and B both die earlier, C thus
becoming the last survivor. There are two possible interpretations
at that point. One is that the will is concerned simply with
survivorship as among A, B and C, "*inter se*": if so C at once takes
a vested right, which will not lapse if he then himself dies before
the date of payment. The other is that survivorship refers to the
date of payment, and the legacy only vests if C survives till then.

The second interpretation is normal. But as always one must    **11.57**
look to the precise words of the clause and the whole scheme of
the will. They may displace the *Young* rule by pointing clearly to
survivorship *inter se* as the test. There is no rigid form of words for
this, but it should be made clear that the whole legacy goes to the
one survivor (or "longest liver") when the other legatees die.[51] A
reference to "survivors"—plural—will almost certainly rule this
construction out.[52]

## Destinations-over[53]

In a destination-over, the institute A's right depends on his    **11.58**
surviving to a set age or date. Does the condition "carry over" and
apply to the conditional institute B as well? If it does, the legacy
vests in B at the date originally envisaged for A; but if not, it may
vest as soon as A dies. The answer depends on what the condition
is and who B is.

Take the simplest case: A is to survive to (say) age 18. There is    **11.59**
nothing else to delay payment and thus vesting. The condition is

---

[48] An event which may not take place: see paras 11.21–11.23.
[49] *McAlpine v. Studholme* (1883) 10 R. 837; Henderson, *Vesting*, pp. 56, 266.
[50] See Henderson, *Vesting*, pp. 84 *et seq.*; Elder, *Forms*, p. 128.
[51] *Laing's Trs v. Horsburgh*, 1965 S.L.T. 215; Henderson, *Vesting*, pp. 84 *et seq.*
[52] *Playfair's Trs v. Stewart's Trs*, 1960 S.L.T. 351.
[53] See Henderson, *Vesting*, pp. 92 *et seq.*, 109 *et seq.*, 154; Elder, *Forms*, pp. 128, 130.

purely personal to A: it does not affect B. If A dies earlier, the legacy vests in B at once.[54]

**11.60** More commonly A is to survive until a liferenter dies. The destination-over usually suspends vesting until that date. If A dies earlier, B must still wait till then for vesting. That applies whether B is a named individual or merely A's "heir". For that reason the heir's identity is ascertained, not at A's death, but at the date of vesting, on the fiction that A actually died then.[55]

**11.61** Complications start if B inherits as A's "issue" or "child". One must distinguish two situations.

**11.62** (1) *By itself* this allows A's right to vest on the testator's death, subject to defeasance: it falls when A dies during the liferent leaving issue B. Is there then vesting in B at once, or only when the liferenter dies? Logic and precedent favour the first, but the law is unsettled.[56]

**11.63** (2) Additional words may suspend vesting. Take a survivorship clause: "*to A and B, or (if either dies before the date of payment leaving issue) to his issue,*" or "*(if he leaves no issue) to the survivor of A and B.*" There is no vesting in A or B until the date of payment—the ordinary *Young* rule. But suppose A dies first: can the legacy vest in his issue at once, or must they also live till payment? Here the law contrasts "substitutional" and "original" bequests. In the first (and normal) type A's issue get the same share A would have had had he lived: they must therefore fulfil the same condition, *i.e.* survive till payment.[57] In an original bequest (which is very rare) the shares are not thus linked; there is vesting in the issue at once.[58]

### Accelerated vesting and payment[59]

**11.64** There are two main reasons to postpone vesting or payment of a legacy: to allow accumulation of income arising from it, or to give someone a liferent of it. Both may occur in one will; in each case the property is usually administered by means of a trust. But the period may be cut short: the accumulation becomes illegal; the liferenter renounces the liferent, or forfeits it by claiming legal rights instead. What happens to (firstly) the income which was to be accumulated or taken by the liferenter, and (secondly) the capital sum itself? As a general rule the event does not hasten

---

[54] *Cattanach's Trs v. Cattanach* (1901) 4 F. 205.

[55] *Thompson's Trs v. Jamieson* (1900) 2 F. 470; *Wylie's Trs v. Bruce*, 1919 S.C. 211.

[56] *Davidson's Trs v. Davidson*, 1909 2 S.L.T. 20; *Wardlaw's Trs v. Wardlaw's Exrs*, 1940 S.C. 286.

[57] *Addie's Trs v. Jackson*, 1913 S.C. 681.

[58] *Campbell's Trs v. Dick*, 1915 S.C. 100; criticised in *Robertson's Trs v. Mitchell*, 1930 S.C. 970.

[59] See Henderson, *Vesting*, pp. 297 *et seq.*; Wilson & Duncan, 9.45 *et seq.*

vesting or payment: that must still await the date envisaged in the will.

With accumulations two issues arise. **11.65**

(1) How is the no-longer accumulated income from the fund **11.66** disposed of? The words of the will are crucial. It may give a legatee a "present gift" of the fund so that, in the absence of accumulation, he is entitled to the income. If it does not the income falls into intestacy. This is a question of payment rather than vesting, as *Wilson's Trs v. Glasgow Royal Infirmary* makes clear[60]:

> "Absolute vesting is indeed a condition of success on the part of the legatee, but something more is required. A legatee . . . whose legacy falls to be paid or delivered at a postponed date is not necessarily . . . entitled to receive the intermediate income even although his right to the corpus is absolutely vested in him. It is always a question of intention, depending upon the express or implied directions of the testator."

So in *Wilson's Trs* the legacy was payable on the death of the testator's widow: all income till then went to his heir on intestacy. By contrast, in *Landale's Trs v. Overseas Missionary Fellowship*[61] the legacy was immediate, subject only to accumulation and to payment of an annuity to another beneficiary: when accumulation ended the legatee got all the surplus income left over after deducting the annuity. Alternatively, as in *Stewart's Trs v. Whitelaw*,[62] a liferenter may have a vested immediate right to the income.

(2) The legatee *may* be entitled to immediate payment, not just **11.67** of income arising from the legacy, but of the legacy itself. This applies only if he has an indefeasible vested right and is an adult and no trust purposes remain to be fulfilled. This reflects the general principle in *Miller's Trs v. Miller*[63] that someone with a complete vested proprietary right cannot be denied possession of the item except to protect his own interests (as under age and so incapax) or someone else's (as beneficiary under the trust). *Landale's Trs* illustrates the point in reverse: there the trustees had still to retain sufficient funds to allow them to pay the annuitant.

Analogous points apply where a liferent is renounced. The **11.68** legatee may be able to claim payment under *Miller's Trs* if he already has a vested right. But "where vesting and not mere payment is dependent upon the death of the liferenter, nothing that the liferenter does in the way of abandoning his or her right can accelerate the period of vesting, because the testator has fixed

---

[60] 1917 S.C. 527 at 532, *per* Lord Skerrington.
[61] 1982 S.L.T. 158.
[62] 1926 S.C. 701.
[63] (1890) 18 R.301.

it finally, and it is not for anybody else to make a new will for him."[64] Otherwise one might defeat his scheme and prejudice other beneficiaries. The same applies if someone forfeits a liferent by claiming legal rights instead.[65]

**11.69** On the other hand the will itself may expressly or implicitly link vesting to renunciation.[66] Many cases hinge on what exactly its words mean; their context is decisive. So "lapse" has been held to refer to renunciation, unlike "expiry",[67] while "termination" has gone both ways.[68] Clear precise wording avoids such semantics.

**11.70** If vesting is not accelerated, what happens to the income which would have gone to the liferenter? If the will allows, it may be accumulated or may fall into residue. If the will fails to cover the point (as in *Buyer's Trs v. Nunan*[69] where the liferent was itself of residue) the income must go as it arises to the heirs on intestacy.

**11.71** Under the Commission's proposals forfeiture or renunciation of the liferent will automatically trigger accelerated vesting *unless* the will excludes it.[70]

CLASS GIFTS

**11.72** A legacy to a class—"children", "issue", or other relations—is inevitably more imprecise than one to a named individual. The membership of the class may change through time. So it is important to know at what point they are identified, and when the legacy vests.

**11.73** Often the answer is clear. The facts of life and death may dictate one date when (unless the will says otherwise) the legacy vests and the class must be identified. So "my children" points to the testator's death; some may die later, but the class cannot enlarge.[71] The "heirs" of the testator or of a legatee, being the people entitled to inherit from him, are normally ascertained at the date of vesting.[72]

**11.74** However, take a legacy to *"the children [or issue] of X."* X may outlive the testator. The class is open-ended: it may grow or wither

---

[64] *Jacks's Trs v. Jacks*, 1913 S.C. 815 at 826, *per* Lord Kinnear.

[65] *Munro's Trs*, 1971 S.C. 280.

[66] *Muirhead v. Muirhead* (1890) 17 R. (H.L.) 45.

[67] *Whitelaw's Trs v. Whitelaw's Trs*, 1981 S.L.T. 94; *cf. Middleton's Trs v. Middleton*, 1955 S.C. 51.

[68] *Chrystal's Trs v. Haldane*, 1960 S.C. 127; *Hurll's Trs v. Hurll*, 1964 S.C. 12.

[69] 1981 S.C. 313, *sub nom. Collie & Buyers*, 1981 S.L.T. 191.

[70] Report No. 124, para. 9.17.

[71] Except for posthumous children who are treated as already born when the testator died: see paras 1.33–1.35.

[72] *Wylie's Trs v. Bruce*, 1919 S.C. 211; *Barr's Trs v. Inland Revenue*, 1943 S.C. 157; Henderson, *Vesting*, pp. 92 *et seq.*, 225 *et seq.*

after the testator dies. The law takes a pragmatic approach. The class is finally fixed at the date of payment: later-born children are excluded.[73] (Otherwise one could not know how much to pay each child.) Four main results are possible:

(1) If payment is at the testator's death, the legacy vests then in **11.75** the children then alive.

(2) If it is later (say, the end of a liferent) the legacy initially **11.76** vests in children alive at the testator's death (or, if none, the first born afterwards), subject to *partial* defeasance in favour of any others born before the date of payment.[74] So all children alive at any time between the testator's death and payment are in the class (they need not survive the whole period), though their exact number and shares are not known till payment.

(3) Suppose the legacy is conditional on children reaching (say) **11.77** age 18. If so it vests in the first who does, subject to partial defeasance in favour of those who later reach 18. The class is finally ascertained at the point when the eldest child's share is payable: later-born children are again excluded.[75]

(4) The legacy may depend on X *"leaving issue"*. Some issue **11.78** must outlive X for the class to exist. But, provided that happens, the effect of *Hickling's Trs v. Garland's Trs*[76] is that the legacy vests in all the issue, including (retrospectively) any who had survived the testator but died before X. The decision is bizarre; plainly the testator wanted only the surviving issue to inherit, and where possible that is the interpretation the courts prefer.

There may also be a destination-over: *"to the issue of X, or failing* **11.79** *issue* [or *if X dies without leaving issue*] *to Y"*. Y's initial right is defeated when the legacy vests in the issue. The form of wording determines when they are identified.

(1) With *"failing issue"* the legacy vests in the issue as soon as **11.80** any exist. Again there is partial defeasance in favour of other issue born before payment. After vesting, they need not live till payment.

(2) With *"leaving issue"* only issue who outlive X get a vested **11.81** right. The destination-over rules out "retrospective" vesting and allows the courts to distinguish *Hickling's Trs*, which did not contain one.

As always, these rules yield to a contrary direction in the will. It may, for instance, suspend vesting until the date of payment: explicitly, or by a survivorship clause, or by a destination-over to heirs or a named legatee.

---

[73] *Wood v. Wood* (1861) 23 D. 338; Henderson, *Vesting*, pp. 188–215.
[74] *Carleton v. Thomson* (1867) 5 M. (H.L.) 151.
[75] *Scott's Trs v. Scott*, 1909 S.C. 773.
[76] (1898) 1 F. (H.L.) 7.

**Further reading**

G.L. Gretton, "Vesting, Equitable Compensation and the Mystery of the Shadow Liferent", 1988 S.L.T. (News) 149.

R. Candlish Henderson, *Vesting*.

G.L.F. Henry, "Vesting Subject to Defeasance" (1959) Conv. Rev. 173.

C. de B. Murray, *Laws of Wills*, Chap. XV.

*Stair Memorial Encyclopaedia*, Vol. 25, paras 900—956.

# Chapter 12

# TAXATION

## INHERITANCE TAX[1]

### BACKGROUND AND PURPOSE

At least since the 1600s taxes have been levied on people's **12.01**
property at their death. Death is inevitable: it is an ideal occasion
for governments to raise revenue. Death taxes were gradually
extended to include property transferred within a limited period
before death. This reflected the need to make their avoidance
more difficult, and (during this century) the avowed aim of using
taxation to redistribute wealth within society.

From 1894 to 1975 the main tax was estate duty. This was **12.02**
"progressive", like income tax: the larger the estate, the higher the
rate of duty. It applied to transfers on death and within the
previous seven years, to property the deceased owned or had a
liferent of. Certain transfers were exempt; transfers between
spouses were not, *but* if the surviving spouse was only given a
liferent and duty was payable on the property, it was exempt when
that spouse subsequently died.

Capital transfer tax replaced estate duty in 1975. This was **12.03**
cumulative throughout life and on death, so that each successive
transfer attracted tax at a higher rate. A special 10–yearly charge
applied to trusts where no beneficiary had an "interest in possession" in the trust funds: discretionary trusts, except for (among
others) accumulation and maintenance trusts.[2] Gifts between
spouses were now exempt.[3]

Capital transfer tax was severely modified in 1986 and renamed **12.04**
inheritance tax (IHT). Lifetime transfers are now cumulated for

---

[1] Some aspects were covered earlier: common calamities and survivorship, deeds of
arrangement, and legitim (paras 1.30–1.32, 4.66–4.68 and 5.54 et seq). This book
only briefly touches on Trusts. For trusts see Norrie & Scobbie, *Trusts, passim*.
[2] See paras 11.10–11.14, above; Norrie & Scobbie pp. 21–37.
[3] But the estate duty liferent exemption is preserved where the liferent began before
November 13, 1974: IHTA 1984, Sched. 6, para. 2.

only seven years, and the tax has a flat rate.[4] It applies to transfers made by individuals domiciled[5] in the U.K. (wherever the item is located) and of property situated in the U.K. (wherever the owner is domiciled).

### Chargeable transfers

**12.05**    IHT is charged on the *value transferred* by a *chargeable transfer*. A chargeable transfer is any *transfer of value* made by an individual except for an *exempt transfer*. A transfer of value is a disposition made by a person as a result of which the value of his estate immediately afterwards is less than it would be but for the disposition; the value transferred is the amount by which it is less.[6] It thus comprises, not just gifts, but deliberately selling assets at below their true value; also failure to exercise an enforceable right (*e.g.* to money due under a contract). On death a person is treated as if he made a transfer of value of his whole estate.[7]

**12.06**    A person's *estate* is the aggregate of all the property to which he is *beneficially entitled*. That is wider than ownership: it includes property over which he has a power of disposal, and trust property in which he has an interest in possession as a beneficiary, such as a liferent. Conversely certain *excluded property* is disregarded and debts are deducted.[8]

**12.07**    Thus IHT is charged on the loss to the transferor's estate. This has three implications.

### (a) Omissions

**12.08**    Where the value of his estate is diminished by his omission to exercise a right, he is treated as making a disposition at the latest time when he could have exercised the right, unless he shows the omission was not deliberate. Two omissions are ignored: waiving remuneration which would be taxable under Schedule E income tax, or waiving a dividend within 12 months before the right to it arose.[9]

### (b) Commercial transactions

**12.09**    A disposition is not a transfer of value if it is shown that it was not intended to give anyone a gratuitous benefit *and* (1) it was an arm's length transaction between two people who were not *con-*

---

[4] Currently (2001/02) 20 per cent on lifetime transfers in excess of £242,000 in cumulative total; 40 per cent on death.
[5] "Domicile" has a special wide meaning for IHT: IHTA 1984, s.267.
[6] IHTA 1984, ss.1–3.
[7] IHTA 1984, s.4(1).
[8] IHTA 1984, ss.5, 6, 49(1). See para. 12.26.
[9] IHTA 1984, ss.3(3), 14, 15. For legal rights renunciations see paras 4.66–4.68, 5.54 *et seq.*, above.

*nected persons,* or (2) it was what one would expect in such a transaction. Relatives, trustees and settlor, partners (and their relatives), and companies controlled by one person are instances of connected persons.[10]

IHT might be minimised by artificially splitting one transfer into **12.10** several which, taken individually, are worth less than the undivided transfer. For instance, one gift of 60 per cent of a company's shares is worth more than two separate transfers each of 30 per cent. To prevent this, "transaction" has a wide sense, including a series of transactions or *associated operations*: essentially operations which are interdependent or relate to the same property.[11]

### (c) Gross and net transfers

IHT is levied on the gross—total—loss to the donor's estate. **12.11** Now suppose X gives Y £100,000. If Y agrees to pay the IHT, that is the relevant figure; it is a *gross chargeable transfer*; the IHT comes out of it. If X is to pay, his total loss is £100,000 *plus* IHT; the £100,000 is a *net chargeable transfer* which must be *grossed up* to obtain a total figure on which the IHT is levied. The gross figure is therefore that which, after IHT is deducted from it, will leave the net cash sum.[12]

The difference can be large. Take the above case, with IHT at 20 **12.12** per cent.[13] A gross chargeable transfer produces IHT of £20,000. A net one gives a bill of £25,000 (20 per cent of a £125,000 total, in effect 25 per cent of the cash sum). Grossing up is complex, and is usually done by using published tables of figures.

Lifetime gifts are grossed up if the donor pays the IHT, but not **12.13** if the donee pays. If the donor dies less than seven years after making the gift, liability for the IHT on it always falls primarily on the donee; so there is no grossing-up at the time of death and the gift's original gross value is used.

In principle the estate is not grossed up on death, because **12.14** plainly the IHT must come out of it. However, a specific (non residuary) legacy may be left "free of tax": it gives rise to IHT (unless exempt), but that is paid out of the residue of the estate. The legacy must therefore be grossed up to determine what the IHT attributable to it amounts to.[14]

---

[10] Taxation of Chargeable Gains Act 1992, s.286.

[11] IHTA 1984, s.268; two exceptions concern (a) operations straddling March 27, 1974, and (b) leases.

[12] A dividend displays the same idea. The shareholder receives it net of basic rate tax, but the gross figure (including the "tax credit") must go in his income tax return.

[13] For simplicity this ignores annual exemptions and assumes that the £242,000 threshold has already been exceeded.

[14] See "Calculation of tax", paras 12.56 *et seq.*

**Cumulation**

**12.15**    Once any applicable exemptions have been deducted from transfers of value,[15] the resulting chargeable transfers are cumulated for seven years. It is a rolling period: new transfers are added on (as the "top slice" of the total) while old ones drop out of the cumulative total seven years after they were made. The tax due on each new transfer thus depends critically on the total gross value of any transfers in that prior period. But, once the IHT is paid, only the donor's death can usually reopen it; later fluctuations in the gross total will not affect it retrospectively.

**Calculation of IHT**

> The procedure is in principle simple:
>
>   (i) Take total of previous seven years' chargeable transfers (at existing gross values);
>   (ii) *Add* latest transfer as "top slice" of total;
>   (iii) *Calculate* IHT on (ii) at current rates;
>   (iv) *Calculate* IHT on (i), again at current rates;
>   (v) *Deduct* (iv) from (iii).
>
> For instance: suppose X made the following chargeable transfers[16]:
>
> | July 1993 £50,000 | Total = £50,000 |
> | IHT = nil | |
> | July 1995 £232,000 | Total = £282,000 |
> | IHT = 20% × £40,000 = £8,000 | |
> | July 2001 £90,000 | Total = £322,000 |
> | IHT = 20% × £80,000 = £16,000 | |

**12.16**    Some transfers are chargeable (and cumulated) at once. The main type is a gift to a simple discretionary trust. If the donor dies within seven years IHT is recalculated at the death rate applying at date of death.

**12.17**    But many gifts are *potentially exempt transfers* (PETs): gifts by one individual to another, to a trust in which someone has an interest in possession, an accumulation and maintenance trust, or a trust for a disabled person. They are neither charged nor cumulated at once. If the donor dies within seven years they are then retrospectively cumulated as at their original date, but charged at the death rates in force at the date of death: as a result they not only bear IHT themselves,[17] but (by raising the total) may cause more IHT to be payable on later gifts.

---

[15] *e.g.* annual exemption: see paras 12.40–12.45.
[16] For simplicity this uses 2001/02 rates and nil rate band of £242,000.
[17] At the rate in force at the date of death.

In each case (1) IHT is calculated on the lifetime gross value: the **12.18** gift is not grossed-up afresh on death; (2) "taper relief" reduces the extra tax if the interval till death was between three and seven years. Changes in IHT rates, coupled with taper relief, may mean no extra tax is in fact due.[18]

## Gifts subject to reservation

A gift is *subject to reservation* if, during the seven years before **12.19** the death, the recipient did not at all times have possession and enjoyment of the item to the entire or virtually entire exclusion of the donor.[19] For instance, the donor gifts shares to a discretionary trust but is a potential beneficiary; or he receives the dividend from shares or occupies a house rent-free. "Virtually" disregards minimal benefits to the donor such as staying in the house on short visits, but otherwise the rule applies if the donor retains *any* benefit from the gifted item.[20]

There is no "reservation" if the donor pays a commercial rent **12.20** for his occupation, nor if he is later unexpectedly compelled by old age or infirmity to move in with the recipient because he cannot cope for himself. Conversely it is probably reservation to occupy as a guest without an enforceable contract.[21]

Reservation has two IHT consequences. The initial gift is treated **12.21** in the normal way, *e.g.* as a chargeable transfer if it is to a discretionary trust. However a second charge could arise on the donor's death: if he waived the reservation while alive he made a PET, and if it lasted until his death the item is charged as part of his estate. IHT is not payable twice, but only on whichever of the two transfers produces the higher IHT bill.

VALUING THE ESTATE

## Assets included in the estate

The executor must submit a valuation of the deceased's estate **12.22** when he obtains confirmation to it. The IHT return is submitted along with the inventory for confirmation. But the estate to be

---

[18] For who is liable to pay the extra tax, see paras 12.62–12.63.

[19] Finance Act 1986, s.102, affecting gifts made after March 17, 1986. From March 9, 1999 the rules on reservation of benefit were made more stringent to reverse the effect of *Ingram v I.R.C.* [1999] 1 All E.R. 297, and it is now made clear that someone giving land must pay full consideration (*i.e.* rent) if they then occupy it: Finance Act 1996, s.102A—C. See Davies, *Principles of Tax Law* (4th ed., 2000) 18.07.

[20] Finance Act 1986, ss.102–102C.

[21] *Chick v. Stamp Duties Commissioner* [1958] A.C. 435; but the case law, which concerns analogous estate duty rules, is not consistent.

itemised for IHT differs from that which requires confirmation or which the deceased owned:

**12.23** (1) Items passing under a survivorship destination do not need confirmation, but IHT is due on the deceased's share (usually half the value).

**12.24** (2) The estate for IHT consists of all the property to which he was beneficially entitled immediately *before* he died. That includes property of which he merely had an interest in possession (such as a liferent) or which he had a power to dispose of (such as a tenancy, if assignable).[22] But it omits items to which he had legal title as trustee, though these may need confirmation if he was the sole trustee, in order to transmit the title.[23]

**12.25** (3) A gift under reservation divests the donor of ownership, but the item is deemed to remain part of his estate for IHT.

**12.26** Conversely some assets are *excluded property*. For IHT purposes they do not form part of the estate on death[24]:

(a) Property situated abroad, if the deceased was domiciled there.

(b) A *reversionary interest*, such as that of a fiar in liferented property. With some exceptions[25] his interest is free from IHT if he dies during the liferent.

(c) A liferenter's interest in possession, if it reverts on his death to the settlor or his spouse.[26]

(d) The executor may elect to exclude woodlands.[27]

(e) Pension benefits are included if they *must* be paid to the executors. More usually the pension fund trustees are to pay a widow or dependant but may have discretion to pay the executor; such benefits are not part of the estate.[28] A similar point applies in relation to life assurance policy proceeds.

### Debts and liabilities

**12.27** The deceased's legally enforceable liabilities are deducted in valuing his estate. Not every liability may be deductible:

(a) It must have been incurred for some consideration—not gratuitously—or imposed by law (*e.g.* taxes or rates).[29]

---

[22] IHTA 1984, ss.5(1), (2), 49(1).

[23] See para. 13.44.

[24] They also attract no IHT if gifted *inter vivos*. Only the main types are listed here.

[25] *e.g.* if he had paid for it: IHTA 1984, ss.47, 48.

[26] Unless they paid for it: IHTA 1984, s.54.

[27] IHTA 1984, ss.125–129.

[28] If the scheme was approved by the Inland Revenue for income tax or personal pensions: IHTA 1984, ss.58, 151; Finance (No. 2) Act 1987, s.98.

[29] IHTA 1984, s.5(3), (5).

(b) All or a proportion of the consideration may be property which had itself come from the deceased. If so the same proportion of the debt may be disallowed.[30]

(c) One deducts only so much of a guarantee as is unlikely to be reimbursed. An existing IHT liability is deducted but any reimbursement will be added to the estate.

(d) Reasonable funeral expenses are allowable, including the cost of a gravestone.[31]

(e) Other executry expenses are not deductible, with one exception: extra costs relating to foreign property, to five per cent of its value at most.[32]

So far as possible a secured debt reduces the value of the item it **12.28** is secured over. In the case of heritage it may be deducted from the original inventory value or the IHT account: either produces the same IHT but the first may reduce the confirmation dues payable.

**Basis of valuation**

Property is valued at the price which it might reasonably be **12.29** expected to fetch if sold in the open market. Sale may in fact be impossible: private companies only permit restricted transfer of their shares. A hypothetical sale is nevertheless assumed.[33]

Though the estate is defined as that immediately before the **12.30** death, valuation takes account of changes resulting from it. Thus it includes life assurance policy proceeds payable to the executors.[34] Nevertheless it also includes interests which lapse on death (such as liferents) or pass by survivorship.

Lifetime gifts may fall in value before the donor dies. If so the **12.31** date-of-death value may be used if the donee (or spouse) still owns it or has made an arm's length sale to an unconnected person.[35] This is not allowed if the gift is a "wasting asset": tangible moveable property with a predictable life of at most 50 years (such as a car or machinery).

*Related property* must be taken into account in valuing items. The **12.32** main example is property in the estate of the deceased's spouse. Aggregating the two may give a higher value than taking them separately: *e.g.* 60 per cent of a company's shares as opposed to two holdings of 30 per cent. If so the deceased's value is his proportion of the aggregate.

---

[30] The rules are complex: Finance Act 1986, s.103.

[31] IHTA 1984, s.172; Inland Revenue Statement of Practice 7/87.

[32] They may be deductible for income tax: see para. 12.84.

[33] IHTA 1984, s.160; *I.R.C. v. Crossman* [1937] A.C. 26.

[34] If payable to someone else, *e.g.* the widow, they fall outwith the estate.

[35] IHTA 1984, ss.131–132. For "connected person" see para. 12.09.

**12.33**    Publicly-quoted shares are valued at the lower of (a) one quarter of the difference up from the lower to the higher of the two quoted prices, or (b) halfway between the highest and lowest recorded prices. If the stock market was closed on the date of death one may use the previous or next trading day. Unquoted shares must be valued on the "open market" basis.[36]

**12.34**    The executor must enter the most precise valuation he can, relying on an expert where necessary: a stockbroker (for quoted shares), the company (unquoted shares), an accountant (a partnership), and the like. For a house one can consult local house prices, a surveyor, or (if the Capital Taxes Office raises queries) the district valuer. If an estimate is necessary (with items like income tax repayments) the inventory should say so; the executors must undertake to give the exact figure when possible. A "nil" value may occur (*e.g.* for shares of a company in liquidation): the item must still be included in order to get confirmation.

**12.35**    Post-death changes in value usually do not affect the IHT valuation. But if assets fall in value and the executors[37] sell at a loss they can in three cases use the sale price for IHT. This may make it wiser to sell assets rather than transfer them to residuary legatees in specie (in kind) and lose this relief.

**12.36**    (1) Sale of quoted shares or unit trusts within 12 months after death. There must be a loss on the aggregate total of all the investments. The relief now includes shares suspended from Stock Exchange quotation or cancelled within this period.[38]

**12.37**    (2) Sale of land within four years after death.[39]

**12.38**    (3) Sale within three years of property valued on death under the "related property" rules.[40]

EXEMPTIONS AND RELIEFS

**12.39**    Certain transfers are disregarded entirely for IHT and do not enter into the cumulative total.[41] Others receive partial relief and only a proportion is deducted. Their careful use in a will and in lifetime transactions can minimise IHT.

### Exemptions: lifetime only

**12.40**    (1) *Annual exemption* of gifts to a total of £3,000. Where several gifts are made in a year, the earlier ones benefit first. To the extent that the exemption is unused in a particular tax year (because £3,000

---

[36] These are the rules for CGT: Taxation of Chargeable Gains Act 1992, s.272.
[37] Usually, strictly, the person liable to pay the IHT.
[38] IHTA 1984, ss.178–189; Finance Act 1993, s.198.
[39] IHTA 1984, ss.190–198, amended by Finance Act 1993, s.199.
[40] IHTA 1984, s.176.
[41] IHTA 1984, ss.18–42.

worth of chargeable transfers were not made), it can be carried forward for use in the next tax year, but no further. That year will therefore have a £6,000 exemption. Any chargeable transfers in that year will be set against the carried-forward exemption (but only once that year's own exemption has been used).

Suppose a PET is retrospectively "added in" on death, what effect has that on the annual exemption? Strictly speaking the PET should be ignored when made, leaving the exemption available to carry forward; when the PET is added in, the exemption could be carried back and set against the PET. To minimise such reallocations, PETs are regarded as made later in the tax year than any immediately-IHT chargeable gifts.[42]

(2) *Small gifts* of up to a total of £250 per recipient. Unlike (1) **12.41** this cannot be used to partly exempt a larger gift: if the total is exceeded the whole exemption is lost in respect of that person.

(3) *Normal expenditure out of income* which does not harm the **12.42** spender's standard of living; to be "normal" each payment must conform to an established pattern of expenditure. This usually exempts premiums he pays on a life assurance policy in another person's favour (which the law treats as gifts).[43] Indeed the policy can be designed to pay off the IHT on the estate.

(4) *Dispositions for the maintenance of relatives*: to a spouse or **12.43** ex-spouse, for the education of either spouse's child, or to care for a dependent relative.

(5) *Gifts in consideration of the recipient's marriage*. The max- **12.44** imum exemption is £5,000, depending on how and whether the donor is related to the donee.

(6) *Dispositions allowable for income tax or conferring retirement* **12.45** *benefits*.

### Exemptions: lifetime and death

(1) *Transfers between spouses* by gift, intestacy, legal rights, or **12.46** will. This does not apply if the transfer only takes effect after a specified period or a liferent, or depends on a condition which is not met within 12 months. It is limited to £55,000 if the recipient is not domiciled in the U.K.

To minimise tax one should also consider the IHT position on the second spouse's death. Using the exemption may sometimes make that worse: it simply raises the subsequent IHT charge on the

---

[42] IHTA 1984, s.19(3A). Current Inland Revenue practice is however different, setting a PET against the annual exemption immediately when made (and whether or not it ever becomes chargeable): see *Tolley's Inheritance Tax*, para. 38.2 for fuller discussion.

[43] Except for "back to back" schemes where the spender draws an associated annuity: IHTA 1984, s.263. For "normal expenditure" see *Bennett v I.R.C.* [1995] S.T.C. 54.

spouse's estate. Efficient tax planning will make maximum use of both spouses' exemptions and £150,000 nil-rate bands: thus if one's spouse is already well off it may be better in the long run to transfer directly to children or grandchildren.[44]

**12.47**  (2) *Gifts to charities* or political parties, or to trusts for the benefit of employees.

**12.48**  (3) *Gifts for national purposes* (to specified bodies like universities and museums). Certain nationally important property—land, pictures, and the like—may be exempted if given to non-profit making bodies which will hold it for the public benefit. An analogous exemption covers gifts to individuals and trusts: it is conditional on making undertakings about upkeep and public access, and IHT falls due if there is a later non-exempt transfer or a breach of the undertakings.[45]

**12.49**  (4) *Death on active service* gives rise to no IHT charge.

### Reliefs

**12.50**  (1) Business property attracts relief of (depending on the type of asset) either 50 per cent or 100 per cent. The main examples are:

(i)  a business or interest in a business (including a partnership);

(ii)  controlling shareholdings in quoted companies;

(iii)  shareholdings in unquoted companies;

(iv)  land, buildings, machinery or plant used for a business by company controlled by the transferor, or in which he was a partner.

An analogous relief applies to *agricultural property*. There are stringent conditions such as using or occupying the property for two years before death. If property is eligible for both reliefs, agricultural property relief is the one given.[46]

With woodlands which are not part of "agricultural property" the executor can elect within two years after the death to treat them as excluded property.

**12.51**  (2) *Mutual transfers* occur when a donor receives an asset back from the donee and later dies. Without relief he could pay IHT

---

[44] Post-death rearrangement can achieve this result.

[45] The conditions were tightened in 1998, *e.g.* to prevent access being restricted to by prior appointment only; exemption can be withdrawn if the access rules are breached.

[46] IHTA 1984, ss.105–124; extended to all agricultural property by F.A. 1995, s.155. The reliefs are effectively wasted unless used for non-exempt transfers. Especial complexities occur with partly-exempt transfers: IHTA 1984, s.39A.

twice, on the initial gift and on death. To avoid this IHT is charged on whichever one event creates the larger tax bill.[47]

(3) If the donor dies between three and seven years after making **12.52** a PET, *taper relief* reduces the resulting IHT on that PET by between 20 per cent (in year four) and 80 per cent (in year seven). Taper relief does *not* reduce the overall value of the estate cumulated on death: it is effectively wasted if the PET falls into the IHT nil-rate band, as there is no IHT to relieve. Similarly if the transfer had originally borne IHT at lifetime rates: but the relief cannot exceed the extra death-rate tax, so there can be no refund of tax already paid at lifetime rates.[48]

(4) If the deceased had received property less than five years **12.53** previously through a chargeable transfer or PET, *quick succession relief* applies on his death. This is a percentage of the IHT on the *proportion* of the first transfer which actually increased his estate, ranging from 100 per cent (death occurring less than one year after receipt) to 20 per cent (occurring between four and five years after). To illustrate: A inherited property worth £100,000; after IHT on that sum he only received £80,000. On A's death the relief is based on eight-tenths of £20,000. It does not matter if the deceased disposed of the property in the interval between receipt and death.[49]

The initial transfer to the deceased (X) may have been a PET which, when he dies, is still not chargeable because the original donor Y is still alive. If it later becomes chargeable on Y's death, X's estate will at that point have to pay the IHT; quick succession relief will then be available.

### CALCULATION OF TAX

**Ordinary procedure**

This is relatively simple. The order is:                                   **12.54**

(a) Calculate estate for confirmation (in inventory).
(b) Deduct the deceased's debts.
(c) Add other chargeable assets (*e.g.* liferent).
(d) Add chargeable transfers made in previous seven years.
(e) Deduct exemptions and reliefs.
(f) Compute IHT on resulting total at death rates.
(g) Compute IHT on lifetime transfers at death rates.

---

[47] Finance Act 1986, s.104.
[48] IHTA 1984, s.7, for transfers after March 17, 1986.
[49] IHTA 1984, s.141.

(h) IHT chargeable on estate is (6) minus (7). Quick succession relief can now be deducted from (8).

(i) To compute extra tax due on lifetime gifts, from (7) deduct taper relief and then IHT already paid on them while the deceased was alive. The gifts' recipients pay the extra tax.

**12.55**    The main complication is the effect of death on lifetime transfers. The following example illustrates a simple IHT calculation (exemptions are ignored and it is assumed that IHT rates and bands remained constant over the period).

### Calculation of IHT on death

In the 11 years prior to his death X has made the following transfers:

Year 1 (January) to a friend Y £60,000
Year 4 (June) to a friend Z £250,000
Year 7 (January) to a discretionary trust £300,000

Year 11 (May) X dies leaving estate £200,000

*IHT on transfers*

(a) *Chargeable during lifetime*

Year 1: a PET—not cumulated or chargeable at the time
Year 4: a PET—ditto
Year 7: cumulative total is £300,000
   IHT = 0% × £242,000 (nil rate band)
   20% × £58,000 = £11,600

(b) *IHT payable on X's death*

Year 1: outwith 7 year period: never cumulated or chargeable
Year 4: PET becomes chargeable. Cumulative total = £250,000
   IHT due from Z = 0% × £242,000
     40% × £8,000 = £3,200
     less taper relief: IHT = 20% × £3,200 = £640
Year 7: cumulative total = £550,000. Gift falls entirely outwith nil rate band.
   IHT = 40% × £300,000 = £120,000
   less taper relief: IHT = 60% × £120,000 = £72,000
   less IHT already paid (£11,600)
   extra IHT due from trustees = £60,400

Year 11: Cumulative total on death is £750,000. Estate on death falls entirely outwith nil rate band.
       IHT on death estate = 40% × £200,000 = £80,000

If the transfer in Year 1 went to a discretionary trust:

(a) it would be immediately chargeable to IHT at 20%;
(b) it would not enter into the cumulative total at death (being more than seven years previous), but *would* enter into the cumulative totals in Years 4 and 7 and thus affect the IHT due on the gifts in those years.

## Incidence of tax

**12.56** On which assets (and therefore which beneficiaries) does the resulting IHT fall? That is a distinct issue from *liability*: whom can the authorities compel to pay the tax? The person liable can, after paying, insist on reimbursement from the person on whom incidence falls.

**12.57** IHT is a testamentary expense and falls primarily on the residue of the estate. Thus "specific" (in this sense, non-residuary) legacies do not bear their own tax: that falls on the residue. They are "free of tax". Settled property bears its own tax. That said, a testator may vary these rules by instructing that a legacy bears its own tax. He may leave a *share* of residue free of tax (thus casting its IHT on the rest of the residue) but not *all* the residue, because some part of it must ultimately bear the IHT.[49a]

**12.58** "Free of tax" does not mean exempt from IHT. It merely reallocates the IHT due. The specific legacy must be grossed-up, thus increasing the overall value of the estate and the IHT. The procedure varies depending on the composition of the estate.

**12.59** (1) Exempt specific legacy and chargeable residue: the legacy is simply deducted and IHT is due on the residue.

**12.60** (2) Tax-free specific legacy and exempt residue: the legacy is the only chargeable item. No IHT is due on the residue itself but it bears the IHT due on the grossed-up legacy. If the IHT exceeds the residue the legacy abates to pay the excess.

**12.61** (3) Tax-free specific legacy and chargeable residue (or another gift which bears its own tax): the legacy is not the only chargeable item. One must (a) gross-up as in (2) and total up the estate; (b) find out the IHT rate for the estate; and (c) gross-up again at that rate to arrive at the actual tax payable.

Legal rights are (for the purpose of this calculation) treated as a gift bearing its own tax. Now only at age 16 can a child elect whether to claim legitim; but the executor must make a provisional election for IHT purposes within two years after the death. The IHT can be recalculated if the child, before reaching age 20 (or later if the Inland Revenue permit), subsequently reverses the executor's choice.[50]

LIABILITY AND PAYMENT

## Liability to pay tax

**12.62** If extra tax is payable on lifetime transfers the order of liability is:

---

[49a] For recent case law see *Re Benham's Will Trusts* [1995] S.T.C. 210, *Re Ratcliffe (decd.)* [1999] S.T.C. 262; Tiley, *Revenue Law* (4th ed., 2000) 75.3.3.
[50] Age of Legal Capacity (Scotland) Act 1991, s.1; IHTA 1984, ss.42, 147. For election by 16 or 17 year olds see Barr & Edwards, 1991 S.L.T. (News) 77; para. 9.12, above.

(a) the person who received the item, had an interest in possession or vested right in it, or took the benefit of it under a trust.

(b) the executor, but only if (a) does not pay within 12 months after the death or need not pay because his liability is limited. Although executors' liability is secondary, they should take care to find out about PETs and to retain sufficient funds to pay the IHT on them in the event of the donee being untraceable or defaulting. Even when the Capital Taxes Office issues a clearance certificate on completion of the executry, they are still liable in respect of a PET which subsequently comes to light.[51]

**12.63** Those liable for IHT on transfers on death are:

(a) The executor, in respect of (i) property which was not part of a settlement immediately before the death and (ii) settled land within the U.K. which vests in the executor.[51a]

(b) The trustee, in respect of property which was part of a settlement before the death. So the executor need not pay IHT on the deceased's liferent assets, though he will often agree with the trustee to do so and be reimbursed.

(c) Anyone in whom the property vests after the death, or who takes an interest in possession—except a purchaser.

(d) If property was held in trust before the death, anyone who gets the benefit or income from it after the death.

Executors' and trustees' liability is limited to the value of the assets they receive in that capacity, or would have received but for their neglect or default. Others' liability is limited to the value of the property in question.

**The tax return**

**12.64** If tax is payable the executor sends the IHT account/inventory[52] to the Capital Taxes Office (CTO); they return it and he lodges it with the commissary department of the local sheriff court. If no tax

---

[51] The C.T.O. may waive the executors' liability: for C.T.O. practice see (1991) 36 J.L.S. 243.

[51a] See C.T.O. guidance IHT 14, "The Personal Representatives' Responsibilities". Tax materials are generally available at www.inlandrevenue.gov.uk.

[52] Forms C1 (the Inventory) and IHT 200 (the Inland Revenue IHT account), with payment of the tax once provisionally calculated. Guidance notes C3 and IHT 210 explain fully.

is payable, the CTO may sometimes require the inventory, but often it can go direct to the sheriff court. He must do this within 12 months after the end of the month in which death occurred, whether IHT is due or not; if he fails to, the CTO can demand an account from anyone in whom any of the estate vests. He must lodge a corrective inventory if the valuation is later amended. After confirmation the CTO may challenge the valuation, and will formally assess the tax payable.

For smaller estates the executor simply lodges an inventory with **12.65** the sheriff court.[53] This is done in two cases:

(1) *Excepted estates*: estates where (i) the total gross value does **12.66** not exceed £210,000, no more than £50,000 being situated outwith the U.K.; (ii) all the property passed under the deceased's will, intestacy, nomination, or survivorship; (iii) the deceased died domiciled in the U.K. and had made no lifetime gifts chargeable to IHT; and (iv) in the previous four years she had not transferred money or shares worth more than £75,000. So there must be no settled property, or PETs on which IHT is due. The CTO may ask for the inventory within 60 days after confirmation.

(2) *Small estates*: where the "small estates" confirmation pro- **12.67** cedure is used and the gross estate for IHT purposes is no more than £25,000.

### Payment

The executor must pay the IHT when he lodges the account, and **12.68** at any rate within six months after the end of the month when the death occurred. But for certain assets he may instead opt to pay by 10 equal annual instalments[54]: land; controlling shareholdings; some unquoted minority holdings; and a business or interest in one. He will be wise to opt: it avoids borrowing to pay before confirmation, and once estate funds are available he can then pay in a lump sum if he chooses.

When the executry is finished the executor can ask the CTO for **12.69** a "clearance certificate" covering any or all of the estate assets. This certifies that the due IHT has been paid and (in the absence of fraud, non-disclosure of material facts, or subsequent changes in the valuation or distribution of the estate) discharges any possible liability. With "excepted estates" discharge is automatic 60 days after confirmation. Even if the executry administration is otherwise complete, the executor should remember that IHT may still arise:

(i) if a child elects for legal rights as against a legacy (or vice versa);

---

[53] Using Form C1 again.
[54] Starting at the six month point.

(ii) where the deceased received a PET and the donor dies later than him; and

(iii) where PETs by the deceased only come to light after the executry is complete.[55-56]

## CAPITAL GAINS TAX

### Capital gains before death

**12.70** If any CGT remains unpaid in respect of disposals made by the deceased, it is payable by the executors as a debt of the estate. The annual exemption applies.[57] There may be a net gain or loss in the year of death. If a gain, it can be set against the deceased's previous losses; if a loss, conversely, it is "carried back" for up to three tax years and set against gains.

**12.71** Because CGT is chargeable on lifetime gifts although no actual profit is made, a gift by the deceased may already have borne CGT. To avoid a double tax charge it is possible to set off the CGT and IHT liability against each other.[58] The exact calculation depends on who paid the CGT:

(i) if the *transferor* (the deceased), the sum paid in CGT is not treated as a loss to his estate: so IHT is calculated only on the actual gift itself;

(ii) if the *recipient*, the amount of CGT is deducted from the value of the gift for IHT purposes.

**12.72** A different method of set-off applies to business assets on which the CGT had been deferred by "roll-over relief".

### Capital gains during executry administration[59]

**12.73** Death is not a chargeable disposal: no CGT arises on any unrealised gains, and no reliefs can be claimed on unrealised losses. The executors are treated as acquiring the deceased's assets at their market value at the date of death. This is the IHT value; if the executors subsequently opt for a later lower value for IHT,[60] it applies for CGT as well. In lowering IHT they can thus raise the CGT on a subsequent disposal, and they should weigh the overall effect with care.

---

[55-56] See paras 12.53, 12.61, and 12.62.

[57] Currently (2001/02) £7,500.

[58] IHTA 1984, s.5(4); Taxation of Chargeable Gains Act 1992, s.282.

[59] Taxation of Chargeable Gains Act 1992, ss.62, 64, 65.

[60] *e.g.* they sell shares at a loss in the next 12 months.

The date of death value is the base point for computing later **12.74** gains and losses. If the executors dispose of assets (except to legatees) they are chargeable as a single self-contained body, distinct from themselves as individuals. They cannot set their gains (or losses) against losses (or gains) made by the deceased or by beneficiaries. They have the annual exemption for three years only, and other exemptions where appropriate; for a long-lasting executry taper relief may reduce the gain. As well as ordinary expenses, they may deduct an appropriate proportion of the costs of obtaining confirmation and of administration.[61] The rate of CGT is now (as for discretionary and accumulation trusts) 34 per cent.

It is not a disposal for CGT if the executors in course of **12.75** administration transfer assets to a legatee. "Legatee" means anyone who acquires (for himself or as trustee) under a testamentary disposition or intestacy: including a post-death deed of arrangement, *mortis causa* donation, or (it seems) legal rights. The legatee acquires as at the date of death and the value then; he, not the executry, takes all gains and losses on a subsequent disposal.[62] The same goes for disposals under intestacy or (it seems) legal rights.[63]

So the executors must consider whether to hand over assets to a **12.76** beneficiary or to sell them and give the proceeds. Their choice—if they have one[64]—may involve several factors. Would the executry suffer heavy CGT? Beyond that, who can best minimise CGT: executors or beneficiaries? Which can best set gains against losses? Which has most exemptions? The executry has only one aggregate annual exemption; each beneficiary has his own.[65]

INCOME TAX

### The deceased's income

The executor must inform the Inland Revenue of the death and **12.77** submit an income tax return for the period from April 6 last to the date of death. They can make an assessment within three years after the January 31 following the end of that tax year (*i.e.* the appropriate filing date); it may relate to any tax year whose January 31 filing date was no more than five years before the death.

---

[61] *I.R.C. v. Richard's Exrs*, 1971 S.C. (H.L.) 60. They may use the true cost or a standard scale of costs: Inland Revenue Statement of Practice 7/81.
[62] And can deduct the cost of transferring the asset to him.
[63] See Scobbie (1988) 33 J.L.S. 341.
[64] *e.g.* with residue or legal rights; *cf.* a specific legacy which must be transferred in specie, physically.
[65] Note that the Finance Act 1989, s.124 abolished the general CGT "hold-over" relief on gifts. Reliefs may be available in respect of business assets.

**12.78** If tax is due, that is a deductible debt of the estate. Conversely there may be a tax repayment: among other reasons the deceased gets a full year's personal reliefs on death, but only a pro rata amount will have been set against tax under PAYE while alive. This is an asset of the estate and should be confirmed to. In both cases an estimate may be needed, with a corrective inventory later if necessary.

**12.79** The deceased may have run a business as a sole trader. Accounts will have been prepared on the now-normal "current year basis" (*i.e.* for the accounting period ending in the relevant year of assessment). The period to death will be taxed under the rules for cessation of business.

**12.80** If the deceased had been in partnership, similar rules apply in taxing his share in the partnership; the partnership as a whole will however be treated as continuing despite his death.[66]

**12.81** Investment income received after death is usually executry income (even though it may be in the deceased's estate for IHT purposes). Dividends and most bank and building society interest are received net of lower rate tax or the special rate for dividends, but higher rate tax may be due on the grossed-up amount.

**12.82** Conversely, if the deceased had no tax liability, he may have registered with the bank to have interest paid gross, or (if not) a tax repayment will be due.

**12.83** Some forms of investment give Income Tax and CGT exemption: such as a PEP (Personal Equity Plan) and ISA (Individual Savings Account). These are closed automatically on death but the accrued tax advantages are not lost.

**12.84** Some executry expenses are tax deductible. They are (1) interest on a loan raised to pay IHT before confirmation (for moveable property and for one year only) and (2) mortgage interest on the deceased's only or main residence, if it is also the surviving spouse's (or will be when she leaves job-related accommodation).[67]

**Executry income**

**12.85** The executry is taxable as a separate entity from the deceased and from the executor as an individual. It pays the lower or basic rate on income arising during administration and receives no personal reliefs.

**12.86** Income bears income tax, but capital receipts are chargeable to CGT. Classification is difficult where the deceased had a business. Income tax is due if the executors actively continue trading; CGT if they merely realise the assets. Each case is decided on its facts.[68]

---

[66] ICTA 1988, s.113. Formerly the business was treated as ceasing unless the partners elected to treat it as continuing.

[67] ICTA 1988, ss.358, 364.

[68] *I.R.C. v. Donaldson's Trs*, 1955 S.C. 320.

Liferenters will be entitled to the free income[69] of the estate **12.87**
from the date of death. Residuary legatees will also get income
which the residue produces (with the complication that they also
receive capital, and the executors must distinguish the two for tax
purposes). The executors pay the income net after deduction of
basic or lower rate tax[70]; the beneficiary includes the gross amount
in his tax return so, after crediting the deduction, he may be liable
for higher rate tax. But where the income had already been subject
to IHT (as having accrued before death) the IHT is credited
against this extra income tax.[71]

If complex the executry administration may take two or three **12.88**
years. At its end the residue is paid out or the executry converts
into a continuing trust. Beneficiaries are taxed at the point they
receive the income, even if it accrued to the executry in an earlier
tax year. Liferenters and residuary legatees use different
procedures.[72]

If an executor receives any income after the close of the **12.89**
administration he passes it on to an entitled beneficiary or the trust
(as appropriate), in whose hands it is taxed. For this purpose—and
for CGT—the administration is complete at the point when debts
and prior legacies have been paid or provided for and the residue
has been ascertained.[73]

**Further reading**

Foster, *Capital Taxes Encyclopaedia*, esp. sections B, D and E.
B. McCutcheon, *Inheritance Tax*.
A.R. Mellows, *Taxation for Trustees and Executors*.
E. Scobbie, "Tax-efficient Executry Administration" (1988) 33
J.L.S. 341.

Numerous books cover tax law in detail. Most relevant Law Society
P.Q.L.E. publications contain useful detailed surveys of the
practical problems.

---

[69] *i.e.* after deducting debts and legacies, and apportioning executry expenses
between income and capital.
[70] Along with a certificate stating the income and tax (Form R185 (Estate Income)).
[71] ICTA 1988, s.699. The residuary beneficiary now incurs IT liability in the year she
is paid: ICTA 1998, ss.695–702 am by F.A. 1995, s.75, Sched. 18.
[72] ICTA 1988, ss.695–701.
[73] ICTA 1988, s.702(a).

CHAPTER 13

# EXECUTRY ADMINISTRATION

STRUCTURE AND BACKGROUND

**13.01** When a person dies his property must be gathered in and then distributed to his beneficiaries. The executor is responsible for this. He is appointed either by will (an *executor-nominate*) or by the sheriff (an *executor-dative*). A second step is essential to allow him to administer the estate: he must obtain from the sheriff *confirmation* of his title. Administration without confirmation is an unauthorised "vitious intromission" which may make him liable for all the deceased's debts.

**13.02** Before 1964 only moveables passed via the executor; heritage went directly to the heir by *service*. The Succession (Scotland) Act abolished the separate rules for heritage.[1] They remain relevant for two purposes: administering estates of those who died before the Act was in force, and reviving a "lapsed trust" through the heir of the last surviving trustee.[2]

**13.03** In the case of moveables, the rules evolved over centuries. Before the Reformation in 1560, church officials—"commissaries"—dealt with succession under canon law. They were then replaced by commissary courts under royal control; by the 1800s these had jurisdiction over executries within their area or *commissariot*. Ultimately the sheriff took over their functions, with the sheriff clerk responsible for the administrative aspects.

**13.04** The deceased's domicile determines which sheriff has jurisdiction to grant confirmation or appoint an executor-dative. That is the sheriff in whose commissariot he was domiciled[3] when he died. The Edinburgh commissary office deals with those who had a Scots domicile but no known local domicile within Scotland, or who left property within Scotland but were domiciled elsewhere.

**13.05** Commissary jurisdiction is primarily administrative and non-contentious. The sheriff himself is only involved in appointing

---

[1] Succession (Scotland) Act 1964, s.14(1).
[2] 1964 Act, s.37(1)(d); Law Reform (Miscellaneous Provisions) (Scotland) Act 1980, s.6.
[3] On domicile see paras 14.02–14.04, below.

executors-dative or, where legal difficulties occur, issuing a special warrant for confirmation. Confirmation says who is entitled to be executor. It makes a holograph will probative,[4] but otherwise does not determine the validity of a will or of a beneficiary's right to inherit: that may require separate litigation.

## THE OFFICE OF EXECUTOR

### Executors and trustees

A will may appoint the same people both as executors and as **13.06** testamentary trustees. In practice the two functions tend to overlap. Legally, and for tax, they are distinct. The executor's duty is to collect the estate and distribute it to beneficiaries; the trustee's is to hold it and administer it according to the trust purposes, (say) during a liferent. The executry administration is complete once debts and legacies are paid; at that point the trust takes over.

Furthermore an executor, unlike a trustee, represents the **13.07** deceased: *eadem persona cum defuncto*, he stands in his shoes; if he pursues a debt he can be met by the same defences as the deceased. As such his personal liability for his actions is normally limited to the value of the estate confirmed to.

That said, trustees and executors have much in common. Being **13.08** an executor is an administrative duty, not a benefit: he is not entitled to payment unless the will allows.[5] Executors have the same powers and, conversely, restrictions, as the law imposes on trustees. So—executors-dative apart—they can assume new executors or resign.[6] Conversely, if the will only appoints a trustee, he is entitled to be confirmed as executor.[7]

### Entitlement to be appointed executor

*(a) Executors-nominate*

A testator may expressly appoint someone to be executor. **13.09** Usually he names him, but it is enough if he can be identified: such as "the same executor as X has".[8] The will may ask someone else to make the choice. Alternatively appointment is implicit if the person is given powers which an executor would have: "to collect and divide my estate" or "to give effect to this will".

---

[4] Similarly, under the Requirements of Writing (Scotland) Act 1995, p. 4, a will—unless already presumed valid—has to be declared valid. Succession (Scotland) Act 1964, s.32.
[5] See para. 13.104.
[6] Executors (Scotland) Act 1900, s.2; 1964 Act, s.20.
[7] Executors (Scotland) Act 1900, s.3.
[8] See *Martin v. Ferguson's Trs* (1892) 19 R. 492.

**13.10** Suppose the testator appointed no executor, or his choice has failed by his proposed executor either refusing office, being incapacitated or dying (whether before or after him). Under the Executors (Scotland) Act 1900 the deemed executors-nominate are his testamentary trustees or (if none exist) any general disponee, universal legatee or residuary legatee.[9] If there are several such legatees they must all either accept or expressly decline office. If any are untraceable, or have died causing partial intestacy, this last option is barred.[10]

*(b) Executors-dative*

**13.11** Perhaps the deceased left no will; or he did, but an executor nominate was not appointed. In either case an executor-dative is required. If several people compete for appointment they are selected in order of preference; those falling within the same category are entitled to be appointed jointly. An applicant need not notify other potential competitors. If they want to be informed they should lodge a *"caveat"* with the sheriff court: renewable monthly, it simply asks the court to give notification of any applications.

**13.12** The order of preference is:

(a) General disponees (and the like) when the 1900 Act cannot be used. Any of them may be appointed executor-dative without the others' consent.

(b) The deceased's spouse is exclusively entitled if he or she inherits the whole intestate estate under prior rights.[11] If the estate exceeds prior rights the spouse is entitled concurrently along with (c).

(c) Those who inherit the "free estate" from the deceased under section 2 of the 1964 Act. The equivalent before 1964 was the "next-of-kin", which differed in many ways: it excluded the spouse and maternal relatives. It seems that next-of-kin can still be appointed executor-dative even if not entitled to inherit under section 2: this is an anachronism and the Scottish Law Commission favours its abolition.[12]

Those who inherit directly have, if they apply, preference over those who inherit by representation. So a

---

[9] Executors (Scotland) Act 1900, s.3. "Universal legatee" denotes the estate is all moveable; "general disponee" that it includes heritage.
[10] See Currie, 5.79.
[11] Succession (Scotland) Act 1964, s.9(4).
[12] Report No. 124 (1990) paras 8.23–8.27.

surviving child has priority over a predeceasing child's offspring.[13]

(d) The deceased's creditors.

(e) Legatees who receive a specific legacy or a liferent.

(f) The beneficiary's property may already be under the administration of a court-appointed *judicial factor*. Two types are relevant: a factor for a child under 16, and a *curator bonis*[13a] for a person of unsound mind. He may apply to be appointed executor-dative to the person from whom the beneficiary inherits. If a child has no factor, the sheriff may specially appoint a commissary factor in order to be executor and obtain confirmation.[14]

(g) The procurator fiscal, if asked to by someone with a claim on the estate. This is very rare.

(h) The funerator: the undertaker or whoever has paid his bill. This only occurs if next-of-kin are unknown or cannot or will not be executor.[15]

If the entitled person declines to be executor, the next-entitled can take his or her place. For instance, a widow may be exclusively entitled under (b) but prefer her son to be executor. She should formally decline office and his application will explain the facts. If the estate exceeds prior rights he is independently entitled under (c) and no declinature is needed.

*(c) The executor-creditor*

Confirmation as executor-creditor is unusual and differs from **13.13** other confirmations. It is a type of diligence: a way for a creditor to enforce his debt. So, uniquely, it need cover only that amount and not the whole estate. But it is impossible once another executor has been appointed, and ineffective if the estate is sequestrated within twelve months after the death. In practice the creditor simply sues for his debt.[16]

*(d) Disqualification*

Anyone aged over 16 may be an executor.[17] **13.14**

---

[13] Succession (Scotland) Act 1964, s.5(2).

[13a] To be termed guardian from April 1, 2002: Adults with Incapacity (Scotland) Act 2000, Sched. 4.

[14] Currie, 8.68 *et seq.*; Walker, *Judicial Factors*, pp. 88–90.

[15] Currie, 6.116.

[16] Currie, 6.77 *et seq.*; Wilson & Duncan, Chap. 35.

[17] Age of Legal Capacity (Scotland) Act 1991, s.1(1). Previously there was no age limit.

**13.15**   Insanity is a bar. Section 3 of the Executors (Scotland) Act can supply an alternative executor-nominate. Otherwise the executor's *curator bonis* can be appointed executor-dative in his place.

**13.16**   Bankruptcy is no bar. The only guarantee against financial mishaps or fraud is the bond of caution which executors-dative must lodge before confirmation.

**13.17**   Executors need not be resident in the United Kingdom. For convenience they should be.

### Appointing executors-dative—procedure

*(a) The petition*

**13.18**   The applicant lodges a petition in the appropriate sheriff court.[18] This "initial writ" must state:

**13.19**   (1) the date and place of death. Sometimes these are not exactly known. It is sufficient to follow the words of the death certificate and to describe the location: *e.g.* "on the road between X and Y near Z". If death was presumed by virtue of disappearance the court decree specifies a date.[19]

**13.20**   (2) if the deceased died intestate. If he died testate it must mention the will and any declinature of office by executors-nominate.

**13.21**   (3) where the deceased was domiciled, to prove jurisdiction. If it was abroad, the applicant must lodge an expert opinion that he is entitled to be executor under the law of that place.

**13.22**   (4) the applicant's relationship to the deceased, to show his entitlement. It must eliminate potential preferable claimants, in particular any who died before the deceased. If a spouse survives, it must explain why she is not the applicant *or* state that the estate exceeds her prior rights. But the relationship—even if illegitimate—needs no proof by supporting evidence like birth certificates.[20]

**13.23**   Any documents referred to in the petition are lodged along with it. It is displayed in the court or the sheriff clerk's office (the sheriff clerk certifying that this has been done) but other possible claimants are not directly notified unless they lodged a caveat. If the petition is unopposed no hearing is needed and the sheriff grants decree nine clear days after certification.[21]

---

[18] With copies—the number varies—and a fee.

[19] Presumption of Death (Scotland) Act 1977, s.10; see paras 1.07–1.14.

[20] *McLaughlin, Petr*, 1987 S.L.T. (Sh. Ct) 87, disapproving Currie (7th ed., 1973) p. 113.

[21] The exact interval varies between sheriffdoms.

*(b) The bond of caution*

This is a guarantee that the executor-dative will perform his **13.24** duties and not embezzle the estate. It is not required from a surviving spouse who inherits the whole estate by prior rights,[22] nor (except very rarely) from executors-nominate.

The cautioner must be subject to the jurisdiction of the Scottish **13.25** courts, have been approved by the Court of Session, and not be a beneficiary. Almost invariably it is an insurance company. The bond is a standard form and the company makes a charge based on the value of the estate.

Caution is required for the gross estate in the inventory. The **13.26** only debts deductible are those (like mortgages) which are secured over items of heritage and appear as deductions within the inventory rather than the IHT account. In theory the executor can apply by initial writ to reduce the amount of caution, but this is not worthwhile.

All the executors sign the bond and send it to the company for **13.27** completion. It is probative and must be entirely executed, with due authentication, *after* the sheriff's decree. The relevant details (names and addresses and capacity of executor's appointment) must match the initial writ and the inventory precisely.

After being appointed and taking out caution the executor- **13.28** dative can apply for confirmation.

CONFIRMATION

The grant of confirmation is the executor's title to administer the **13.29** estate. It reproduces the inventory[23] of the estate (but not the associated IHT account) and the associated oath sworn by the executor that it is valid.

For convenience one usually also obtains certificates of confir- **13.30** mation for individual items in the inventory. The executor then sends the confirmation or certificate to whoever possesses or registers the item—banks, company registrars, and the like. He can then have it endorsed in his name, encashed, sold, or in due course transferred to a beneficiary.

**The inventory estate: classification**

The concept of confirmation dates back to the Middle Ages. **13.31** Executors were always required to state on oath an inventory of the deceased's estate as far as they knew it. In practice it was common

---

[22] Law Reform (Miscellaneous Provisions) (Scotland) Act 1980, s.5. See S.L.C. Report No. 124 (1990) paras 8.32–8.39.

[23] The IHT form formerly comprised both the inventory and IHT account. They are now separate (Forms C1 and IHT 200 respectively) but are lodged at the same time.

to obtain partial confirmation to save expense, omitting items or minimising their value. The inventory had no tax function.

13.32    Those halcyon days ended with the Probate and Legacy Duties Act of 1808, which introduced an inventory duty and, with it, the modern distinction between estate subject to confirmation and that to be declared for tax purposes. By its terms:

13.33    "before [anyone] shall be confirmed executor he shall exhibit upon oath or solemn affirmation, in the proper commissary court in Scotland, a full and true inventory . . . of all the personal or moveable estate and effects of the deceased . . . distinguishing what shall be in Scotland and what elsewhere."[24]

13.34    At that time confirmation affected only moveable property located within Scotland. For items elsewhere the executor had to obtain the local equivalent—in England, probate or letters of administration; vice versa for an English executor in Scotland. Though Scots law determined who *inherited* a domiciled Scot's moveable estate, wherever located, each country's executry procedure was quite separate.

13.35    Modern law considerably extends the scope of confirmation.

(a)  It includes heritage.[25]

(b)  It is recognised throughout the United Kingdom and may include property outwith Scotland if the deceased had Scots domicile; otherwise it includes only estate in Scotland. Conversely grants of probate or administration carry Scottish estate: no separate confirmation is needed.[26]

(c)  Confirmation does not in principle affect property outwith the United Kingdom. However the courts in Commonwealth countries have discretion to accept and "reseal" it, giving it the same effect as a local grant of administration. Conversely Edinburgh Sheriff Court may, on certain conditions, reseal a Commonwealth grant for use here.[27] Estate outwith the Commonwealth normally requires a fresh local grant.

For (b) and (c) to apply there must be some confirmable estate in Scotland. If not the executor must get a grant of administration in the country where the property

---

[24] s.38.
[25] Succession (Scotland) Act 1964, ss.14, 15.
[26] Administration of Estates Act 1971, ss.1–6: if domiciled in the place where the grant was issued.
[27] Colonial Probates Act 1892; Currie, Chap. 15.

is. The Scottish Law Commission favours allowing a Scots confirmation in such cases.[28]

The inventory should therefore list and value the confirmable **13.36** estate, item by item, in order under these headings:

Heritable estate in Scotland

Moveable estate in Scotland

Real and personal estate in England and Wales

Real and personal estate in Northern Ireland

A summary for confirmation then gives the total values for each head (lumping Scottish estate together) and the aggregate total. Finally foreign property is itemised and valued.

Itemised confirmable values are extended into the column of values on the form. Values in the summary and foreign values are not extended.

**The inventory: particular items**

The treatment of certain items can raise difficulties.        **13.37**

(1) *Heritage* and (outwith Scotland) *real property*. The description **13.38** must be sufficient to identify the property as a separate item in the estate. A full conveyancing description is not necessary, but can have advantages: it ensures accurate identification if the property is later conveyed to a beneficiary, not by a full conveyance, but by a docket on the confirmation.[29]

Suppose the deceased had contracted to buy or sell a house but died before money was paid and the property conveyed. In either case the house must be confirmed to in order to complete the executor's title and allow subsequent conveyance. In the first case it is entered at full value and the price is a deductible debt for IHT; in the second it is given a nil value and the unpaid sale proceeds go in as an asset.

(2) The deceased's aggregate share of *partnership assets* appears **13.39** as one moveable item. It may include heritage registered in the deceased's name as an individual: that needs an extra separate entry at a nil value in order to complete title. If the deceased had a one-man business its assets appear individually in the inventory and its liabilities are deducted in the IHT account.

(3) The deceased may have been a *co-owner* of property: **13.40** heritage, shares, bank accounts, and the like. Their treatment in the inventory varies.

---

[28] Report No. 124 (1990) para. 8.28.
[29] Currie, 10.102; Succession (Scotland) Act 1964, s.15(2).

(a) *Heritage, company shares, and unit trusts*: one confirms in the inventory to the proportionate share registered in the deceased's name—usually one-half. The exception is a survivorship destination of heritage: the share is omitted from the inventory but listed in the IHT account. (One must check that the deceased had not validly revoked the destination.)

(b) With *bank accounts*, by contrast, joint names do not imply joint ownership. They merely allow each person to operate the account. He owns only the money he paid in, which may be all or none. The inventory therefore states the proportion contributed by the deceased, and that is confirmed to.

Take an account in name of "X and Y and the survivor". The survivor can uplift the money without confirmation: that conveniently covers immediate expenses. But—except for the survivor's own contribution—the executor can reclaim the money for distribution to the appropriate beneficiary.

There are two exceptions. If the funds derived from either spouse's housekeeping allowance the spouses own them in equal shares; similarly items bought with those funds.[30] Or the deceased may have gifted his share to his co-holder: but that needs very clear proof.[31]

(c) Until recently *household goods* belonged to whoever bought them. But spouses are now presumed to own "matrimonial property" in equal shares, unless proved otherwise (and contributing unequally to the cost is not proof enough).[32] This covers most items bought for use in the matrimonial home except cars, money and shares. Thus only the deceased's half-share is confirmed to.

**13.41**   (4) *Life assurance* policy proceeds need confirmation only if payable to the executors; otherwise they are not part of the estate and can be paid on production of the death certificate. The deceased may have assigned the policy in security for a loan which was not repaid before he died. Two complications arise.

(a) The policy proceeds go to the lender to pay off the loan; the estate is entitled to any surplus remaining. The inventory shows the gross proceeds minus loan, and thus

---

[30] Family Law (Scotland) Act 1985, s.26.
[31] *Forrest-Hamilton's Tr. v. Forrest-Hamilton*, 1970 S.L.T. 338.
[32] Family Law (Scotland) Act 1985, s.25. See Clive, 14.096–14.099.

the executor confirms to the net surplus. The entry is headed in the lender's name because the estate's claim is against the lender rather than the insurance company. It is also acceptable to confirm to the gross sum and deduct the debt separately in the IHT account: but the drawback is that the higher inventory total leads to higher caution and confirmation dues.

(b) There is usually a second security: a standard security over a house. When calculating prior or legal rights the loan must be allocated to the two securities in proportion to their values.[33] One may, but need not, use the same method in the inventory; or one can deduct the whole amount from the policy. The latter simplifies the inventory and maximises the heritage on which IHT can be paid by instalments; but in that case one must remember to reallocate at the prior/legal rights stage.[34]

(5) A *lease* is confirmed to (as heritage) unless it ends on the death. Even if the deceased could not assign his interest while alive, the executor can do so.[35] **13.42**

(6) *Stocks and shares* are listed as Scottish or English depending on where the company is registered; government stock is English. One must also include (a) dividends declared before the date of death, though paid later, and (b) interest accrued till then (calculated on a daily basis; special rules apply to government stock).[36] **13.43**

(7) Property held by the deceased as *trustee* passes automatically by accretion to the remaining trustees, without confirmation. But if he was the sole surviving trustee the property is now in limbo. It can be put as a note at the very end of the inventory: this allows his executor to transfer it to a beneficiary or to someone the beneficiary selects.[37] **13.44**

The same applies if the deceased held as a confirmed *executor* on another person's estate. If he was not merely executor but *beneficiary* two entries are needed: that whole executry estate (as a note) and his own beneficial interest (as a confirmable item in the body of the inventory). Other procedures are sometimes possible.[38]

---

[33] *Graham v. Graham* (1898) 5 S.L.T. 319; see para. 4.40.
[34] If two borrowers have a joint policy in respect of a joint loan the debt must be divided between them. This affects how the policy proceeds are treated. See Gretton (1988) 33 J.L.S. 141.
[35] Succession (Scotland) Act 1964, s.16(2): Meston, pp. 86–89.
[36] A beneficiary may suffer income tax on these (because they are paid after death). If so he has a credit for the IHT. See para. 12.87.
[37] Executors (Scotland) Act 1900, s.6.
[38] For procedure when an executor dies see in more detail paras 13.119 *et seq.*

### The oath[39]

*(a) Who swears the oath, and before whom?*

**13.45**  The executor must personally swear an oath that the inventory and associated details are true. He may instead solemnly affirm on grounds of religious belief or non-belief. If there are several executors only one need swear. If the inventory is compiled purely for IHT and no confirmation is required,[40] a relation or beneficiary or anyone with an interest may swear.

**13.46**  The person before whom the oath is sworn must be completely impartial and independent. He should not be the executor's partner, co-executor, or a beneficiary. Subject to that he can be any of the following:

**13.47**  (1) *In Scotland*: a sheriff principal, sheriff, commissioner appointed by either, sheriff clerk or his depute, notary public, magistrate, or justice of the peace.[41]

**13.48**  (2) *In England or Northern Ireland*: anyone in (1), a commissioner for oaths appointed by the English or Northern Irish courts (respectively), or (in England) a solicitor entitled to administer oaths.

**13.49**  (3) *Abroad*: a local magistrate, British consul, notary public practising in that country or admitted and practising in Great Britain or Ireland, someone locally authorised to administer oaths, or certain senior officers in the Forces.

*(b) Contents*

**13.50**  The details must be accurate, consistent, and connect up with any will, initial writ, or related documents such as minutes of declinature. Certain preliminaries precede the oath:

**13.51**  (1) The deceased's full name and address. Previous names, addresses and aliases are included if needed to tie in with the will. Date of birth, date and place of death, and occupation or designation follow.

**13.52**  (2) The names and addresses of all executors being confirmed.

**13.53**  (3) Date and place of the oath. The oath is only valid for six months and must be re-sworn if the inventory is not lodged within that time.

**13.54**  (4) The name and address of the person administering the oath (stating his capacity), and those of the executor swearing it—the *deponent*. The names should link up with their surnames and initials as signed after the oath, while previous names and addresses may tie in with the will or initial writ.

---

[39] See Currie, 10.10 *et seq.*
[40] *e.g.* under para. 13.80.
[41] Executors (Scotland) Act 1900, s.8.

The oath itself states the following: **13.55**

(1) The deceased's name and domicile, to show jurisdiction: **13.56** "domiciled in the Sheriffdom of X in Scotland" or as appropriate if of foreign or unknown domicile.

(2) The deponent's right to act as executor-nominate or dative, **13.57** along with co-executors (using the order in the will). At this point the oath must, as appropriate:

(a) identify the will, when it was recorded, or the decree appointing as executor-dative.

(b) state any special capacity, such as "attorney under power of attorney dated . . ."

(c) explain if any executors-nominate have died or decline appointment.

(d) state the executor-dative's capacity as per the initial writ. For small estates there is no separate initial writ and the oath must also eliminate anyone with a preferable right to be appointed.[42]

(e) reiterate if the deponent's or deceased's name or address were different in the will.

(3) Who the other executors are. **13.58**

(4) Where the estate is and whether confirmation is required. **13.59** The deponent and the person administering the oath sign it.

### Associated documents and procedure

Except for an executor-dative's decree of appointment, all **13.60** documents referred to in the oath must be lodged along with the inventory. They must be docketed to identify them. The docket is a note written on the document (*not* on a separate sheet):

"[Place, date] Referred to in my deposition of this date to the **13.61** inventory of the estate of the late [X]."

It is signed by the deponent and the person administering the **13.62** oath. The date must of course match that of the oath.

Unless the will is in English, attested, and clearly names the **13.63** executor, additional procedure is needed to establish the executor's right to appointment.

(1) *An attested will* (under the pre-Requirements of Writing **13.64** (Scotland) Act 1995 rules)[42a] may have been defectively executed, or its testing clause left uncompleted. The defect can be curable by

---

[42] Using Form C1 with no initial writ; see para. 13.68. For larger estates these details go in the initial writ.

[42a] *i.e.* executed before August 1, 1995.

a petition under section 39 of the Conveyancing (Scotland) Act 1874.[43] While a separate Court of Session or sheriff court action is possible, the point usually arises when seeking confirmation.

The executor applies by initial writ for (a) proof that the will was duly executed *and* (b) special authority for appointment as executor nominate or (if the will named no executor) as executor-dative. The initial writ must state how the will is defective (itemising any missing details), that the will is subscribed by the testator and bears to be[44] attested by two witnesses, and that the subscriptions are genuine.

Proof is by affidavits. They are sworn, before a notary public or justice of the peace or anyone else locally authorised, by the two witnesses, anyone else present when the will was executed, and (if the will has several pages) whoever found it or had custody of it. Those swearing docket the will appropriately to link with their affidavits. The initial writ, will (or extract),[45] affidavits, and inventory are lodged with the sheriff clerk's office. The sheriff rarely requires a full hearing before granting decree and confirmation.

**13.65** (2) The will may omit to name the executor and merely identify him as, say, "my son". Confirmation should be sought by initial writ, with affidavits that the executor is in fact the person referred to.

**13.66** (3) A (pre-Requirements of Writing (Scotland) Act 1995) will which is *holograph* or adopted as holograph always requires to be validated by affidavits from two people who knew the testator and can swear that the handwriting and signature are genuinely his. They should see the original will before it is sent for registration and extract. Furthermore the initial writ procedure is used if there is some question whether the writing or signature is genuine and valid.

An informal writing does not need to be "set up" if it was adopted by another formally valid will which is itself lodged.

For wills executed under the Requirements of Writing (Scotland) Act 1995—*i.e.* on or after August 1, 1995—there is an analogous validation requirement under section 4 of the Act. This applies where the will was signed (and therefore formally valid) but, because unwitnessed, cannot be automatically presumed valid under section 3. (If it was not signed at all, it will be invalid unless the relatively narrow "adoption" mechanism in section 8 applies.)[45a]

**13.67** (4) A will executed *abroad* but not meeting Scots formalities is effective if executed validly under the law of the place of execution

---

[43] See paras 6.20–6.21. Section 38 may also cure the testing clause.

[44] *i.e.* is on the face of it attested.

[45] See para. 13.81.

[45a] See Currie, 4.20, 4.92–4.93; Act of Sederunt (Requirements of Writing) 1996 (S.I. 1996 No. 1534). See para. 6.68 above.

or of the testator's domicile, habitual residence, or nationality.[46]
The inventory should refer to and be accompanied by an opinion
by someone qualified in that local law that it is valid and that the
named executor is entitled to administer the estate. An initial writ
is not necessary.

Similarly a will in a foreign language must be lodged along with
a translation certified by an expert as accurate.

A foreign will may be unavailable because it is deposited
permanently with a local notary. It is acceptable to lodge a copy
certified by him, if accompanied by an opinion by another expert as
to local validity. A British consul or a notary public should also
authenticate the copy.[47]

### Small estates

A "small estate" is one whose gross value, without deducting **13.68**
debts and funeral expenses, does not exceed £25,000.[48] An optional
simplified confirmation procedure is available.[49] The sheriff clerk
administers the oath and completes the inventory; there is no
separate initial writ for executors-dative, but a bond of caution is
still needed.

The sheriff clerk must be satisfied of several points: **13.69**

(a) There must be no competition for the post of executor.

(b) The value is no more than £25,000. The executor should
give him a list which itemises and values the estate.

(c) The executor is entitled to appointment, either under the
will or by relationship to the deceased. The details go in
the oath. In intestate cases he can be asked for proof of
identity and relationship: two witnesses attend the sheriff
clerk's office with him and swear affidavits (not all clerks
require this). If there is a will the clerk checks its validity.

### Additional confirmations

It may emerge that property was omitted or wrongly valued in **13.70**
the original inventory. The executor must lodge an additional or
corrective inventory (or "eik") if IHT is payable and confirmation
is required.

If confirmation is not needed the matter is usually simply **13.71**
resolved by correspondence with the Capital Taxes Office.

---

[46] Wills Act 1963, ss.1 and 2; see paras 14.36–14.41.
[47] See Currie, 2.63A *et seq.*, 10.60.
[48] Confirmation to Small Estates (Scotland) Act 1979, s.1(3); Confirmation to Small
Estates (Scotland) Order 1999 (S.I. 1999 No. 290).
[49] Using Form C1.

**13.72** For confirmation purposes the inventory or eik states the new or revalued items. These are confirmed to. The executor also needs an eik where, though the estate is no larger, items were wrongly described originally so that he cannot obtain title to them without correction. In that case the eik adds on the item as corrected and deducts the value of the original entry from the estate.

**13.73** Only the original executor can use an eik. If he has died or become incapable a new executor must apply afresh for confirmation *ad omissa*.[50] Nor is it available if the "small estates" procedure was originally used: the executor must repeat that procedure or (if the new items take the estate above £25,000) get confirmation *ad omissa*.

### Payment without confirmation

**13.74** Not until the executor has been confirmed can he insist that the executry assets be paid or handed over to him. Whoever holds the assets can require to see the confirmation. If the holder chooses not to and pays earlier he takes the risk of paying the wrong person; the true confirmed executor will be entitled to demand payment again.

**13.75** Confirmation is however dispensed with in several (largely statutory) situations. The claimant must instead produce proof of the death.

**13.76** (1) Property subject to a *survivorship destination* belongs automatically to the survivor without confirmation. But the destination must be in a title deed. Contrast a destination in a bank account. There the survivor can operate the account and so demand payment without confirmation; but he does not necessarily own the funds and may have to hand them over to the executor.[51]

**13.77** (2) The deceased may have *nominated* someone to receive funds on his death. The method and maximum amount differ between funds under various statutes. The nominee can insist on payment: usually he is also beneficially entitled to the money and can keep it, but in rare cases the nomination is (like the bank account) for mere administrative convenience and he must pass it on to the executor.[52]

13.78

(3) In other cases payment is a privilege, not a right. Building societies, pensions, and company shares are examples. The holder has discretion whether to pay, but it must treat all claimants on the estate alike. It will usually require evidence of the claimant's entitlement to inherit. It may ask the claimant to grant an

---

[50] See paras 13.119 *et seq.*
[51] See paras 5.02–5.06.
[52] See Currie, 13.10 *et seq.*

indemnity in case a confirmed executor later appears, and may also require evidence that no IHT is payable on the item.[53] For numerous public bodies a blanket statutory maximum of £5,000 is laid down.[54] Others, such as banks and companies, set their own limits on both the individual item and the total estate.

(4) If the Crown takes as *ultimus haeres* it requires no confirmation. **13.79**

Though assets pass without confirmation they must still be included in an appropriate inventory for IHT purposes. If no confirmation is required and no tax is payable, then (by concession) one may instead lodge a simpler form to have the estate certified free of IHT. **13.80**

### Recording documents[55]

It is common to *register* the will at the start of the executry *for preservation* in the Books of Council and Session.[56] While not essential it avoids the risk of losing the will, and is particularly wise if the estate is large or there is to be an ongoing trust. The original document is kept in the register and an *extract* is issued—an official authenticated copy which is probative evidence of its terms. A special certified extract can be obtained for use abroad. If the will has to be validated with affidavits, these should be obtained before sending for registration. **13.81**

When seeking confirmation, the inventory and associated documents (including the will or extract but not the IHT accounts) are recorded in the Commissariot Books of the sheriff court. The inventory and IHT account are forwarded to the Capital Taxes Office; the documents are returned to whoever lodged them. The executor can then obtain the following: **13.82**

(a) confirmation (in respect of the whole inventory);

(b) certificates of confirmation (one for each separate item);

(c) a certified copy of the confirmation, to use for foreign estate;

(d) an ordinary copy, for private records: this lacks the force of an extract.

Both types of register are open to public inspection.

---

[53] The C.T.O. can certify this using a Form 20.
[54] Administration of Estates (Small Payments) Act 1965; S.I. 1984 No. 539.
[55] See Currie, Chap. 18.
[56] In the registers at Meadowbank House, Edinburgh. Registration of a living person's will is also to be made possible: Administration of Justice Act 1982, ss.23–25 (not yet in force).

## THE EXECUTOR'S DUTIES

### Funeral arrangements

**13.83**    Funeral arrangements are not specifically the executor's responsibility: they fall to the next-of-kin or other close relatives. But in
practice they may sometimes be delegated to the executor. If so he
will of course have to act according to the relatives' wishes so far as
possible.

**13.84**    The deceased may have given his own instructions, possibly in a
will: *e.g.* for his body to be cremated or given to medical research.
Relatives *may* wish to follow these, but cannot be compelled to do
so. Whoever is in lawful possession of the body *may* (but need not)
authorise removal of organs for medical research, provided the
deceased had requested it (orally before at least two witnesses, or
in writing) and had not withdrawn the request. An undertaker
cannot grant authorisation; the procurator fiscal can veto removal
to allow criminal investigation.[57]

### To gather in the estate

**13.85**    The executor must uplift the deceased's assets to allow him to
pay his debts and distribute the remaining assets to his beneficiaries. Confirmation is his title to do so. Though any dealing with
the assets before confirmation is vitious intromission, he "purges"
it by being confirmed within a year and a day. In any case he can
take preliminary steps beforehand. He can sue for a debt owed to
the deceased; but he needs confirmation to be able to extract the
court decree, discharge the debt, or enforce it.

**13.86**    The executor is in breach of duty if he negligently fails to pursue
debts or other assets. A beneficiary has several remedies. He can
sue the executor to make him account for the assets. He can sue a
debtor in the executor's name, provided he gives the executor an
indemnity against possible court expenses. If he is due a specific
legacy, he can bring an action against whoever has the item, to
have it delivered.

### To pay the deceased's debts

**13.87**    The executor must pay debts in order of preference: privileged
debts; preferential debts; lastly, ordinary debts.[58] He should not pay
ordinary debts till six months after the death unless he is sure there
are assets enough to pay the others: if he gets it wrong he must
compensate the others personally. If necessary he will advertise
inviting creditors to notify claims.

---

[57] Human Tissue Act 1961, s.1. Medical research apart, special procedures must be
followed (as regards certifying cause of death) if cremation is proposed.
[58] See Chap. 3.

He must check the incidence of the debts: on what assets do they **13.88** fall? IHT and secured debts raise the point. Whoever inherits an asset burdened by a security (say, a house) takes *cum onere*— subject to the security—unless the will says otherwise, and must pay the estate the value of the debt secured on it.

The executor need not pay debts exceeding the value of the **13.89** confirmed estate. If the estate is absolutely insolvent, and likely to remain so, he should take steps to have it sequestrated or a judicial factor appointed.[59]

## To distribute the estate

Creditors must be paid before beneficiaries. But the executor **13.90** need not wait indefinitely. If the estate is solvent he can start distribution after 12 months (at most); earlier if, after due inquiry, he is satisfied outstanding debts have been met. Any creditor who chooses to delay till later cannot sue an executor who has in the meantime distributed the estate with due care.

Potential legal rights claimants should be notified and asked to **13.91** elect to claim or not. A child aged under 16 cannot validly elect; if aged 16 or 17, he may be able to re-open his election before age 21. The executor should retain funds to meet a possible claim.

The beneficiaries can then be paid. If they are short of money **13.92** the executor will often make a payment to account as soon as he is certain that funds permit. If legacies exceed the value of the estate they must be abated in order of preference, residue first and specific legacies last.[60]

A specific legacy is transferred in specie—physically. Moveables **13.93** are delivered. For heritage a docket[61] can be noted on the confirmation or certificate of confirmation which is given to the beneficiary. Alternatively it can be formally conveyed. If so the disposition links up with the deceased's title: title is *deduced* through the confirmation. The will may instead be an acceptable link, but that may soon cease to be possible, and it is best avoided.[62]

General legacies are paid in kind or in cash according to their **13.94** terms. Residuary legatees can take their legacies in kind if they agree collectively, but otherwise they cannot insist on particular items. Their primary right is to cash, and the executor can sell the items and distribute the proceeds; he will have to weigh up the CGT consequences. Complex rules govern the transfer of leases, including agricultural leases and crofting tenancies.[63]

---

[59] Bankruptcy (Scotland) Act 1985, s.8(3). See Walker, *Judicial Factors*, pp. 42–46; McBryde, *Bankruptcy*, pp. 32–33, 41 and 236–238.

[60] See paras 10.71–10.74.

[61] Succession (Scotland) Act 1964, s.15(2). Notice of title is also an option.

[62] Opinion of the Professors of Conveyancing (1965) 10 J.L.S. 153; (1966) 11 J.L.S. 84; Scot. Law Com. Report No. 124 (1990), paras 8.21–8.22.

[63] Succession (Scotland) Act 1964, s.16; Meston, pp. 109–113.

**13.95**     Due care must be taken to ascertain and pay the correct beneficiaries. If the wrong person is paid four distinct issues arise:

**13.96**     (1) The beneficiary can sue the executor in an action of accounting to enforce his legacy. (This is also his remedy if the executor is simply unduly slow to pay.) But the executor has no liability to illegitimate or adoptive relations of whom he had no notice when he distributed the estate; he need not check first if they exist.[64]

**13.97**     (2) Can the beneficiary sue the solicitor who administered the estate? In *Loretto School Ltd v. Macandrew & Jenkins*[65] the solicitor's liability to account was said to be owed only to the executor. A delictual remedy was not argued, on the authority of *Robertson v. Fleming.*[66]

**13.98**     (3) Can the executor recover the asset from the payee? That depends on general principles of restitution, which are developing rapidly. In principle it should now be recoverable whether the error relates to the surrounding facts (is X the person named as legatee?) or the law (is X entitled to inherit?).[67]

**13.99**     (4) Can the beneficiary sue the payee for payment or delivery of the legacy? It seems he can if he brings in the executor as a defender.[68] Payees may also be liable for delictual damages if they know that the payment is wrong but nevertheless permit or facilitate it.[69] But a purchaser in good faith *cannot* be challenged. In the case of heritage he is protected by section 2 of the Trusts (Scotland) Act 1961 or section 17 of the 1964 Act depending on whether he bought directly from the executor or from another beneficiary. Section 17 only applies if his title rests on the executor's confirmation: not if it derives from a will or special destination. Section 2 extends to moveables as well.[70]

**Fiduciary duties**

**13.100**     The executor is a trustee and has the same powers and duties. As a fundamental principle he must not be *auctor in rem suam*: he must not allow his own personal interests to prevail over the

---

[64] Succession (Scotland) Act 1964, s.24(2); Law Reform (Miscellaneous Provisions) (Scotland) Act 1968, s.7. The Scottish Law Commission favours a generalised rule: Report No. 124 (1990), paras 8.15–8.18.

[65] 1992 S.C.L.R. 108.

[66] (1861) 4 Macq. 167; see discussion at paras 6.70–6.72 above, regarding negligently preparing a will.

[67] *Morgan Guaranty Trust Co. of New York v. Lothian R.C.*, 1995 S.C. 151.

[68] *Armour v. Glasgow Royal Infirmary*, 1909 S.C. 916.

[69] As in *MacDougall v. MacDougall's Exrs*, 1994 S.L.T. 1178 where they obtained a charter to make up title to a house on the basis of a will which (it was argued) they knew was invalid.

[70] Similarly in *MacDougall v MacDougall's Exrs*, 1989 S.L.T. 1178, where title passed through a charter given by the intestate's feudal superior, s.17 gave no protection to the recipient. The Scottish Law Commission proposes extending the scope of s.17 to protect everyone (not just purchasers) acquiring any assets bona fide from an executor: Report No. 124 (1990) paras 8.19–8.20.

interests of the executry estate. So he must derive no personal advantage at the expense of the estate.

It is quite acceptable in law for the executor to be a legatee **13.101** (though for a solicitor it breaches professional ethics). But there must be no transactions between himself (as an individual) and the executry: he may not purchase assets of the estate. It matters not that the price was fair: the conflict of interest is plain, and a beneficiary can have the sale set aside.[71]

Such transactions are allowed only if clearly authorised by the **13.102** testator or, subsequently, by all the affected beneficiaries. Authorisation need not be express, but by necessary implication: *e.g.* because the deceased must have known that the executor would face an unavoidable conflict of interest. Thus in *Sarris v. Clark*[72] the testator's wife had been his partner in managing a farm; she was one of his executors. To dispose of the farm the executors had necessarily to buy out her share: this was allowed. By contrast, in *Inglis v. Inglis*[73] the executor's deliberate self-selection as assignee of a farm tenancy (when there were other candidates) was impermissible. Fair price or not, he had to account for any profit he made from the transaction.

In *Inglis* the *auctor* principle was held to override section 16 of **13.103** the 1964 Act which governs transfer of the deceased's interest in a lease. The Scottish Law Commission proposes that it should no longer do so provided the interest in the lease is (failing agreement) fixed by the Lands Tribunal or Scottish Land Court.[74]

The executor can recoup his out-of-pocket expenses from the **13.104** estate. Beyond that he must act gratuitously: unless the will allows he cannot charge a fee, nor (since he benefits indirectly) can his partners if he is in a firm. He can however appoint an outsider to act as factor or solicitor.[75] The typical will, avoiding the problem, authorises executors to "appoint one of their number to act as solicitor, with his usual professional remuneration".

Executors make decisions by majority. Each is liable only for his **13.105** own acts and omissions, not his co-executors'—though blatant and continued neglect of executry affairs may itself be a breach of duty. If they wish to appoint agents, such as solicitors, they must choose them with care and should (however slightly) supervise their activities. But provided they do that they need not answer to beneficiaries for their agents' mistakes.

Beneficiaries are entitled to see accounts up to the end of the **13.106** executry detailing the executor's dealings with the estate. At that

---

[71] *Johnston v. Macfarlane*, 1987 S.L.T. 593; *Clark v. Clark's Exrs*, 1989 S.L.T. 665.
[72] 1995 S.L.T. 44.
[73] 1983 S.L.T. 437; 1983 S.C. 8.
[74] Report No. 124 (1990), paras 8.40–8.46.
[75] Trusts (Scotland) Act 1921, s.4(f).

stage he can also ask the beneficiaries to give him a discharge for his actions. It is not necessary, and they can still sue if a breach of duty is discovered, but by it they will acknowledge having duly received their entitlement from the estate.

**13.107** The beneficiaries cannot demand that the executor's solicitor account directly to them for alleged wrong payments. His duty is to account to the executor.[76]

**13.108** All these rules are primarily to protect the beneficiaries. A breach of duty cannot be challenged if they *all* authorise it in full knowledge of the facts. But, that aside, the obligation to account and to hand over legacies never lapses by prescription.

CESSATION OR LAPSE OF OFFICE

### Declinature

**13.109** An executor can decline appointment. A written minute is needed: either written on the will, in a separate document, or excerpted from minutes of a meeting where he attended and recorded his declinature. A sole executor should if possible first appoint an alternative and then resign, recording this in a combined minute of assumption and resignation.

**13.110** In principle executors-nominate are all entitled to be confirmed jointly. So if only some apply, the others' declinature must be produced along with the inventory, referred to in it and docketed to link the two. The initial writ for an executor-dative must likewise be accompanied by declinature from anyone with a preferable exclusive right to appointment, (say) an executor-nominate or a widow who takes the whole estate under prior rights.

**13.111** If the potential executor is mentally incapable his curator bonis[76a] can decline on his behalf. Otherwise a medical certificate stating his incapacity is needed. If he is abroad or untraceable the sheriff may still grant confirmation: but delays will result, a special warrant will be required, and possibly caution as well.

### Resignation

**13.112** An executor-nominate can resign. If acting alone he should first appoint a new executor. An executor-dative can neither resign nor assume new executors.[77]

### Removal

**13.113** An executor is regarded as a trustee and can be removed by the courts for the same reasons:

---

[76] *Loretto School Ltd. v. Macandrew & Jenkins*, above at n. 65.

[76a] To be termed guardian as from April 1, 2002: Adults with Incapacity (Scotland) Act 2000, Sched. 4.

[77] Succession (Scotland) Act 1964, s.20.

(1) If an executor is insane or physically or mentally disabled, or **13.114** disappears or leaves the U.K. for a continuous period of at least six months, beneficiaries or co-executors can ask the Court of Session or the sheriff court where confirmation was granted to remove him.[78]

(2) An executor cannot be removed merely because of a **13.115** potential conflict of interest with the estate: so he can be a beneficiary. But he can if he actively pursues his own interests against the estate (say by claiming legal rights) or if he causes deadlock by obstructing his co-executors.[79] Beneficiaries or co-executors should petition the Court of Session.

In many cases the other executors will continue the administra- **13.116** tion. But that will be inappropriate if there are none, or if financial problems are suspected: the court can then appoint a judicial factor to complete the executry.[80]

Confirmation makes a will probative but says nothing as to its **13.117** essential validity; the will can be reduced in the Court of Session if invalid. So can the confirmation itself, if it emerges that the wrong person was confirmed. In either case the original executor's appointment lapses.[81] However, the law protects those to whom the executor had sold heritage or securities over heritage: if they acquired in good faith and for value their title cannot be challenged on grounds of the reduction.[82]

An executor-dative's appointment can be recalled at any time **13.118** before confirmation. If a new executor seeks appointment (either to remove the existing one or after his death) he applies by initial writ. In cases of simple recall the applicant seeks the sheriff's consent by writing a minute on the original initial writ: *e.g.* if the initial writ was incorrect, one of several executors-dative has died or wishes to withdraw, or no executor-dative is required because a will has turned up.[83]

## Death

If one of several executors dies, the others continue in office **13.119** unless (rarely) they were expressly appointed to act jointly.[84] But if a sole executor dies the executry lapses. There are several ways to revive it and dispose of the estate: the choice depends on when the

---

[78] Trusts (Scotland) Act 1921, s.23.
[79] See *Meek v. Thompson's Exx*, 1991 G.W.D. 14–873: removal justified by combination of inordinate delay (18 years), conflict of interest, and being undischarged bankrupt.
[80] See Walker, *Judicial Factors*, pp. 33–37; Wilson & Duncan, 22.37 *et seq.*, 31.24.
[81] Currie, 19.72 *et seq.*
[82] Succession (Scotland) Act 1964, s.17.
[83] See Currie, 7.56.
[84] Executors (Scotland) Act 1900, s.4; McLaren, *Wills*, Vol. II, p. 898.

lapse occurs. One must envisage four people: an original deceased A, his executor B (who has died), B's own executor C, and an executor D who concludes A's executry.

**13.120** (1) Suppose B had confirmed to A's property. *His* executor C, by noting it in B's inventory, can recover it and transfer it to a beneficiary, anyone chosen by the beneficiary, or someone entitled to carry on the executry administration.[85] This covers most cases, but not all. If A's estate requires further administration, it needs a new executor D; mere noting does not allow C to do it. Moreover a beneficiary cannot compel C to note and transfer. ((2) answers each problem.)

**13.121** (2) Alternatively a new executor D is confirmed directly to A's estate: *confirmation ad non executa*.[86] He *may* undertake the administration. He can be anyone who has a beneficial interest in the estate: a legatee, heir on intestacy, or their executor representing their claim. (So he *may* coincidentally be the same person as C.) This procedure is also available if B did not die but was merely incapacitated.

**13.122** (3) If B omitted some of A's assets from his confirmation, a new executor obtains confirmation *ad omissa* to them. He is chosen as in (2), but procedure differs: there will be fresh confirmation dues and IHT because B did not report the items.

**13.123** (4) If B was appointed but died before confirmation, a new executor must confirm to A's estate. The rules are similar to (3).

**13.124** (5) A beneficiary can petition the Court of Session to transfer assets directly to him if the executor through death or incapacity failed to do so.[87] Being relatively costly this is a last resort.

There is the complication that where A died before the 1964 Act the old law governs how his estate is wound up.[88] In that event the above procedures will not apply to heritage: the heir may have to make up title by "service".

**13.125** It is worth noting how the rules for *lapsed testamentary trusts* differ. (1) and (5) both apply to trustees. (2) applies only if the last trustee had also been confirmed executor. Otherwise there are two options if further trust administration is needed:

(a) to ask the court to appoint a new trustee.[89]

(b) the last trustee's heir inherits the office if the trust deed says so. He is then entitled to be "served heir of

---

[85] Executors (Scotland) Act 1900, s.6.
[86] Executors (Scotland) Act 1900, s.7.
[87] Trusts (Scotland) Act 1921, s.24.
[88] Succession (Scotland) Act 1964, s.37(1)(d). See McDonald, *Manual*, paras 32.8–32.13; Meston, pp. 105–107.
[89] Trusts (Scotland) Act 1921, s.22; Wilson & Duncan, Chap. 21, 22.02 *et seq.*

provision in trust"—a quaint relic of pre-1964 procedure.[90]

**Further reading**

Currie, *Confirmation of Executors, passim,* and Forms in Supplement.

G.L. Gretton, "Trust and Executry Conveyancing" (1987) 32 J.L.S. 111.

Halliday, *Conveyancing Law & Practice*, Vol. IV.

McDonald, *Conveyancing Manual*, Chap. 31.

Meston, *The Succession (Scotland) Act 1964*, Chap. 8.

Morley, *Accounting*, Chaps 1, 2.

Wilson & Duncan, *Trusts, Trustees and Executors*, Chaps 28–32.

Law Society of Scotland Post-Qualifying Legal Education papers regularly touch on substantive law and taxation as well as executry practice. They included detailed case studies. Among recent articles on executries:

N.R. Allan: "Conveyancing" (1981), pp. 34–43.

A.M.C. Dalgleish: "Insurance Policies" (1988), pp. 83–100.

C. Glasse: "Commissary Considerations" (1986), pp. 72–211.

W. Jones: "Commissary Considerations" (1988), pp. 65–82.

C.B. Miller: "Executry Conveyancing" (1988), pp. 5–29.

"Registration of Death; Procedure on Sudden Death" (1981), pp. 7–13.

---

[90] Revived by Law Reform (Miscellaneous Provisions) (Scotland) Act 1980, s.6. But the "heir" is identified under the 1964 Act as the law in force when the trustee dies: *MacMillan, Petr*, 1987 S.L.T. (Sh. Ct) 50.

# CHAPTER 14

# PRIVATE INTERNATIONAL LAW

## INTRODUCTION

**14.01** Problems of private international law or "conflict of laws" arise commonly in practice. If a person, whether a Scot or a foreigner, dies leaving property in Scotland, the Scottish courts may in various circumstances have to decide to what extent foreign law governs succession to his estate. Foreign law may be relevant in the administration of the estate and in ascertaining to whom it passes under rules of intestate succession. If a will was made, questions may arise of the deceased's capacity to test; the formal validity of its execution or its revocation; the essential validity of its provisions, for instance as regards rules of public policy; and the construction to be placed on those provisions. Certain fundamental rules should be borne in mind in this context.

## GENERAL ASPECTS

### Domicile

**14.02** The concept of domicile is fundamental to questions of choice of law. In essence it denotes "a legal relationship between a person and a place governed by a single system of law. The central idea is that it is the place where [he] has made his home."[1] The concept is difficult to define precisely—a permanent physical dwelling is not required. Every person must have a domicile; he may only have one at any one time. This may be acquired by birth—a domicile of origin—or by choice; acquisition of a domicile of choice requires actual residence but also a settled intention to change one's permanent home. In most questions of succession the domicile at date of death is relevant.

---

[1] Anton, p. 125; see generally at pp. 124–146. For possible changes see Scot. Law Comm. Report on Domicile (No. 107, 1987); (on domicile of children) Report on Family Law (No. 135, 1992) paras 17.12–17.13; E. Crawford, *Private International Law* (1998), 6.26–6.27.

A child derives its domicile from its father or (in some cases **14.03** where the child is illegitimate, the father dead, or the parents separated) its mother: a domicile of dependence. A child aged over 16[2] can acquire its own domicile. Before 1974 a woman automatically took her husband's domicile on marriage, but no longer.[3]

Note that domicile has a wider meaning for inheritance tax **14.04** purposes, extending to residence in the United Kingdom in 17 out of the previous 20 years of assessment.[4]

## Characterisation

Characterisation of a legal question is the process of determining **14.05** the juridical category into which it falls.[5] This will decide the appropriate class of conflict of law rule to apply. For instance, are presumptions of death substantive or procedural for purposes of private international law? Is property moveable or immoveable? The problem arises because different legal systems' conflict of law rules themselves conflict: they classify such questions differently.

The general principle is to characterise from the standpoint of **14.06** the *lex fori*, the place where the question is being litigated; but in doing so account is taken of any potentially relevant rules of foreign law in the context of their own legal system. So Scots law will decide whether a question in a Scottish executry is a matter of executry administration or of rights of succession.

However, this must be qualified in three respects. **14.07**

(1) Legislation may dictate how a rule is to be characterised. So, **14.08** section 3 of the Wills Act 1963 provides that where a law in force outside the United Kingdom falls to be applied in relation to a will, any requirement of that law whereby special formalities are to be observed by testators answering a particular description, or witnesses to the execution of a will are to possess certain qualifications, shall be treated as a formal requirement whatever that law says to the contrary.

(2) The *lex situs*—the law of the place where the property is **14.09** located—determines whether property is moveable or immoveable.[6] Thus in *Macdonald v. Macdonald*,[7] where a domiciled Scotsman died leaving land in various Canadian provinces, it was held that because land was immoveable according to their law, it was not subject to Scottish legal rights over moveable estate.

Classification as moveable or immoveable is based, broadly speaking, on the physical nature of the property; it is distinct from

---

[2] Age of Legal Capacity (Scotland) Act 1991, s.7.
[3] Domicile and Matrimonial Proceedings Act 1973, ss.1, 3, 4.
[4] IHTA 1984, s.267.
[5] See generally Anton, pp. 65–72; Morris, pp. 416–423.
[6] See Anton, pp. 597–601.
[7] 1932 S.C. (H.L.) 79. See also *Lashley v. Hog* (1804) 4 Pat. App. 581.

the internal rules of classification as heritable and moveable (in Scots law) or real and personal (in English law) which a legal system applies in disputes where no foreign element arises. So, in English law, leases are personal for domestic purposes but immoveable in international law; debts secured on land, in Scots law, are moveable for most purposes but probably immoveable in international law.

Similarly the doctrine of conversion, whereby heritable property devolves *as if* moveable where the deceased intended its conversion (*e.g.* by selling it and giving the beneficiaries the cash proceeds), does not alter its immoveable status in international law. Take *Re Berchtold*[8]: a domiciled Hungarian owned a house in England; it was immoveable under English choice of law rules; English internal law applied; by its rule of conversion the house then devolved as if personal.

**14.10**   When the Crown or a foreign government takes as *ultimus haeres* in the absence of other beneficiaries, is that (a) a true right of succession or (b) an instance of its right to all ownerless property—*bona vacantia*—situated within the state?[9] If the former, only immoveables may fall to the Crown, moveables going to the state where the deceased was domiciled; if the latter, the Crown takes both. Some states favour (a), others (b). For United Kingdom purposes both Scotland and England follow (b) (despite the term *ultimus haeres*): the Crown's claim is caduciary (*i.e.* by way of lapse), arising from the royal prerogative by failure of the normal succession.

**14.11**   In international law the position is less clear. The problem arises when a domiciled foreigner leaves moveables in Britain which his own government claims. In England, *Re Maldonado*[10] allowed the claim to be characterised under the foreign law: as that law applied (a), the foreign government inherited; had (b) applied, the British Crown would have obtained the items. In Scotland the point has not arisen, though in *Goold Stuart's Trs v. McPhail*[11] it was implied that *Maldonado* might be followed if it did. If so this would overturn current Scots practice, which favours approach (b). The Scottish Law Commission, which initially recommended that Scots law adopt (a) for all purposes now proposes no change.[12]

**14.12**   Numerous cases show how important characterisation is.

**14.13**   (1) Does the claim concern executry administration or rights of succession? If the former, the *lex fori*—as the law of the place where administration is taking place—applies; if the latter the *lex*

---

[8] [1923] 1 Ch. 192.
[9] Anton, pp. 678–680; McMillan, pp. 10–13.
[10] [1954] P. 233.
[11] 1947 S.L.T. 221.
[12] Memorandum No. 71, paras 6.8–6.13; Report No. 124, para. 10.10.

*situs* or *lex domicilii*[13] depending whether the rights involve immoveables or moveable property. The *lex fori* decides the initial question of characterisation (*Scottish National Orchestra Society Ltd. v. Thomson's Exr*[14]).

(2) Is the question one of succession or matrimonial property? If **14.14** the latter, the spouses' *lex domicilii* as at marriage—not death—will apply. This problem has arisen in two contexts: legal rights and revocation of wills. Since *Lashley v. Hog*[15] Scots law has treated legal rights arising on the death of a spouse or parent as a right of succession. By contrast, if proprietary rights arise on marriage—by an express marriage contract or under a regime of community of spouses' property—English and South African law[16] characterise the matter as one of matrimonial property; so, probably, will Scots law.[17] Where it is argued that a will has been revoked by marriage (*e.g.* under English law) Scots and English courts[18] both refer the question to the domiciliary law at date of marriage: unlike South Africa[19] we do not explicitly characterise the issue as concerning matrimonial property, but the result is the same.

(3) Are rules of evidence or substantive rights of succession at **14.15** issue? If the former, the *lex fori* applies exclusively and foreign rules are ignored. In *Re Cohn*[20] two domiciled Germans were killed in a bomb blast in London: their moveable property devolved under German law. English law presumed that the elder died first; the German Civil Code, that they died simultaneously. Uthwatt J., considering the German rule in the context of the Code, held that it was substantive rather than merely procedural, and thus must be given effect by the English courts.

### Renvoi

Having characterised the problem the Scots courts may, follow- **14.16** ing Scots choice of law rules, decide that a foreign law applies. Suppose that that law, under its own—different—choice of law rules, does not consider its own internal rules applicable but transmits the question to a third legal system or remits it back to Scots law. For instance, Scots law holds that the law of the deceased's domicile applies, but that law refers the question to the law of his nationality. That is the problem of *renvoi*.[21]

---

[13] Law of the deceased's place of domicile.
[14] 1969 S.L.T. 325.
[15] (1804) 4 Pat. 581.
[16] Corbett, pp. 617–620; Morris, p. 370.
[17] Anton, pp. 573–575, 584–586, 672–673.
[18] Anton, pp. 694–695; Morris, p. 360; *Westerman's Exr v. Schwab* (1905) 8 F. 132.
[19] Corbett, pp. 618–620; *Pitluk v. Gavendo*, 1955 (2) S.A. 573 (T).
[20] [1945] Ch. 5.
[21] Anton, pp. 85–94.

**14.17**    Several solutions are possible. The simplest is for the Scots
courts to apply only the *internal* law of the foreign legal system:
thus ignoring its choice of law rules and preventing *renvoi*. This is
the purpose of the provision in section 1 of the Wills Act 1963 that
a will is treated as properly executed if its execution conformed to
the internal law in force in, *inter alia*, the territory where it was
executed.

**14.18**    Alternatively the courts may accept the foreign choice of law and
its *renvoi* back to Scots law. Or they may apply the whole foreign
law including its internal rules. There is no uniform doctrine.[22]

### Incidental questions

**14.19**    Once the courts have decided to apply a foreign law in a
question of succession, a subsidiary issue may then emerge concerning some other area of law: for instance, a beneficiary's
legitimacy. What legal system governs that? Logically the foreign *or*
the Scots choice of law rules could decide, but again there is no
universal principle.

**14.20**    In deciding legitimacy the Scots courts usually apply the parents'
domiciliary law as at the date of the child's birth, except for
succession to heritage where legitimacy under the *lex situs* is also
required.[23]

INTESTATE SUCCESSION

### General

**14.21**    The general rule is that intestate succession to immoveables is
governed by the *lex situs*, to moveables by the law of the deceased's
last domicile.[24] Characterisation as moveable or immoveable is
made by the *lex situs*.[25]

**14.22**    The Succession (Scotland) Act 1964 largely abolished the distinction between heritable and moveable property in succession:
henceforth heritage devolves in the same way as moveables. The
old distinction is preserved for purposes of legal rights and private
international law.[26] Immoveables therefore do not become moveables for these purposes; they merely devolve as if moveable in
ordinary domestic Scots questions. In particular, immoveables still
devolve by the *lex situs*, not the *lex ultimi domicilii*.

---

[22] *Re Annesley* [1926] Ch. 692; *Re Ross* [1930] 1 Ch. 377.
[23] *Fenton v. Livingstone* (1859) 3 Macq. 497; Anton, pp. 484–492.
[24] The *lex ultimi domicilii*. Anton, pp. 675–676.
[25] *Macdonald v. Macdonald*, 1932 S.C. (H.L.) 79.
[26] Succession (Scotland) Act 1964, ss.1 and 37(2).

## Legal rights

**14.23** Scots law treats legal rights as rights of succession; they are indefeasible except by *inter vivos* disposition and so arise on both testacy and intestacy.

**14.24** The existence, nature and extent of legal rights[27] over moveables is governed by the *lex domicilii*. So *jus relictae, jus relicti* and legitim may be claimed out of the deceased's moveable property, wherever situated, if he died domiciled in Scotland. Conversely moveables in Scotland belonging to a domiciled foreigner are subject to any appropriate foreign legal rights.

**14.25** Rights over immoveables are governed by the *lex situs*; since such rights were abolished in Scots law in 1964 the point will only arise in connection with analogous rights recognised by foreign legal systems over immoveables situated outwith Scotland.

**14.26** Note that English law recognises no such legal rights. Payments may be made out of the deceased's estate under the Inheritance (Provision for Family and Dependants) Act 1975 to dependants of the deceased for whom he has not made reasonable provision: but the deceased must have been domiciled in England (so immoveables in England belonging to a domiciled Scot are not affected); and payments are at the discretion of the High Court (so the Scots courts apparently could not make payments out of the moveables in Scotland of a domiciled Englishman).

## Prior rights

**14.27** Again the *lex domicilii* and *lex situs* apply in respect of moveables and immoveables respectively. The existence of three types of prior rights makes for complexity[28]:

**14.28** (1) In respect of the deceased spouse's interest in a dwelling-house: this (being immoveable) applies to dwelling-houses situated in Scotland but not abroad, whatever the deceased's domicile. Where a cash sum is given in lieu, this is a surrogate for the house and so probably to be treated as immoveable likewise.

**14.29** (2) In respect of furniture and plenishings: though these are moveable, the right *may* only apply if they are in a Scottish house. The answer is unclear and depends on how one interprets section 8 of the 1964 Act.

**14.30** (3) Cash sum: this is borne by and paid out of heritage and moveables in proportion to their relative values. In the case of a domiciled Scot, his heritage in Scotland and his moveables everywhere are affected. If the deceased was domiciled elsewhere, only his heritage in Scotland is affected: only that is subject to Scots law,

---

[27] Anton, pp. 670–674.
[28] Meston, pp. 116–117, Leslie, 1988 S.L.T. (News) 105.

so it bears the whole cash sum however large the rest of his estate may be; immoveables outwith Scotland and moveables everywhere are disregarded.

**Law reform**

**14.31** The current rules have been widely criticised. Their *raison d'être*—the need for each state to control ownership of its land lest its dignity and independence be threatened—is suspect; their principles outdated, since in many legal systems the *lex domicilii* governs both moveables and immoveables; and their effects arbitrary, since relatives' succession rights differ greatly depending on the chance of where property is located. Consequently the Scottish Law Commission advocated[29] that both moveables and immoveables devolve according to the law of the deceased's last domicile, in line with its proposed abolition of the heritable-moveable distinction in domestic Scots law.

TESTATE SUCCESSION[30]

**Capacity**

**14.32** Capacity to make a will may depend on age, understanding, or status (such as marriage or legitimacy). Capacity to make a will of moveables is governed by the domiciliary law at the time the will is made; of immoveables, by the *lex situs*. The Scottish Law Commission thinks[31] that section 28 of the Succession (Scotland) Act 1964, by which minors have "the like capacity to test" on heritage as moveables, might suggest that minors' capacity is always judged by their domiciliary law; it is hard to see how this stands with the express preservation (by section 37(2)) of existing choice of law rules.

**14.33** The moveable-immoveable distinction has been widely questioned, and again the Commission advocates that the *lex domicilii* govern wills of both types of property.[32]

**14.34** Capacity of a legatee to take under a will is judged by his, rather than the testator's, domiciliary law: presumably at the date of the testator's death.[33]

---

[29] Memorandum No. 71, paras 6.2–6.7. The Hague Conference on Private International Law later issued a draft Convention on Succession (Oct. 1988); to avoid overlap the Scot. Law Comm. Report omitted most of the points considered in Memorandum No. 71.

[30] See generally Anton, pp. 680–699.

[31] Memorandum No. 71, para. 6.14.

[32] Memorandum No. 71, para. 6.14; Report No. 124, para. 10.4.

[33] Anton, pp. 664–665; Corbett, pp. 640–641.

## Formal validity

### (a) The common law

In *Purvis's Trs v. Purvis's Exrs*[34] it was held that a will of **14.35** moveables was valid if executed according to the law of the place of execution or that of the testator's domicile. This might be the domicile at the date of execution, validity being unaffected by a later change of domicile, or—as was confirmed in *Chisholm v. Chisholm*[35]—at date of death. English law accepted only the last. The Wills Act 1861, of importance in England, was little used in Scotland because of the breadth of the Scots rules. Similar rules governed wills of heritage—not permitted at common law—after the Titles to Land Consolidation (Scotland) Act 1868 allowed their execution in the same way as wills of moveables.

### (b) The Wills Act 1963

The Wills Act 1963 implemented the 1961 Hague Convention on **14.36** Conflicts of Laws relating to the form of testamentary dispositions and other calls for reform. By its main provisions:

(1) A will is treated as properly executed if (section 1) its **14.37** execution conformed to the internal law of either (a) the territory where it was executed, (b) the territory of the testator's domicile or habitual residence at the time of its execution or his death, or (c) a state of which he was a national at either time; or (section 2(1)(b)) in the case of wills of immoveables only, the territory where the property was situated.

(2) A will executed on board a vessel or aircraft is treated as **14.38** properly executed if its execution conformed to the internal law of the territory with which, having regard to registration and other relevant circumstances, the vessel or aircraft was most closely connected (section 2(1)(a)).

(3) A will exercising a power of appointment is properly **14.39** executed if its execution conforms to the law governing the essential validity of the power: despite its failure to comply with formal requirements specified in the instrument creating the power (sections 2(1)(d) and (2)).

(4) Conformity to a law is judged by its requirements at the time **14.40** of execution, but account is taken of subsequent changes if they enable the will to be treated as properly executed (section 6(2)).

(5) If a state or territory has more than one legal system—as **14.41** does the United Kingdom—the system applicable is that indicated by the state's rules or, failing that, with which the testator was most closely connected at the time in question (section 6(3)).

---

[34] (1861) 23 D. 812.
[35] 1949 S.C. 434.

*(c) The Administration of Justice Act 1982*

**14.42**    The Act gives effect *inter alia* to the 1973 Convention providing a Uniform Law on the Form of an International Will. Schedule 2 to the Act, which sets out the Annex to the Convention, establishes a new form of "international will". Such a will, apart from being valid for purposes of internal Scots law alongside existing methods of execution, will be recognised in any state which has signed and ratified the Convention, and may be recognised in other countries whose choice of law rules so permit. The place of execution is irrelevant. The will need not be "international" in, say, the sense of involving a foreign testator or foreign property.

**14.43**    Schedule 2 stipulates the formalities to be followed by such a will. Invalidity as an international will does not affect validity as a will of another kind, *e.g.* under domestic Scots law.

**Essential validity**

**14.44**    Rules of essential validity must be distinguished from those of formal validity. The Wills Act 1963 will, of course, only apply to the latter. *Irving v. Snow*[36] illustrates the contrast. A will was notarially executed in Carlisle by a solicitor on behalf of a domiciled Scot; under the will the solicitor was entitled as executor to charge for his services. Such execution would have been formally invalid had it happened in Scotland, but was valid by English law which Scots law accepted as the *lex loci actus*. Quite separate was the question whether Scots law would give effect to a bequest in a will: the solicitor's charges might still be struck down under the principle that a notary must not take an interest under a will he executes.

**14.45**    The essential validity of a will of immoveables is governed by the *lex situs*; of a will of moveables, by the law of the testator's last domicile. Again the Scottish Law Commission proposed that the domiciliary law should apply to both.[37] In some cases the validity of a legacy is instead judged by the law of the place where it is to take effect.[38]

**14.46**    The law of the testator's last domicile will govern whether a legatee is required to elect between a legacy and other benefits such as legal rights. This is the rule even if those benefits concern immoveables situated abroad. See, for instance, *Brown's Trs v. Gregson*[39]: a will purported to create a trust over Argentine land; under Argentine law the trust was invalid and the beneficiaries took the land as outright owners; as the legacy was null by the *lex situs* Scots law did not require election.

---

[36] 1956 S.C. 257.
[37] Memorandum No. 71, para. 6.15.
[38] Anton, pp. 688–691.
[39] 1920 S.C. (H.L.) 87.

## Construction

As a general principle a will must be construed according to the **14.47** intention of the testator.[40] The courts must ascertain by which legal system he intended its provisions to be construed. The tendency is to presume that a will of moveables is to be construed by the testator's domiciliary law. This is determined as at the date of the will, not of the testator's death; under section 4 of the Wills Act 1963 the construction of a will is not altered by reason of any subsequent change of domicile. The presumption may be rebutted by circumstances pointing to a different intention, such as the location of the property and the technical legal terms used in the deed.

Where the will is of immoveables, the Scots courts tend to **14.48** construe according to the *lex situs*. Thus in *Mitchell and Baxter v. Davies*,[41] where a domiciled Englishwoman disposed of heritage in Scotland by a deed which used Scots legal terms, these factors displaced the usual presumption of construction by the domiciliary law. Again the rule is not conclusive: use of English legal forms may—even in respect of Scottish heritage—lead to construction by English law.[42]

Where foreign property is owned jointly by the testator and **14.49** others, the title may be construed according to the foreign law. Thus shares in an English company will be joint property, with the deceased's portion passing to the survivor, whereas under Scots rules of construction it would pass as common property to the deceased's estate: *Connell's Trs v. Connell's Trs*.[43] The Scottish Law Commission point out[44] that this will scarcely square with the deceased's intention, which would be given better effect by application of Scots law as the domiciliary law.

What legal system decides who the "issue" or "heirs" are? This **14.50** matters partly because the concept of illegitimacy varies between countries. Issue are identified under the law of the testator's domicile (even if they are someone else's issue); heirs, by contrast, by the law of the domicile of the person whose heir they are.[45]

## Revocation

There is little Scottish authority on questions whether a will has **14.51** been validly revoked. The position may vary according to the method used.[46]

---

[40] *S.N.O. Society Ltd. v. Thomson's Exr*, 1969 S.L.T. 325.
[41] (1875) 3 R. 208.
[42] *Studd v. Cook* (1883) 10 R. (H.L.) 53.
[43] (1886) 13 R. 1175.
[44] Memorandum No. 71, paras 6.17–6.22; Report No. 124, paras 10.5–10.9.
[45] *Smith's Trs v. Macpherson*, 1926 S.C. 983; *Allan Petr*, 1991 S.L.T. 203. See Crawford, 1994 S.L.T. (News) 225.
[46] See Morris, pp. 358–360.

**14.52** (1) Revocation by later will or codicil: the usual tests will decide the validity of the second deed. In addition, under section 2(1)(c) of the Wills Act 1963, a will (so far as it revokes a will or provision in a will) is also treated as properly executed if its execution conforms to any law by reference to which the revoked will or provision is so treated. Note too that where revocation is by implication, insofar as inconsistent with the earlier will, the extent of revocation must be determined by construing according to the *lex domicilii* at date of execution.

**14.53** (2) Revocation by destruction or deletion: probably the *lex domicilii* at date of revocation applies, but there is no United Kingdom authority. It would be odd if a later change of domicile revived the will. The issue arises because some legal systems prescribe formalities for destruction, such as the testator being present.

**14.54** (3) Revocation by operation of law: this may be by marriage (as in English law) or by the birth of a child (Scots law). Probably the rule in (2) applies. The only Scots authority, *Westerman's Exr v. Schwab*,[47] concerned the effect on an English spinster's will of her later marriage to a domiciled Scotsman: taking the spouses' (and therefore at that time the husband's) domicile at date of marriage to be the criterion the court held that the will was not revoked. In fact that is probably a question, not of succession, but matrimonial property (and English law so regards it); if so the *lex domicilii* applies to wills of any property, both moveables and immoveables.

**Administration of estates**[48]

*(a) Appointment of executor*

**14.55** (1) *Right to appointment.* In Scotland a deceased's estate is administered by an executor, whose title to ingather and deal with the property derives from a grant of confirmation by the sheriff court. While the English system of a grant of probate or letters of administration is similar, many foreign legal systems are radically different. The estate may pass directly to heirs, or through the medium of a public administrator; where there is an office of executor his role may be merely to advise the heirs.

The Scots courts can grant confirmation only if the deceased left property located in Scotland. His domicile determines which sheriff court makes the grant.[49]

By contrast, the law of the deceased's last domicile determines who has the right to be confirmed executor.[50] It will be necessary to

---

[47] (1905) 8 F. 132.
[48] See generally Anton, pp. 647–666.
[49] See para. 13.04.
[50] *Marchioness of Hastings v. Marquess of Hastings' Exrs* (1852) 14 D. 489.

aver the foreign law, prove his entitlement, and also the validity of any will from which it derives.[51] It is unnecessary to have previously obtained a grant of administration in the country of domicile. Nor need the executor reside in Scotland: he may grant someone resident here a power of attorney to seek confirmation in his name and administer the estate on his behalf.

The exception is an executor-creditor. He is regarded as doing diligence in order to realise the estate for the benefit of the deceased's creditors. Consequently Scots law determines who is entitled to be appointed.

(2) *Recognition of foreign appointments.* It is obviously convenient **14.56** for the person entitled to administration under the domiciliary law to deal with the whole estate wherever situated. But in principle confirmation gives no title to administer property outwith Scotland, and a separate grant of confirmation must be sought afresh within each jurisdiction where property is located.

The major exception concerns England and Wales and Northern Ireland.[52] Under the Administration of Estates Act 1971 a grant of confirmation in Scotland, stating the deceased's Scottish domicile, is automatically treated in England and Wales and Northern Ireland as a grant of representation; and an English or Northern Irish grant of representation has the same effect in Scotland as a grant of confirmation.

The 1971 Act only applies if the deceased was domiciled (if outside Scotland) in England, Wales or Northern Ireland. Otherwise a grant of representation in respect of property there will not dispense with the need to obtain separate confirmation in Scotland. The Act does not extend to the Channel Islands or the Isle of Man. Resealing is possible of grants of representation made in Commonwealth countries.[53]

### (b) Administration

Questions of executry administration (as opposed to rights of **14.57** inheritance) are governed by the law of the country where the administration takes place; the deceased's domicile is irrelevant. Thus Scots law will govern the rights and duties of executors in a Scottish executry, such as their duty to find caution. It also dictates the order of priority in which they pay the deceased's debts.

These points were illustrated in the complex case of *Scottish* **14.58** *National Orchestra Society Ltd. v. Thomson's Exr.*[54] The testatrix, born in Scotland, made a will in Sweden while separated from her

---

[51] Currie, 2.34 *et seq.*
[52] Currie, 14.22 *et seq.*, Chap. 15.
[53] Colonial Probates Act 1892. See Currie, Chap. 15.
[54] 1969 S.L.T. 325.

Canadian husband. Though she was thus then domiciled in Canada, all the circumstances pointed to it being her intention that Scots law should govern the construction of the will (and in particular a legacy "free of Government duties"). She died domiciled in Sweden leaving property in Sweden and Scotland, to which separate executors or administrators were appointed. Swedish law decided who the beneficiaries were. Scots law decided whether the Scottish executor could remit Swedish inheritance tax to the Swedish administrator: under normal rules he could not (foreign taxes are unenforceable in Scotland), but this case was an exception, since until he did so he could not fulfil his duty to pay the legatees.

**Further reading**

A.E. Anton, "The Formal Validity of Wills", 1958 S.L.T. (News) 217.

M. Brandon, "U.K. Accession to the Wills Conventions" (1983) 32 I.C.L.Q. 742.

R.D. Leslie, "Prior Rights in Succession: the International Dimension", 1988 S.L.T. (News) 105.

M.C. Meston, "Prior Rights in Scottish Heritage" (1967) 12 J.L.S. 401.

J.H.C. Morris, "Intestate Succession to Land in the Conflict of Laws" (1969) 85 L.Q.R. 339.

C. Robertson, "International Succession Law" (1989) 34 J.L.S. 377.

"The Wills Act 1963", 1963 S.L.T. (News) 161 and (1964) 9 J.L.S. 75.

# CHAPTER 15

# LAW REFORM

## INTRODUCTION

The Scottish Law Commission issued its Report on Succession (Scot. Law Com. No. 124) in January 1990, with a draft Bill annexed. This chapter sets out its main proposals, which seem unlikely to be enacted in the near future. To assist cross-reference, headings contain the relevant paragraph numbers. References marked [ ] are to the clauses in the draft Bill.

## DEATH AND SURVIVORSHIP

**Paragraph 1.27**

To be able to inherit property from the deceased, a beneficiary **15.01** must survive him for at least five days from the beginning of the day on which the deceased died. This applies to testate and intestate succession, legal shares, special destinations, *mortis causa* donations, and nominations. Otherwise he is deemed to have predeceased the deceased, as regards any third person's right to inherit that property. However, a testator is permitted to stipulate a longer or shorter period of survivance. (The latter is best avoided: the effect may be that the beneficiary, while surviving for the purpose of inheriting under the testator's will, "predeceases" him for purposes of legal shares.) [Clause 28.]

A presumption of survivorship will rarely now be needed; the above rule will cover the typical "common calamity". But it will not deal with every case; so there is a new, simplified, presumption. Where two or more persons die in such circumstances that it cannot be established whether either survived the other for five days (or any other period required under a will), each person's estate is disposed of as if the other(s) predeceased [clause 28(4)].

The five-day rule is concerned with the order in which A (a beneficiary) and B (someone from whom he inherits) die. By contrast, property may pass directly to either A or B from a third person, C, depending on who lives longer. This may occur (say) under a will (by a destination-over) or under life assurance. In this case the five-day rule will not apply. If A and B die simultaneously, or the order is uncertain, the property is divided equally between the estates of A and B [clause 28(5)].

Clause 28(4) and (5) both apply *unless* the will (or other document regulating the transfer) makes some other provision for the event.

The new rules will apply to all deaths occurring after the proposed Act comes into force. If it is uncertain whether someone died before or after that date, he will be deemed to have died afterwards [clause 34(1), (2)].

### ENTITLEMENT TO INHERIT

#### FORFEITURE

**Paragraph 2.18**

15.02   The Parricide Act 1594 will be repealed. A new forfeiture rule will apply when someone has been convicted of murder or culpable homicide in the United Kingdom, Channel Islands or Isle of Man (or of an analogous crime elsewhere) and the conviction is no longer open to appeal. In that case the killer:

> (a) automatically forfeits any rights to inherit from his victim, or to property which was previously held in trust and which would have gone to him on the victim's death, or to property which he received from the victim by a *mortis causa* donation;
>
> (b) is deemed for this purpose not to have survived the victim.

So the killer's issue, or alternative beneficiaries under the victim's will, can inherit in his place. For other purposes—such as the disposal of his own estate—the killer is of course still alive [clause 19, Schedule 2].

The common law rules of public policy are not repealed, and will govern cases where the killer has not been convicted under the above criteria.

The civil courts may grant relief from statutory or common law forfeiture. The time limit will be six months after the conviction ceases to be appealable; where there is no conviction there is no time limit. Relief may now be complete or partial [clause 20].

**Paragraph 2.23**

15.03   Judicial separation of spouses will no longer affect their right to inherit from each other. Section 6 of the Conjugal Rights (Scotland) Amendment Act 1861 will be repealed, but existing decrees of separation will remain effective [Schedule 2].

ADOPTION

**Paragraph 2.24**

Sections 23 and 24 of the 1964 Act, together with section 5 of **15.04**
the Law Reform (Miscellaneous Provisions) (Scotland) Act 1966,
will be re-enacted as section 39A of the Adoption (Scotland) Act
1978. Two minor amendments are to be made. To answer previous
doubts about the scope of section 23A, it will now clearly cover
references in deeds to "issue". Section 24(1A), which dealt with the
relative seniority of adopted children, is to be repealed.

PAYMENT OF DEBTS

**Paragraph 3.09**

The draft Bill abolishes the right of the deceased's family to **15.05**
claim an allowance for mourning expenses. Similarly the right to
aliment from his estate disappears [clauses 25–27].

**Paragraph 3.37**

Anyone succeeding to property under a special destination will **15.06**
be personally liable for the previous owner's debts, up to the value
of the property when the owner died. Thus his own assets may be
subject to diligence by the previous owner's creditors. This reverses
the effect of *Barclay's Bank v. McGreish*.[1] He can avoid liability by
disclaiming his right to the property [clause 29(6)].

INTESTATE SUCCESSION

**Paragraph 4.01**

There are substantial changes. To summarise: prior rights in **15.07**
their current form disappear; the surviving spouse gets more
extensive rights in the intestate estate; the rules for dividing the
"free estate" remain largely unchanged. Legal rights of spouse and
issue are renamed and re-shaped as a "legal share"; they become
primarily a means to protect against disinheritance by a testator,
and cease to provide (as at present) a means for dividing up the
intestate estate after prior rights and before the free estate.

**The intestate estate**

The relevant estate is the "net intestate estate": this is any "net **15.08**
estate" which is not disposed of by will or special destination. Legal
shares are not deducted first. The "net estate" is the deceased's

---

[1] 1983 S.L.T. 344. *McGreish* has since been overruled: *Fleming's Tr. v. Fleming*, 2000
S.L.T. 406.

estate less his debts (other than IHT) and funeral expenses [clause 36(1)].

IHT and expenses of administration will thus be deducted from the estate *after* ascertaining its value and division for purposes of intestacy and legal share. As regards IHT, the Inheritance Tax Act 1984 will, as before, govern its incidence on the assets of the estate. Expenses of administration will fall on the assets in the intestate estate and residue, implicitly pro rata in accordance with their values; then on the legal shares and general legacies pro rata; lastly on special legacies [clauses 10, 36(5)].

The estate is valued at the date of death; but where estate is realised in ordinary course and without due delay after the death, the realised value is used, except insofar as the estate could be accurately valued as at the date of death. This simply aims to make the existing common law explicit [clause 24].

**Rights of spouse and issue**

15.09    Where the deceased is survived by a spouse and no issue (or vice versa), the spouse or issue (respectively) inherit the whole intestate estate. If both spouse and issue survive, the spouse takes the first £100,000 and—if applicable—half the excess estate over that figure; the issue take the other half of the excess. The Secretary of State will have power to raise or lower the figure by statutory instrument [clauses 1(2), (3)].

Thus prior rights are replaced by a blanket cash sum. But the surviving spouse has a new right, reminiscent of the old prior right under section 8 of the 1964 Act, but wider. Suppose she is entitled to a share of intestate estate—or to residue under the deceased's will—which includes his interest in the matrimonial home and furnishings. In that event she will have the option to acquire that interest in satisfaction (in whole or in part) of her entitlement; she can do so even if the interest exceeds her entitlement, provided she pays the estate the difference between the two figures. "Matrimonial home" is wider than the section 8 "dwelling-house" test: it clearly includes caravans and other structures (there was doubt under section 8), and the home may have been a family residence even if the surviving spouse was not ordinarily resident in it at the date when the deceased died.[2] The exclusion from section 8 of certain tenancies, property used for trade, and (as regards contents) business assets and heirlooms is broadly reproduced [clause 23].

The right to the matrimonial home is not automatic. The surviving spouse has six months after the executors' confirmation to intimate to them her intention to claim. She cannot claim if, in the

---

[2] Matrimonial Homes (Family Protection) (Scotland) Act 1981, s.22.

meantime, the executors have disposed of the property. As under section 8, there is provision for valuing the claim, by arbitration if need be.

If the spouse is herself the sole executor, she intimates to any children who have claimed legal shares and to all beneficiaries whom she can trace by reasonable inquiry. Her transaction with the estate will not be voidable on the grounds (applicable at common law) that she is *auctor in rem suam* and has a conflict of interest as beneficiary and executor.

### General rules

The order of succession to the intestate estate otherwise remains **15.10** much the same [clauses 1, 2, 4]. The rules of *per stirpes* division are now spelled out clearly in plain English [clause 3].

Collaterals of the full blood will no longer have preference over those of the half blood; all will have equal rights [clause 1(4)].

WILL SUBSTITUTES

SPECIAL DESTINATIONS

### Paragraph 5.18

The proposed Act will restrict the scope of special destinations **15.11** in two complementary ways [clause 29]:

(a) Simple survivorship destinations will remain valid. But where a document of title to property—moveable or heritable—contains a destination in favour of some person other than the original grantee or (if there was more than one grantee) the survivor, the destination is invalid in respect of that person. The grantee or the survivor, as appropriate, has an outright title which simply passes as part of his estate by the ordinary rules of succession. This rule does not apply to destinations to "X in liferent and Y in fee", nor to "X as trustee [or as an officeholder] and his successors in office".

(b) Destinations-over in wills may instruct conditional institution or substitution. The first remains valid. The second will be ineffective in respect of the substitute beneficiary; the original institute will, by analogy with (a), take an outright right.

The Act will govern title deeds and wills (respectively) executed after its commencement, with one exception: deeds after the Act which implement a provision contained in a pre-Act will [clause 34(4)].

In all cases where a post-Act title deed contains a destination, the owner may validly evacuate it either by will or during his lifetime. If the destination is contractual, that would not prevent evacuation: it would merely leave the owner liable for damages for breach of contract [clause 29(3)].

Special rules will cover destinations in leases. More generally, special destinations will include "class" destinations [clause 36(1)].[3] Property subject to a destination will be excluded from the deceased's estate for the purpose of administration under the 1964 Act—unless a transfer by the executor is necessary—only if, in the circumstances the destination actually takes effect [Schedule 1, paras. 12 and 14].[4]

The Bill provides that the construction of title deeds to moveable property will—unless the document says otherwise—be determined in accordance with the law of the deceased's last domicile. This aims to reverse the rule in *Connell's Trs v. Connell's Trs*[5] that English law applied to shares held by a Scotsman in English companies, so that where shares were held in joint names there was an implied survivorship destination.

Donations mortis causa

**Paragraph 5.34**

15.12    These will not be deemed to be part of the donor's estate for the purpose of legal shares, so will not be forfeited if the recipient claims on the estate. They will be returnable if the recipient forfeits his rights by killing the donor, or fails to survive him for five days [clauses 19(1), 28(8), 36(1)].

Wills: Formal Validity

**Paragraph 6.61**

15.13    The Court of Session and the sheriff court will have power to declare formally valid a writing which purports to be a will, an alteration to one, or a revocation of one, notwithstanding failure to comply with the normal requirements for formal validity. The court must be satisfied that the testator intended it to take effect as his

---

[3] Reversing the effect of *Cormack v. McIldowie's Exrs*, 1975 S.C. 161.
[4] Amending Succession (Scotland) Act 1964, ss.18(2), 36(2).
[5] (1886) 13 R. 1175.

will (or alteration or revocation); extrinsic evidence will be permitted for this purpose. In validating the will, the court may also declare when (or within what period) and where the will was made [clause 12].[5a]

The validating power would apply so long as the testator dies after the Act comes into force, whatever the date of the will.

## REVOCATION OF WILLS

### Paragraph 7.32

Marriage will not revoke a previous will. But divorce or annul- **15.14** ment of marriage is to have the effect of revoking provisions made by one spouse in the other's favour—*e.g.* legacies, nominations and special destinations, and appointment as trustee, executor, tutor or curator, or donee of a power of appointment—unless the document indicates that provision is to take effect nevertheless. The benefiting ex-spouse will be deemed not to have survived [clause 14].

However, suppose someone, unaware of the new rule, sells property which she believes she has inherited from her ex-spouse under a destination. The destination does not reveal the true position. The buyer, if he bought in good faith, has a protected title [clause 14(4), (5)]. The seller must pay over the proceeds of her ex-spouse's share (if she still has them) to his estate.

The *conditio si testator sine liberis decesserit* will be abolished [clause 15].

If a will is revoked in whole or in part, the will (or part) is not revived unless (a) it is subsequently re-executed, or (b) another document which expressly revives it is executed or is validated by a court order [clause 16].

## WILLS: ESSENTIAL VALIDITY

### Paragraph 8.13

Neither the courts nor *curators bonis*[5b] are to be given power to **15.15** make a will on behalf of someone who lacks testamentary capacity.

### Paragraph 8.42

The Court of Session and sheriff court will have a limited power **15.16** to order a will to be rectified so as to give effect to a testator's instructions, if satisfied that it fails to do so. The will must have

---

[5a] The need for such a power has largely—though not entirely—disappeared as a result of the more liberal formality requirements in the Requirements of Writing (Scotland) Act 1995: see Chap. 6 above.

[5b] or guardians under the Adults with Incapacity (Scotland) Act 2000: see para. 8.15 above.

been prepared by someone other than the testator. An application for rectification must be brought within six months after the executor is confirmed, unless the court on cause shown allows one later. A trustee or executor shall not be personally liable for having distributed, in good faith, estate which vested in him under the unrectified will [clause 13].

TESTAMENTARY FREEDOM

LEGAL SHARES

### Paragraph 9.01

**15.17** "Legal rights" are replaced by "legal shares" in favour of the surviving spouse and issue. As before, these will be fixed proportions of the estate, rather than discretionary awards made by the courts on the English model. They will be exigible from both heritage and moveables.

The surviving spouse's legal share will in all cases be 30 per cent of the first £200,000 of the net estate, and 10 per cent of any excess estate over that figure.[6] The issue take a similar share if there is no surviving spouse. If there is, then (a) their share is halved; (b) they cannot claim out of the first £100,000 of any net estate of which the spouse inherits the fee (as opposed to a liferent) under the deceased's will or intestacy. The purpose of (b) is to avoid the position in *Kerr, Petr*[7] where the spouse inherited the whole estate under a will, but was worse off than under intestacy (because she had no prior rights with which to defeat the legal rights of issue): (b) gives the spouse the same protected right as she would take under intestacy [clauses 5, 7].

Legal shares will not vest automatically by mere survivance of the deceased. They must be claimed within two years after the death by the spouse or child, or (if legally incapacitated for some reason) by someone entitled to act on his behalf in the management of his affairs: *e.g.* a parent or a *curator bonis*.[7a] If the spouse or child dies before claiming, his own executor may claim within the two years or within six months after his death, whichever ends later. Where the court grants a decree under the Presumption of Death (Scotland) Act 1977, it may extend the period for up to six months after the decree [clause 6].

Legal shares may be renounced before or after the deceased died, by or on behalf of the spouse or issue. If a share is renounced

---

[6] The Secretary of State can amend the figure by statutory instrument.
[7] 1968 S.L.T. (Sh. Ct) 61.
[7a] or guardians under the Adults with Incapacity (Scotland) Act 2000.

or merely not claimed, it does not pass to any other potential claimant. Nor does that constitute a transfer of value under the Inheritance Tax Act 1984 [clauses 5(5), 7(5); Schedule 1, para. 24].

Anyone claiming a legal share forfeits all rights under the deceased's will (unless the will provides otherwise) and under intestacy. The claimant is treated as failing to survive, but only so as to debar his own rights: they do not pass to his issue (under intestacy or the *conditio si institutus*) or to a conditional institute (under a destination-over), as they would have done had he really not survived. But a claimant may withdraw his claim before payment and keep his rights [clause 8].

The net estate is calculated before the legal share is divided. The different parts of the estate bear the share in the following order, unless the deceased's will stipulates a different order: (a) intestate estate; (b) residue; (c) general legacies; (d) special legacies, and property passing by nomination or special destination. Assets within each class bear the share pro rata according to value. Conversely, the spouse's "protected £100,000"—free from the issue's legal share—is attributed to the estate in the reverse order; the effect is to minimise the conflict between legal share and protected sum. Finally, the legal share will now bear expenses of administration (throughout the executry) pro rata along with general legacies [clauses 5(4), 9,10].

Legal rights will be abolished and, along with them, collation *inter liberos* [clause 5(6)].

Where legal shares are payable out of agricultural property, it will be possible to pay by 10 equal annual instalments starting from the date of death. Each instalment bears interest at seven per cent from its due date, or such other rate as the Secretary of State may prescribe [clause 11].

FORFEITURE AND EQUITABLE COMPENSATION

**Paragraph 9.19**

If property is left in liferent and fee, and the liferent for any 15.18 reason lapses before the liferenter's death, the Bill allows accelerated vesting in the fiar. Unless the document creating the liferent expressly provides otherwise, the fee vests on the date when it would have done if the liferenter had in fact died at the date of lapse (which may of course not be at once: other conditions may have to be fulfilled) [clause 18]. In that situation there will presumably be no opportunity for equitable compensation to occur.

**Paragraph 10.59**

**15.19**    The *conditio si institutus sine liberis decesserit* survives in an altered form.[8] It will apply only to direct descendants, and then only unless "the will clearly intends otherwise". A survivorship clause or destination-over will be taken to show clear intention, thus defeating the *conditio*. The beneficiary's issue will take the share he would have taken had he survived, including accresced shares. Finally, the rules for per capita and *per stirpes* division among a predeceased beneficiary's issue are set out in clear English [clause 17].

EXECUTRY ADMINISTRATION

**Paragraph 13.11**

**15.20**    The Bill updates the rules which state who is entitled to be appointed executor-dative. Entitlement as "next-of-kin", derived from pre-1964 succession law, is abolished. Instead, anyone entitled to inherit by the rules of intestacy can apply; or, if the sheriff is satisfied that no such person is going to do so, any blood relation of the deceased. (The relation will, as now, be best to get a written declinature from the entitled beneficiary.) If more than one relation applies, the sheriff shall—unless there is good reason not to do so—appoint one or more of those most closely related to the deceased [Schedule 1, para. 2].[9]

**Paragraph 13.24**

**15.21**    Caution will be required for the whole estate administered by the executor-dative: not just that confirmed to by him [Schedule 1, para. 1].

**Paragraph 13.34**

**15.22**    It will be competent for an executor to be confirmed to the estate of someone who died domiciled in Scotland, even if none of that estate was in Scotland [clause 21].[10]

**Paragraph 13.93**

**15.23**    It will remain competent for an executor or trustee to use the deceased's will as a link through which to deduce title in a conveyance to a third party or to complete title in his own name by

---

[8] The change applies only to wills executed after the new Act becomes law [clause 34(3)].

[9] Inserting new Confirmation of Executors (Scotland) Act 1858, s.2.

[10] Inserting new Succession (Scotland) Act 1964, s.14A.

notice of title [Schedule 1, para. 4]. That option will now be open to legatees and general disponees under the will—thus avoiding the need to seek confirmation if no other property has to be transferred. But, as before, only a purchaser acquiring in good faith from a confirmed executor will get a protected title under section 17 of the 1964 Act, so the new option may be little practical use if the heritage is to be sold.

### Paragraph 13.95

Replacing the rules which apply in the case of illegitimate **15.24** beneficiaries, there is a new general protection for a trustee or executor distributing the estate. He is not personally liable for any error in distribution based on ignorance of the (non-) existence of persons, or their (lack of) relationship to any other person; *provided* he acted in good faith and made such inquiries as a reasonable and prudent trustee or executor would make in such circumstances [Schedule 1, para. 7].[11]

### Paragraph 13.99

Section 17 of the 1964 Act, which protects the title of those who **15.25** acquire heritage from a confirmed executor, is to be extended to moveables. It will also be made clear that it is not confined to purchase; it will, say, apply where someone acquires assets in lieu of an alternative claim on the estate, *e.g.* a house or moveables instead of a legal share or intestacy [Schedule 1, para. 11].

### Paragraph 13.100

New rules govern the transfer of a lease by an executor, and **15.26** (reversing the effect of *Inglis v. Inglis*[12]) permit him to acquire it for himself without the transaction being challengeable as being in breach of the common law *auctor in rem suam* rule [clause 22].[13]

---

[11] Inserting new Trusts (Scotland) Act 1921, s.29A.
[12] 1983 S.L.T. 437.
[13] Amending Succession (Scotland) Act 1964, s.16.

# INDEX